Gothic Cinema

Katharina Rein

Gothic Cinema

An introduction

palgrave
macmillan

Katharina Rein
Berlin, Germany

ISBN 978-3-658-40720-9 ISBN 978-3-658-40721-6 (eBook)
https://doi.org/10.1007/978-3-658-40721-6

This Palgrave imprint is published by the registered company Springer Fachmedien Wiesbaden GmbH, part of Springer Nature.
The registered company address is: Abraham-Lincoln-Str. 46, 65189 Wiesbaden, Germany

Genrediscourses

Series published by
Marcus Stiglegger, University of Mainz, Mainz, Germany

From today's perspective, the ideal conception of the film genre as a phenomenon that can be clearly defined in terms of motif and aesthetics belongs to the past of the American studio system. What has always borne cross-border traits in an international context must today be regarded as hybridity. Only a few film productions can still be assigned to classical genre models. Instead, current productions are dominated by the overlapping and constantly changing recombination of these established elements. The same applies to television series, which for a long time still functioned according to classical patterns, but which in recent years have also become genre hybrids.

Consequently, today it must be about discourse if genres are to be discussed in a new and fruitful way. The series Discourses of Genres in Film and Television Series is therefore not about volumes on individual genre models, but about broader discourse reflections such as: "fantasy", "crime" or "melodrama", but also aspects such as "music" and "gender". This opens the field for multimodal approaches, transmedial hybridity models and intercultural perspectives. In this way, the series edited by the Berlin film scholar Prof. Dr. Marcus Stiglegger will close a gaping hole in German-language film research, complementing the *Filmgenres* handbook that is being produced in parallel.

Other volumes in the series: http://www.springer.com/series/15873

V

Contents

Part I   Introduction 1

1   Definition of the Term 5
   1.1   Gothic vs. Dark Romancism............................. 7
   1.2   Gothic vs. Gothic 9
   1.3   Gothic vs. Horror Film 12
   References 17

2   Elements, Motifs, Themes 21
   2.1   The Past.. 24
   2.2   Media 26
   2.3   Spaces 30
   2.4   Monsters 32
   2.5   Reccurency 35
   2.6   Ambiguity... 39
   References 41

Part II   Historical Overview: Gothic Cinema 1896–2000 45

3   Gothic Cinema Before 1960................................. 47
   3.1   Early Film and Illusionism 47
   3.2   German Expressionism.................................. 51
   3.3   The Universal Horror Cycle 54
   3.4   Female Gothic... 65
   References 72

4   Gothic Cinema After 1960 77
    4.1   Gothic in Transition 77
    4.2   Television Gothic 81
    4.3   Hammer Film Productions 83
    4.4   Roger Corman's "Poe Cycle" 88
    4.5   International Gothic 91
    4.6   Postcolonial Gothic....................................104
    4.7   Queer Gothic..106
    4.8   Body Gothic 108
    References 113

5   Gothic Cinema Around 2000: Old Monsters in a New Guise. 121
    5.1   New Zombies 122
    5.2   New Vampires...123
    5.3   Family-Friendly and Mainstream Gothic 126
    5.4   Tim Burton's Gothic....................................128
    References 131

Part III   Gothic Cinema After 2000 135

6   Between the Old and the New 137
    References 142

7   The Haunting of Hill House (2018) 145
    7.1   Haunted Media and Mediums...........................145
    7.2   The Hill House from Jackson's Novel to Netflix 147
    7.3   The Haunted House as a Dysfunctional Storage Medium 149
    7.4   Ambiguity, Disorientation and Unreliability 156
    References 160

8   Dracula (2020). 163
    8.1   The Vampiric Palimpsest................................163
    8.2   Medial Transmission...................................165
    8.3   The Drinking of Blood and Its Consequences 171
    8.4   (Homo)Sexuality......................................174
    8.5   Society and Transgression...............................177
    References 184

9 Crimson Peak (2015) 185
  9.1 The Old and the New World 186
  9.2 Allerdale Hall 189
  9.3 Colors and Costumes 193
  9.4 The Ghosts of Crimson Peak 195
  9.5 Ghostly Media.......................................197
  9.6 Tyrannical Mothers and Incestuous Love...................198
  9.7 Gothic Fiction About Gothic Fiction 200
  References 201

About the Author

Katharina Rein Dr. Katharina Rein currently works as a researcher and lecturer at the University of Potsdam, Germany. She was previously a guest professor at the University of Vienna, Austria and a researcher at the Bauhaus-University Weimar, Germany. She received her PhD in Cultural History and Theory from the Humboldt University of Berlin. Her dissertation on the cultural and media history of stage magic in the late nineteenth century was awarded the Anniversary Prize for Young Researchers by Büchner Verlag. Her academic work has been published in four languages.

Part I
Introduction

Black wheels swirl up a deep puddle before the camera pans up to bring a row of carriages into view, driving through the darkness in the rain. The narrow dirt road leads past a dark lake and toward a castle perched on a hill in the distance. Moonlight struggles to emerge from between the dense clouds. A small street lamp on a black and white striped pole that also serves as a signpost sparsely illuminates the scene. A raven sits on it, its call joining the eerie, polyphonic children's choir singing on the soundtrack. This sequence of only 14 seconds duration contains various canonical elements that create an atmosphere specific to the Gothic. Those who think of horror film when they hear "Gothic" may be surprised to learn that the sequence in question is from the film *Harry Potter and the Prisoner of Azkaban* (00:23), which is cleared by the FSK from age 12 in Germany and by the Austrian JMK from age 6.[1] So what is Gothic cinema?

This volume attempts to answer this question. In the German-speaking world, it has not yet been established as a film genre, and even in Anglophone cultures, which in addition to a long tradition of the Gothic have also established the academic discipline of Gothic Studies, the cinematic form of the Gothic has received comparatively little academic attention until recently. In order to provide conceptual, historical, and contemporary insight, this volume is divided into three parts, the first of which sets a general genre-theoretical focus, while the second provides an overview of the history of Gothic cinema and the third examines individual examples from the past years. First, the term "Gothic" is delineated, including its

---

[1] FSK is the abbreviation of Freiwillige Selbstkontrolle der Filmwirtschaft, i.e. the Self-Regulatory Body of the Movie Industry, a German organisation that rates and approves films, trailers, commercials etc. in Germany. The JMK, Jugendmedienkommission [Youth Media Commission] establishes the suitabilitiy of films and trailers for young people in Austria.

distinction from Dark Romanticism and horror film, before the second chapter of the introduction narrows down Gothic cinema's defining motifs, themes, and topoi.

In three chapters divided in accordance with film-historical caesurae or periods of time, the second part highlights significant points of the history of Gothic cinema. Closer examinations of individual examples supplement the overview. Chapter 3 ranges from early fantastic films beginning in 1896 through German Expressionism and the horror films of the Universal Studios to the Female Gothic of the 1940s. This is followed by a chapter on Gothic cinema from about 1960 onward, which looks at the films of the British Hammer Film Productions and Roger Corman's "Poe-Cycle," among others. In the 1960s, Gothic also migrated to another medium, television, to which a subchapter is devoted. Moreover, Gothic cinema increasingly diversified and internationalized during this period, which is why further subchapters illuminate inter- and transnational variations, including Italian Gothic and Asian Gothic, the Edgar Wallace films as a German variation, and American and Southern Gothic as specifically U.S.-American subtypes. Chapter 5 concludes the historical section by looking at Gothic cinema from around 1990, when it became more differentiated and at the same time gained a clearer foothold in the mainstream, thanks in no small part to the works of Tim Burton, to whom the final subchapter is devoted. In this part of the book, special attention is paid to tracing interconnections and interactions as well as to illustrating caesuras and innovations resulting from developments in film and production technology. For example, Gothic cinema changes significantly with the arrival of film in the studios, with the advent of sound and later color film, with the abolition of the Hays Code, and finally with the appearance of digital special effects and the proliferation of online streaming services.

This historical overview is followed by the third section, which focuses on contemporary Gothic cinema since 2015. It begins by discussing how the series *Penny Dreadful* (2014–2016) illustrates a central dilemma of twenty-first century Gothic cinema, which must reconcile outdated values and norms of canonical works with the views and interests of contemporary audiences. The following three chapters examine in detail one post-2015 case study each. On the one hand, these close readings exemplify the characteristics of Gothic cinema identified in the first part as well as its references back to its own history outlined in the second part. On the other hand, they allow for a deeper understanding than could be offered by an overview of films in which variations of typical motifs, characters, or plots can be found. The fact that, with the popularity of online streaming service providers such as Netflix or Amazon Prime Video, the Gothic has also conquered this media area is reflected here in such a way that series distributed via these services are examined along with feature films.

The term "Gothic cinema" is thus applied in a way that goes beyond the motion picture. While "Gothic film" mostly refers to the audiovisual artifacts themselves, "Gothic cinema" also includes the contexts and paratexts of cinematographic production and performance practices. Due to the importance of television series and streaming services in the twenty-first century, neither can be limited to the reception of audiovisual products in the screening context of the movie theater. To avoid neologisms of conceptual monsters, "Gothic cinema" in this volume therefore refers to audiovisual artifacts across media.

The analyses in the third part focus on reflections on media theory: Chap. 7 examines *The Haunting of Hill House* (2018), the first season of an anthology series created by Mike Flanagan, who adapted Shirley Jackson's seminal haunted house novel for the streaming service Netflix. If the haunted house is a paradigmatic site of the Gothic, here it is interpreted as a place that idiosyncratically stores and replays events and characters, thereby disrupting the continuum of time – a recording medium gone wild. Chapter 8 is devoted to a recent adaptation of the paradigmatic vampire novel, Bram Stoker's *Dracula* (1896), in the form of a miniseries produced for BBC One and Netflix by Mark Gatiss and Steven Moffat in 2020. In addition to some of the central themes of the vampire film, blood comes into particular focus here, presented in the series as a univiersal medium that conveys the nature and knowledge of humans. The final chapter analyzes Guillermo del Toro's feature film *Crimson Peak* (2015), a colorful representative of the neo-Victorian Gothic that proves to be a catalog of Gothic motifs, characters, and topoi, as well as quotations from canonical films. However, del Toro manages not to place these unconnectedly next to each other, but to skillfully merge them into a harmonious whole, while at the same time developing a striking aesthetic of his own. Because of this film's referential character, this chapter can stand in place of a summary.

Definition of the Term

1

Genre definitions are as helpful as they are problematic. Historically, genres go back to the Hollywood studio system and the film production of the Weimar Republic, but established themselves especially since 1930, together with sound film (see Stiglegger 2020, p. 4). Assigning films to individual genres comes with the risk of slipping into debates about inclusion and exclusion of single works. These are often tautological, as the defining elements of a genre are distilled from a group of works assigned to it. This classification, in turn, is based on characteristics that have been set as defining for the genre because they occur in works that belong to it. When one gets bogged down in such debates, it often seems tempting to quote United States Supreme Court Justice Potter Stewart, who, in the context of a case concerning obscenity in film, sidestepped a concrete genre definition of the hardcore pornographic film by saying, "I know it when I see it" (378 U.S. 184 1963, p. 197). Particularly in postmodernism, unambiguous assignments to just one genre are the exception rather than the rule, for "[s]ince the 1980s at the latest [...]," writes Marcus Stiglegger (2020, p. 4), "the fragile boundaries of genre cinema began to visibly dissolve." Instead of arguing for the abolition of genres, however, it is necessary to adapt conceptions, for the concept of genre is not only firmly anchored in discourse, but also remains fruitful. Genre assignments not only help to classify works and render them discursive – whether in academia, film journalism, or leisure. They also enable comparison with more or less similar works and thus also the identification of individual peculiarities (see Grant 2007, p. 2).

This volume does not so much attempt to provide a dogmatic definition as to give an idea of what can be understood as Gothic cinema. As others have often noted, the Gothic is notoriously difficult to define, but we do know it when we see it. Gothic cinema is usually not regarded as a distinct film genre analogous to

K. Rein, *Gothic Cinema*, https://doi.org/10.1007/978-3-658-40721-6_1

horror, western, or musical. Rather, researchers speak of the idea (Neibaur 2020, p. 13) or the gesture of the Gothic (Bronfen 2014, p. 112), of its indexicality (Aldana Reyes 2020b, p. 77), of Gothic as an (aesthetic) mode (Aldana Reyes 2020a, pp. 16–17; Hutchings 1996, p. 89) or as a visual sign system (Kavka 2002, p. 210). It is thus an umbrella term for a specific aesthetic, atmosphere, and repertoire of motifs and characters.

"It may come as a surprise, in view of the generic force of the term *Gothic*," writes Misha Kavka (2002, p. 209) "that there is no established genre called *Gothic cinema* or *Gothic film*. There are Gothic images and Gothic plots and Gothic characters and even Gothic styles within film, [...], but there is no delimited or demonstrable genre specific to film called the Gothic." This is surprising because, as I also tried to illustrate by the scene at the beginning of this chapter, there is such a thing as the "Gothic" in film, identified by audiences, critics, and scholars.

The distinctive aesthetic of the Gothic, a genre that emerged in literature in the second half of the eighteenth century, is predestined for a translation into the audiovisual. "[O]nly with the advent of cinema," writes Christopher Frayling (2013, p. 5), "did 'the Gothic' come into its own. Before that, as a literary form it was waiting in the wings: not quite respectable, reviled by the Victorian academic establishment". But in film of all places, where the Gothic unfolds its full potential, it has hardly been concretely formulated as a genre – unlike in architecture and literature. And "if there has to date not been a genre called Gothic film," Kavka (2002, p. 209) therefore concludes, "then we must strive to invent it". Gothic film, she argues, should then be understood as the recognizable visual language of the historically variable Gothic, which has coagulated into a visual code especially in the course of the twentieth century (Kavka 2002, p. 210).

The elements and visuality of the Gothic have long since arrived in mainstream film and television. Beginning with *The Munsters* (1964–1966) and *The Addams Family* (1964–1966), they have become especially prevalent through the work of Tim Burton, but also through the films of Guillermo del Toro, the *Harry Potter* films (2001–2011), and most recently in series such as *True Blood* (2008–2014), *Penny Dreadful* (2014–2016), *True Detective* (2014–2019), or *Chilling Adventures of Sabrina* (2018–2020) as so-called Quality TV permeated popular visual culture. The Gothic not only spread from literature into audiovisual media, but also into youth culture in the 1980s, when Goth developed as a new subculture from Punk and New Wave. It in turn split into several subcultures, each with specific styles of dress and dance, forms of music, spaces, and in some cases political and religious beliefs (see, e.g., Hodkinson 2007; on Goth and Gothic fashion, see Spooner 2004, 2017, pp. 67–82; on Goth as a lifestyle, see Spooner 2013). In the twenty-first century, the Gothic aesthetic has become part of mass culture. "Like a malevolent virus," writes Catherine Spooner (2006, p. 8),

> Gothic narratives have escaped the confines of literature and spread across disciplinary boundaries to infect all kinds of media, from fashion and advertising to the way contemporary events are constructed in mass culture. Gothic musicians such as Nick Cave and Robert Smith of The Cure have become critically acclaimed broadsheet staples, exemplars of middle-class taste, while teenage Goths continue to preoccupy the media and even appear as regular characters in *Coronation Street*.

Commercialized under the conditions of the twenty-first century, the Gothic has permeated the mainstream as well as niche markets, exerting its influence on fiction, film, television, fashion, design, video games, youth culture, and advertising (Spooner 2006, p. 23). In particular its striking visuality came into effect as it unfolded, established itself, and spread primarily in film (and previously in art) over the course of the last century. In the 21 years since Misha Kavka's statement that there is no "Gothic film" genre, the research literature has grown in volume, but the detailed examination of Gothic in film has just begun. Whereas for a long time, only individual essays were available, Justin D. Edwards' and Johan A. Höglund's 2019 examination of the Gothic in B-movies was followed in 2020 by a single-author monograph, *Gothic Cinema*, by Xavier Aldana Reyes, and a few months later by the anthology *Gothic Film*, edited by Richard J. Hand and Jay McRoy.

1.1   Gothic vs. Dark Romancism

Although the tradition of the Gothic in literature and film can be identified at points in Germany – from the horror story [*Schauergeschichte*] to the Expressionist fantastic films to the Edgar Wallace films – Gothic is not an established cinematic genre (on genre cinema in Germany see Alexius and Beicht 2018).[1] Even beyond German film production, "Gothic" is not widely used in the German-speaking world as a designation of a film genre. While the German *Schauergeschichte* and Dark Romanticism [*Schwarze Romantik*] are related to Gothic fiction, respectively Gothic art, they denote different movements. The English term "Gothic" is associated in German primarily with the music and fashion style of the subculture referred to in English as "Goth."

---

[1] There is a focus on the German-language discourse and a possible German term for "Gothic" here because this book originally appeared in German.

A direct translation is difficult, since "Gotik" in German refers to the period of architecture and art between the twelfth and fifteenth centuries and is not applied in the same sense to literature or film, as "Gothic" has been in English since the eighteenth century. A related genre in art and literature is Dark Romanticism, of which E. T. A. Hoffmann is considered the most prominent literary representative. In his standard literary work *The Romantic Agony,* which was first published in 1963 in a German translation (*Liebe Tod und Teufel. Die schwarze Romantik*) of the 1930 Italian original (*La carne, la morte e il diavolo nella letterature romantica*), Mario Praz defines the dark side of Romanticism with reference to the Gothic novel. The term "Dark Romanticism," writes Felix Krämer (2012b, p. 15), also "cannot be reduced to a specific historical period, but can only be understood through its characteristics". These are quite similar to those of the Gothic: Dark Romanticism interlinks love, eroticism, and death. It revolves around the indistinguishability of imagination and reality, inexplicable events and hidden realities, dark forces, isolation, and the Uncanny. We often encounter religious motifs, characters, and places, such as monks, nuns, (ruinous) convents, and cemeteries. "The late Romantic artists of the late nineteenth century," writes Marcus Stiglegger (2018, p. 42), "lived in awareness of a decaying culture, which they reflected in their art in a nightmarish way: degeneration, deformation, illness, death, erotic extravagance, vampirism [...]. And also the contemporary cinema celebrates a return of the *Gothic fiction,* the irrationality of Dark Romanticism."

Upon closer inspection, however, the terms "Gothic" and "Dark Romanticism" [*Schwarze Romantik*] are not translations of one another. If Romanticism defined itself as a countermovement to the Enlightenment, and therefore especially through a reference to dreams and fantasy as the flip side of reason, such a focus is found in Gothic fiction at most implicitly, but not programmatically. In terms of literature, the British Gothic novel is also distinguished in academic discourse from the German *Schauerroman* – although similarities can be found internationally, including with French literature (for example, the works of Charles Baudelaire or Victor Hugo), differences are also clear.[2]

In the visual arts, Dark Romanticism primarily refers to a gloomy movement oriented toward physicality, loneliness, melancholy, and nightmares in the roughly 60 years around 1800. It is represented by artists such as Henry Fuseli, Caspar David Friedrich, Eugène Delacroix and Francisco Goya. It, too, refers to the irrational, to imagination, fantasy and nightmares or dreams and is therefore often regarded as a predecessor of Surrealism. In the book accompanying the exhibition

---

[2] The Gothic novel is also not to be confused is the French *roman noir*, a subcategory of the detective novel that emerged as an analogy to Film Noir in the 1940s.

Dark Romanticism at the Städel Museum Frankfurt from 2013, Felix Krämer (2012a) argues for expanding the concept of Dark Romanticism in art beyond this epoch, including works of the Decadent movement around 1900 and Surrealism. Although these two periods coincide with the traditional Gothic novel, respectively with that of the Gothic Revival in Great Britain, the art movement that the German term "Schwarze Romantik" denotes is called "Dark Romanticism" in the English-speaking world. "Gothic" as an art movement, in turn, refers to what in German is called "Gotik", i.e., the art of the Middle Ages that flourished at the same time as Gothic architecture. Thus, even with regard to periods of art history, the terms are not directly transferable.

The visual world of Dark Romanticism may have entered the aesthetics of Gothic cinema via the detour of German Expressionist film, but "Dark Romanticism" denotes a genre of the past. Even the extended time frame of the above-mentioned volume reaches only to the middle of the twentieth century. Accordingly, the contribution on film by Claudia Dillmann contained therein treats the Expressionist fantastic films of the 1910s and 1920s as a cinematic form of expression of Dark Romanticism. Nor is the term applied to contemporary works in visual art or literature. Hardly anyone would describe James Whale's *Frankenstein* (1931), Terence Fisher's *Dracula* (1958), Tim Burton's *Edward Scissorhands* (1990) or Jim Jarmush's *Only Lovers Left Alive* (2013) as works of Dark Romanticism. But they all belong to Gothic cinema, which is very much a contemporary phenomenon – in film as well as in art, literature, and popular culture.

1.2   Gothic vs. Gothic

If definitions of Dark Romanticism often remain vague (see e.g. Krämer 2012b, p. 15), the English term "Gothic" is also multi-layered. The chaos surrounding it is revealed, for example, by the entry in the *Oxford English Dictionary,* which lists six different meanings, some of which are completed by up to four sub-entries, as well as two additions. Most refer to the Goths or Gothic architecture as: "Of, pertaining to, or concerned with the Goths or their language" and "[f]ormerly used in extended sense, now expressed by Teutonic *adj. and n.* or Germanic *adj. and n.*" Only the most recent 2007 addition denotes "a genre of fiction characterized by suspenseful, sensational plots involving supernatural or macabre elements and often (esp. in early use) having a medieval theme or setting." ("Gothic," OED 2020). Further definitions take the probably most common meaning into account: "the style of architecture prevalent in Western Europe from the twelfth to the sixteenth century, of which the chief characteristic is the pointed arch. Applied also to buildings, architectural details, and ornamentation" as well as its return in the nineteenth century as "Gothic Revival *n.* the reintroduction of a Gothic style of architecture towards the middle of the nineteenth century" (ibid.).

This already shows the bewildering breadth of the various facets of the word "Gothic," which have little in common, if they are not incompatible. The Goths never built a Gothic cathedral nor wrote a Gothic novel, and although Gothic pointed arches and ornamentation are part of the visual repertoire of the traditional Gothic film aesthetic, the architectural concept is not directly indicative of the literary or cinematic one, and vice versa. If we refer to an architectural style as Gothic that flourished between the twelfth and sixteenth centuries, in literature, the Gothic refers to works created several centuries later in a different medium (see Baldick 2009, p. xi). And while in architectural history there may be as many as six centuries between the medieval and historicist styles of the Gothic Revival, in literary historical terms traditional Gothic fiction and the literature of the Gothic Revival are separated by 20–80 years.

In terms of literature, traditional Gothic fiction refers to a body of literary works produced in Britain between the 1760s and the 1820s that share a number of characteristics. These include, according to David Punter's pioneering work *The Literature of Terror* (1996, vol. 1, p. 14)*:* the desire to portray something frightening, the prominence of archaic settings, supernatural elements as well as stereotypical characters, and the attempt to develop and perfect techniques of literary suspense. "'Gothic' fiction," he writes, "is the fiction of the haunted castle, of heroines preyed upon by unspeakable terrors, of the blackly lowering villain, of ghosts, vampires, monsters and werewolves" (ibid., p. 1). Suspense, the central narratological tool of the Gothic novel, was later translated masterfully into the medium of film by Alfred Hitchcock. Among the most influential Gothic novels of the traditional period are Horace Walpole's *The Castle of Otranto* (1764), Ann Radcliffe's *The Mysteries of Udolpho* (1794), Matthew Lewis' *The Monk* (1796), and Mary Shelley's *Frankenstein* (1818).

Catherine Spooner (2006, p. 10) has repeatedly pointed out that the Gothic continues to redefine itself throughout its history, reviving and reinterpreting traditions. If the above-mentioned works positioned the central elements of the Gothic, a little under a century later[3] they were taken up and significantly expanded. This literature of the Gothic Revival of the late nineteenth century, in particular, continues to shape the repertoire of Gothic themes and aesthetics to this day. The influence of the characters, themes, and motifs it introduced can be explained not least

---

[3] Some authors identify an earlier beginning of the Gothic Revival, for instance in the 1840s, according to Alexandra Warwick (2007, p. 30).

by the fact that they became inscribed into the cultural imaginary in the form of countless (more or less loose) cinematic adaptations, which consolidated and canonized themselves therein. Since Gothic cinema (especially before the 1970s) drew to a large extent on works of the Gothic Revival, its aesthetics were more strongly associated with the Victorian era than with the traditional period of the Gothic novel from the second half of the eighteenth century onward. Therefore, mansions, dandies, and lantern-lit urban landscapes with cobblestone streets are as much a part of Gothic film's aesthetic repertoire as medieval castles and ruins.

Like Mary Shelley's *Frankenstein,* Robert Louis Stevenson's *Strange Case of Dr. Jekyll & Mr. Hyde* ostensibly examined the potential consequences of the dizzying scientific advances of the time in the hands of ethically questionable characters. The transformation of the gentleman Dr. Jekyll into the cruel and anti-social Mr. Hyde epitomizes the conflict between individual desire and societal respectability – a theme also addressed by another Gothic Revival classic: Oscar Wilde's *The Picture of Dorian Gray* (1890). Seven years after this milestone of Decadent literature appeared the paradigmatic vampire novel, Bram Stoker's *Dracula.* This metaphorizes the colonial fear of the invasion of one's own culture by the Other, which appears here in the form of the vampire. The latter's status as a count also articulates the bourgeoisie's fear of the return of the aristocracy, which, before losing large parts of its power through peasant liberations and land reforms in the nineteenth century, metaphorically sucked out the blood of the people dependent on them. Not least, the vampire here also becomes a symbol of a sexual licentiousness which was frowned upon in Victorian England.

Like the traditional Gothic novels, the literary works of the Gothic Revival revolve around taboo subjects such as intoxication, madness, violence, sexual assault, incest, and other transgressions. Suspense and shock merge here with spectacular aesthetics to create an atmosphere of terror and the Uncanny. Even looking back to the Victorian era, it is clear that Gothic as a genre is difficult to narrow down – it was gaining complexity, becoming more and more differentiated, and producing offshoots and crossovers. These include, for example, H. G. Wells' scientific romances, which also mark the beginning of the science fiction genre, or the detective story. The latter began as a genre in Edgar Allen Poe's short stories about C. Auguste Dupin and thus came directly from the pen of one of the most important authors of the American Gothic. The central works of the Gothic Revival are among Britain's most important contributions to the world literature of their time. Their motifs and characters are an integral part of the popular culture of the twentieth and twenty-first centuries (Frayling 2013, p. 6).

In the twentieth century, the differentiation of the Gothic accelerated in literature and especially in film, where the central motifs of the genre found their iconic visualization. A film-historical caesura is usually identified in the 1960s: if the aesthetic and motivic elements of Gothic cinema were established, canonized, and formalized in the preceding decades, they were now broken with. Although what is often referred to as the dissolution or decomposition of the Gothic does not become tangible until the 1980s, the first representatives of what is retrospectively referred to as postclassical horror film already manifested themselves in the 1960s, in particular *Psycho*, *Peeping Tom* (both 1960) and *Night of the Living Dead* (1968). Since the 1960s, the aesthetic of Gothic film has also increasingly been diffusing into other genres and media, especially television and later online streaming services. A number of works emerged that contain elements and traces of the Gothic – such as the example of the *Harry Potter* series cited at the beginning of this introduction – without belonging to it in the same sense as, for example, the Universal or Hammer horror films do.

Especially since the 1980s, the episodes, events, characters, as well as the iconography of the Gothic have been less central as characteristics. Rather, they are used across genres in film as tools to evoke the horrors from within. Traditional Gothic and the works of the Gothic Revival have become reference points for the Gothic of the late twentieth century, Catherine Spooner (2007, p. 40) writes: "Gothic, we might say, haunts them". For example, the conflict between social respectability and deviant desire that in *Strange Case of Dr. Jekyll & Mr. Hyde* and *The Picture of Dorian Gray* takes the form of doppelgangers with socially unacceptable behavior, is expressed in twentieth century Gothic in the form of oppressive atmospheres, unconventional aesthetics, or drastic depictions of violence. While the Victorian age entered into open opposition to a pre-Enlightenment past, in modernity it is the internalized mechanisms of the Enlightenment itself that subordinate us to power (Spooner 2007, p. 44). Contemporary Gothic, writes Catherine Spooner (2006, p. 23), is defined by three factors, the first of which is a heightened awareness of its own nature. Secondly, under the conditions of global consumer culture, the Gothic has reached a new level of mass production and distribution, in the context of which, thirdly, disciplinary boundaries are transcended and diverse media are permeated.

1.3   Gothic vs. Horror Film

In the German-speaking discourse, Gothic film – if it is perceived as such at all – is usually considered a subgenre of horror film. This is due to the fact that horror has been a recognized film genre for much longer and is also cited as such in film studies (e.g. Bordwell and Thompson 2001, pp. 102–105; Grant 2007; Langford 2005, pp. 158–181) as well as in the genre selection of streaming services such as Netflix or Amazon Prime Video. While most films that can be categorized as Gothic are also horror films, regarding Gothic as a subgenre of horror falls short of its potential. Rather, Gothic cinema should be understood as a metagenre that, while having a strong affinity with horror, also includes films of other genres.

In the anglophone discourse, due to the long tradition and cultural significance of the Gothic in British literature, architecture and culture, the study of the Gothic is much more pronounced than in German-speaking countries. "Gothic" is a well established term here, reaching well beyond the designation of a literary genre. Gothic Studies have developed into an independent academic research and study discipline during the past decades. Specifically regarding film, however, even anglophone research literature remains relatively scarce, albeit growing. Accordingly, no universally accepted definition of Gothic cinema has yet been established. One of the difficulties is that the films in question can often be assigned to other genres as well, or are not clearly distinguished (or indistinguishable) from horror. Isabella van Elferen (2012, p. 35) writes in this regard:

> Films that are considered Gothic in academic studies of popular culture also appear in discussions of other, more general, genres such as thrillers, psychological thrillers, fantasy and, most often, horror. The three films that are generally considered to mark the birth of horror cinema are in fact all three adaptations of Gothic novels: Tod Browning's *Dracula* with Bela Lugosi (1931), Rouben Marmoulian's *Dr. Jekyll and Mr. Hyde* with Fredric March (1932) and James Whale's *Frankenstein* with Boris Karloff (1932).

Not only are horror films often adaptations of Gothic fiction, but the Gothic novel can also be seen as the first form of horror literature, whose central motifs it processed in an entertaining and exciting way. But where should the line be drawn? Is Gothic a subgenre of horror?

Gothic and horror film overlap extensively. Both deal with cultural fears – sometimes openly, but more often metaphorically. Frequently this is personified by characters who function as manifestations of the Id – the famous, by now formulaic, return of the repressed. Both describe transgressions, remind us of the presence of impending death in life, and revolve around tensions between fear and desire. Accordingly, both are characterized by an aesthetic of ambivalence that oscillates between the attractive and the repulsive, or depicts both simultaneously. Most examples of Gothic films that are discussed in this book and elsewhere belong to the horror genre. If horror is usually defined by the fact that it evokes fear and terror, this is also often cited as a defining characteristic of the Gothic. Nevertheless,

I agree with most anglophone research that argues against considering the Gothic as a subcategory of horror.

A common distinction between the Gothic and horror film is based on the implicit or explicit representation of the object of fear. If the horror film relies on moments of direct shock and scare, the Gothic tends to opt for an insidious suspense and the Uncanny. While horror film explicates, that is, visualizes the object of fear, the Gothic implies it. If the horror genre is often extreme and obscene in its depiction of boundary transgressions, directly confronting viewers with violence, blood, wounds, and mutilation, the Gothic traditionally hints at such transgressions through shadows and camerawork, creating a presence of the object of fear through its absence. While the Gothic thus appeals more to the imagination, the horror genre's explicit aesthetic has a different psychological and emotional effect. Contrary to the obvious assumption that this is more extreme than the reaction to the more subtle Gothic, Isabella van Elferen (2012, p. 35 f.), for example, attests to the opposite: by framing horror in the controlled space of the film image, the horror film paradoxically creates a kind of comfort. Here, the object of fear is concrete and accessible. The Gothic, on the other hand, confronts us with the ambivalent, the implied, and the Uncanny. Here the object of fear is abstract and omnipresent, it is always out there and is only perceptible by virtue of our imagination. Imagination, however, knows no boundaries (ibid.).

This differentiation, which conceives of the Gothic as the more subtle but at least equally disturbing film style, goes back to the distinction in the English-speaking world since the late eighteenth century between *terror* and *horror* (see Townshend 2016). This was taken up by Ann Radcliffe in her essay "On the Supernatural in Poetry" of 1826, in which she differentiates the two effects based on their proximity to the object that triggers them: *horror*, according to Radcliffe's conception, arouses uneasiness and arises from the fact that the recipients are confronted too directly with the object. *Terror*, on the other hand, presents it from an appropriate distance and produces pleasure (Radcliffe 1826; see also Townshend 2016, pp. 35–38). Although the author is more interested in the effect of the supernatural than in the dichotomy of these two sensations, their binary opposition still shapes the belief that the Gothic cannot be based on strong feelings or direct attacks (Aldana Reyes 2020a, p. 7). Xavier Aldana Reyes (ibid., p. 8) paraphrases the common distinction between horror and the Gothic as follows:

> According to the popular dyad, the Gothic is subtle and suggestive; it hints at occluded or only partially visible terrors, thus offering half-glimpses of bloodcurdling images which, because they are seldom fully shown or described, allow our imagination to run wild and fill in the gaps. The Gothic is haunting and favors mood over

grisly spectacle; it is interested in recurring motifs and in setting up atmospheres of gloom and unease that may also play with shadows to create a pervasive sense of threat. It is also highly psychological and preoccupied with hallucinations, vivid dreamscapes (often nightmares) and other provinces of the warped mind. Horror, by contrast, is seen as heavily graphic and explicit: it confronts viewers with terrifying images and cinematic "numbers". Gore (especially of the gratuitous type) and violence are its tools, which in fact makes horror more oppositional or niche as a cinematic form (it is not for everyone and harder to watch) and even dangerous or morally bankrupt, potentially of interest only to sadists or those with a strong stomach.

Aldana Reyes also notes that this differentiation, like Radcliffe's original definition of *terror* and *horror,* privileges the Gothic over horror by constructing the former as more tasteful, subtle, and complex. But it also favors a particular tradition of the Gothic, namely that which does not involve graphic depictions of violence. This overlooks the fact that the Gothic also stands in the tradition of the melodrama and Grand Guignol theater, which certainly worked with shock effects and explicit violence (Aldana Reyes 2020a, p. 10; on melodrama, see, for example, Kappelhoff and Bakels 2018; on the Grand Guignol, see, e.g., Gordon 1988).

Excluding all films from the Gothic in which violence is explicitly visualized, however, does not seem purposeful. Not only has the depiction of violence in film increased over the past four decades, so that the splatter aesthetic can increasingly be observed in mainstream cinema. Even some recognized Gothic classics, such as the films of the British Hammer Film Productions, contain drastic imagery. Although they are not capable of shocking today's viewers, their depictions of violence, with their glaring red blood, can certainly be considered excessive for the time in which they were made. It is not a coincidence that ack Halberstam (1995, p. 25) sees the Hammer horror films as precursors of the splatter film. Elisabeth Bronfen (2014, p. 112) even names visual excess as a defining characteristic of the Gothic when she writes: "The Gothic film gesture is one of rendering intellectual and socio-cultural crises in excessive visceral, as well as visual, terms."

It can be said that the distinction between horror and Gothic film is neither clear nor simple. A more psychoanalytically oriented differentiation is proposed by Misha Kavka (2002, p. 210), who draws on the Uncanny and Julia Kristeva's concept of the Abject (see Sect. 2.6): To her determination that "Gothic is about fear, localized in the shape of something monstrous which electrifies the collective mind," she adds, regarding the differebtiation from horror film, that paranoia is central in the Gothic, which she understands as a projection of the self onto the outside world, which in turn is perceived as hostile as a result of this paranoia. This blurring of the boundary between inside and outside, self and other, is related to the fear of the abject – the return of that which has been repelled and repressed. The

Uncanny, a defining characteristic of the Gothic (see, e.g., Bacon 2018) is discussed in more detail in Sect. 2.5. A possible objection against the return of the repressed as a defining characteristic, which has become formulaic in the meantime, would be that it applies just as well to the horror film.

Kavka proposes a distinction based on visualization and visibility, but one that does not have explicit depiction of violence in mind, as does the differentiation paraphrased by Aldana Reyes in the quote above. Although Gothic is primarily a spectacle, it is characterized by liminality, Kavka (2002, pp. 226–227) writes, whereas horror prefers the head-on collision, so to speak. Kavka uses the example of the serial killer film to illustrate the transition from one to the other when horror becomes explicit. When the paranoia evoked in Gothic through a shadow play and latencies manifests itself in the rational fear of a concrete, psychopathic killer like Hannibal Lecter, we have crossed the line from Gothic to horror, Kavka (ibid., p. 227) says. The point is not that the monster in Gothic films remains offstage – it does not – but rather that the Gothic is interested in the kind of terror that cannot be depicted. What is metaphorically and affectively expressed in the Gothic cannot be translated into direct visualization. Gothic is not about the representation of the object, but about its effect (ibid., pp. 226–227).

Certainly, many films can be described as both Gothic and horror films. However, it is clear that neither can be considered a subgenre of the other. It is also frequently argued that Gothic should not be considered a separate film genre at all. Thus Isabella van Elferen (2012, p. 36) writes: "in cinema, Gothic is no longer separate genre but rather occurs as a possible dimension of the style, subject matter, performativity of a film." Based on the fact that Gothic manifests itself in other genres as well, for example in melodrama or comedy, Aldana Reyes (2020a, p. 16) also argues against considering it a subgenre of horror. Precisely because Gothic is recognizable primarily by its aesthetics, its visual and iconographic elements and motifs appear in other genres as well. This does not mean, however, that all works that draw from the Gothic repertoire are to be counted as belonging to it, nor that the definition of the Gothic can be limited exclusively to its visuality.

In *Gothic Cinema*, Aldana Reyes proposes the following differentiation between horror and Gothic film: While both share a basic atmospheric mood, conditioned by lighting, music, sound, and camera work, horror aims primarily at an emotional or affective response and is not determined by setting or temporality. The Gothic, on the other hand, cannot be defined solely on the basis of the generation of fear, but it can be defined on the basis of aesthetic characteristics. It can be unambiguously determined in particular by its claustrophobic mood and its anachronistic temporality, which – following the history of the term – can be "associated with barbarism, superstition, revenge, and tyranny" (Aldana Reyes 2020a, p. 25).

He thus sees it as crucial to conceive of the Gothic not so much as a genre or as a subgenre, but rather as a shifting, aesthetic mode that emerges as much from an intertextuality as it is determined by a specific temporality and a set of themes, motifs, and characters (ibid., p. 16). With regard to film in particular, these are predominantly, but not exclusively, visual in nature. Aldana Reyes determines three levels of the Gothic as an aesthetic mode: first, the surface level, i.e., the appearance "of a recognizable set of characters, settings, associated motifs and themes" across films (ibid., p. 17). These achieve an effect on viewers that is captured as a second, affective level. Primarily, this concerns feelings such as fear or suspense. The third, cultural level concerns the impact of a "particular implementation, combination or subversion of the Gothic's main aesthetic elements" in a larger context (ibid.). These levels each also capture the sides of (1) production, (2) reception of individual films as well as their influence on (3) other artifacts, discourses, and culture.

Gothic film, then, is neither a subgenre of horror film nor can it be clearly conceptualized as a separate genre equivalent to it. Rather, it is an aesthetic mode that occurs across genres. While it is encountered more often in the horror genre than in others, fantasy, science fiction, comedy, exploitation, splatter films, Film Noir, Western, or road movies can also be subject to the aesthetic mode of the Gothic. The term is therefore often used in place of an attribute in conjunction with another genre, such as Gothic horror or Gothic comedy.

References

Literature

378 U.S. 184, Jacobellis v. Ohio' (No. 11). 1963. Cornell law school. Legal information institute. https://www.law.cornell.edu/supremecourt/text/378/184. Accessed 15 Oct 2020.

Aldana Reyes, Xavier. 2020a. *Gothic cinema*. London: Routledge.

———. 2020b. Gothic cinema from the 1970s to now. In *Gothic film: An Edinburgh companion*, ed. Richard J. Hand and Jay McRoy, 77–86. Edinburgh: Edinburgh University Press.

Alexius, Christian, and Sarah Beicht. 2018. Einleitung: Der Fantastik eine Chance. In *Fantastisches in dunklen Sälen: Science-Fiction, Horror und Fantasy im jungen deutschen Film*, ed. Christian Alexius and Sarah Beicht, 9–18. Marburg: Schüren.

Baldick, Chris. 2009. Introduction. In *The Oxford book of Gothic Tales*, ed. Chris Baldick, 3rd ed., xi–xxiii. Oxford: Oxford University Press.

Bordwell, David, and Kristin Thompson. 2001. *Film art: An introduction*. 6th ed. New York: McGraw Hill.

Bronfen, Elisabeth. 2014. Cinema of the Gothic extreme. In *The Cambridge companion to the modern Gothic*, ed. Jerrold E. Hogle, 107–122. Cambridge: Cambridge University Press.

Edwards, Justin, and Johan Höglund, eds. 2019. *B-movie Gothic: International perspectives.* Edinburgh: Edinburgh University Press.

Frayling, Christopher. 2013. Foreword. In *Gothic: The dark heart of film*, ed. James Bell, 5–7. London: BFI.

Gordon, Mel. 1988. *The Grand Guignol: Theatre of fear and terror.* New York: Amok Press.

Gothic, adjective and noun. 2020. *Oxford English dictionary online.* Oxford: Oxford University Press. https://www.oed.com/. Accessed 10 Oct 2020.

Grant, Barry Keith. 2007. *Film genre: From iconography to ideology.* Reprint. (Introductions to film studies, Vol. 33). London: Wallflower.

Halberstam, J. 1995. *Skin shows: Gothic horror and the technology of monsters.* Durham: Duke University Press.

Hand, Richard J., and Jay McRoy, eds. 2020. *Gothic film: An Edinburgh companion.* Edinburgh: Edinburgh University Press.

Hodkinson, Paul. 2007. Gothic music and subculture. In *The Routledge companion to Gothic*, ed. Catherine Spooner and Emma McEvoy, 260–269. London: Routledge.

Hutchings, Peter. 1996. Tearing your soul apart: Horror's new monsters. In *Modern Gothic: A reader*, ed. Victor Sage and Allan Lloyd Smith, 89–103. Manchester: Manchester University Press.

Kappelhoff, Hermann, and Jan-Hendrik Bakels. 2018. Das Melodram. In *Handbuch Filmgenre*, ed. Marcus Stiglegger, 591–607. Wiesbaden: Springer VS.

Kavka, Misha. 2002. The Gothic on screen. In *The Cambridge companion to Gothic fiction*, ed. Jerrold E. Hogle, 209–228. Cambridge: Cambridge University Press.

Krämer, Felix, ed. 2012a. *Schwarze Romantik – Von Goya bis Max Ernst* [on the occasion of the exhibition at the Städel-Museum, Frankfurt on the Main, 16 Sept. 2012–20 Jan. 2013]. Ostfildern: Hatje Cantz.

———. 2012b. Schwarze Romantik. Eine Annäherung. In *Schwarze Romantik – Von Goya bis Max Ernst* [on the occasion of the exhibition at the Städel-museum, Frankfurt on the Main, 16 Sept. 2012–20 Jan. 2013], ed. by Felix Krämer, 14–28. Ostfildern: Hatje Cantz.

Langford, Barry. 2005. *Film genre: Hollywood and beyond.* Edinburgh: Edinburgh University Press.

Neibaur, James L. 2020. Gothic cinema during the silent era. In *Gothic film: An Edinburgh companion*, ed. Richard J. Hand and Jay McRoy, 11–20. Edinburgh: Edinburgh University Press.

Punter, David. 1996. *The literature of terror. A history of Gothic fictions from 1765 to the present day. 1. The Gothic tradition.* 2nd ed. London: Longman.

Radcliffe, Ann. 1826. On the supernatural in poetry. *New Monthly Magazine* 16 (1): 145–152.

Spooner, Catherine. 2004. *Fashioning Gothic bodies.* Manchester: Manchester University Press.

———. 2006. *Contemporary Gothic.* London: Reaktion Books.

———. 2007. Gothic in the twentieth century. In *The Routledge companion to Gothic*, ed. Catherine Spooner and Emma McEvoy, 38–47. London: Routledge.

———. 2013. Gothic lifestyle. In *The Gothic world*, ed. Glennis Byron and Dale Townshend, 441–453. London: Routledge.

———. 2017. *Post-millennial Gothic: Comedy, romance and the rise of happy Gothic*. London: Bloomsbury Academic.

Stiglegger, Marcus. 2018. Grenzüberschreitungen. In *Exkursionen in den Abgrund der Filmgeschichte: Der Horrorfilm*. Berlin: Martin Schmitz Verlag.

———. 2020. Genrediskurs. Zur Aktualität des Genrebegriffs in der Filmwissenschaft. In *Handbuch Filmgenre. Geschichte – Ästhetik – Theorie*, ed. Marcus Stiglegger, 3–16. Wiesbaden: Springer.

Townshend, Dale. 2016. Gothic and the cultural sources of horror, 1740–1820. In *Horror: A literary history*, ed. Xavier Aldana Reyes, 19–51. London: The British Library.

van Elferen, Isabella. 2012. *Gothic music: The sounds of the uncanny*. Cardiff: University of Wales Press.

Warwick, Alexandra. 2007. Victorian Gothic. In *The Routledge companion to Gothic*, ed. Catherine Spooner and Emma McEvoy, 29–37. London: Routledge.

Film

Chilling Adventures of Sabrina. TV series. USA 2018–2020. Created by: Roberto Aguirre-Sacasa. Archie Comics Publications/Warner Bros. Television.

Crimson Peak. Canada/USA/Mexico 2015. Directed by Guillermo del Toro. Double Dare You/Legendary Entertainment.

Dracula. UK 1958. Directed by Terence Fisher. Hammer Films.

Dracula. TV-miniseries. UK 2020. Created by Mark Gatiss and Steven Moffat. Hartswood Films/British Broadcasting Corporation/Netflix.

Edward Scissorhands. USA 1990. Directed by Tim Burton. Twentieth Century Fox.

Frankenstein. USA 1931. Directed by James Whale. Universal Pictures.

Harry Potter and the Prisoner of Azkaban. UK/USA 2004. Directed by Alfonso Cuarón. Warner Bros. et al.

Night of the Living Dead. USA 1968. Directed by George A. Romero. Image Ten.

Only Lovers Left Alive. UK et al. 2013. Directed by Jim Jarmusch. Recorded Picture Company et al.

Peeping Tom. UK 1960. Directed by Michael Powell. Michael Powell.

Penny Dreadful. TV series. Ireland/UK/USA 2014–2016. Created by John Logan. Desert Wolf Productions/Neal Street Productions.

Psycho. USA 1960. Directed by Alfred Hitchcock. Shamley Productions.

The Addams Family. TV series. USA 1964–1966. Created by David Levy. Filmways Television.

The Haunting of Hill House. TV series. USA 2018. Created by Mike Flanagan. FlanaganFilm et al.

The Munsters. TV series. USA 1964–1966. Created by Allan Burns and Chris Hayward. CBS/Kayro-Vue Productions.

True Blood. TV series. USA 2008–2014. Created by Alan Ball. Your Face Goes Here Entertainment/Home Box Office.

True Detective. TV series. USA, 2014–2019. Created by Nic Pizzolatto. Anonymous Content/HBO Entertainment/Passenger.

Elements, Motifs, Themes

If film-historical caesurae leave traces in the history of Gothic cinema, as will become clear in the following chapter, this is equally true for the history of culture, media, technology, and science. Gothic favors the history of minorities, the forgotten, and the oppressed, and paints bleak apocalyptic scenarios rather than celebrating great achievements. For example, Victorian Gothic processes the groundbreaking revolutions of the time, such as industrialization, urbanization, mechanization, and scientification. In contrast to the euphoric belief in progress dominant at the time, however, Gothic strikes a different note and articulates concerns and fears. The dark alleys of the rapidly expanding cities offer space for dubious undertakings, shady characters, drugs, prostitution and serial murder. Neither the scientists' ethical consciousness nor their sense of responsibility can keep pace with the dizzyingly rapid progress of science. Knowledge and technology are abused or prove to be forces beyond human comprehension.

Gothic, for example, thematises the decisive change in the role of humans in the world as well as in the relationship of species to one another that was brought about by Charles Darwin's theory of evolution by natural selection. Instead of the comparatively manageable biblical time periods, it set the dizzying scale of geological time, in which the human species plays an infinitesimal role. Moreover, it leveraged the notion that the human species is the result of divine design. Instead, it is now ranked as a link in a chain of animal origin – the metamorphic result of an accidental development that is not yet complete and whose future is open. In the Gothic, this fundamental uncertainty translates into diverse transformation scenarios between humans and animals from werewolves to cat people to vampires to Dr. Moreau's chimeras (see Luckhurst 2016, pp. 122–127). In addition to the boundary between animals and humans, the boundary between the dead and the

© The Author(s), under exclusive license to Springer Fachmedien
Wiesbaden GmbH, part of Springer Nature 2023
K. Rein, *Gothic Cinema*, https://doi.org/10.1007/978-3-658-40721-6_2

living also became permeable from about 1850 onward, among other things in the course of the spread of spiritualism, a religious movement that assumes the continued disembodied existence of the deceased among us.

Looking at the history of the twentieth century, for example, the classic horror films of the Universal Studios, which experienced their heyday in the 1930s and early 1940s, can be interpreted as processing the fears and anxieties that were tied to the political atmosphere of the time. The decline in their popularity after the U.S.A.'s entry into the Second World War can be attributed, among other things, to the fact that the enemy now took on a concrete form and fears could be articulated differently and more directly than in the fantastic metaphorics of the Gothic (see Kavka 2002, p. 212 f.). In adaptations of canonical works – first and foremost *Dracula* – cultural-historical influences can be worked out particularly well in comparison. For example, the U.S.-American uncertainty about a resurgence of relations with Europe that followed a phase of political isolation in the second half of the nineteenth century translates in 1931 into Tod Browing's *Dracula,* whose Hungarian lead Bela Lugosi speaks with a distinctive accent in what is the first Gothic sound film. Francis Ford Coppola's 1992 adaptation of the same novel, in contrast, is noticeably influenced by the association of bodily fluids, especially blood, with HIV and AIDS. Here, microscopic images of blood are repeatedly superimposed or inserted, referring more to the laboratory context of testing for communicable diseases than to vampirism. To stop at the correlation of historical events with the monsters of the Gothic would not do justice to its aesthetic and narrative richness or its effect and function (see Kavka 2002, p. 212 f.). Although threats from outside or elements of the cultural imaginary translate into the artifacts of the Gothic, its timeless appeal comes primarily from the fact that its characters and narratives, as Misha Kavka (2002, p. 213) writes, "give[s] voice to anxieties from within".

Gothic fiction draws our attention to the darker sides of human nature and society. Its narratives revolve around power and its abuse, around the tension between old and new structures, systems and ways of thinking, and between the normative and everything that stands in opposition to it. The Gothic favors taboo subjects such as mental illness, violence, emotional dependence, sexual assault, or incest. Mental illness, death and love are closely interwoven here. An absolute sense of threat characterizes Gothic – an inescapable feeling of being at the mercy of tyrannical, or monstrous characters, architectural aberrations, meteorological phenomena or one's own psychological and emotional determinacy.

Fred Botting associates the affinity of the Gothic with the negative sides of human existence with its cultural and scientific devaluation as trash. The lack of recognition given to the Gothic since its inception allowed for greater freedom on the one hand, while on the other, its own status as an outcast genre itself was thematised in the Gothic. "To study the worst that has been thought and said," Botting (1996, p. 3) writes, "manifests a different attitude toward value. […], a recognition that what is cast out by cultures is often as telling us what is celebrated by them." The Gothic has not only a tendency towards sensationalism, violence and *gore*, but also to playful self-parody (Townshend 2014, p. 24). It is also characterized by a high degree of self-reflexivity, self-irony, and intertextuality.

Traditional Gothic fiction, writes David Punter in *The Literature of Terror* (1996, vol. 1, p. 1), is the genre "of the haunted castle, of heroines preyed on by unspeakable terrors, of the blackly lowering villain, of ghosts, vampires, monsters and werewolves". In addition, there is an opulent aesthetic that Jack Halberstam (1995, p. 2) has called "ornamental excess" and that is particularly effective in film, where it can unfold visually. An element that establishes a clear association with the Gothic can be as simple as a dark cloud passing in front of a full moon. However, enumerating such concrete markers of the Gothic is not the concern of this chapter. It is more useful to identify its characteristics on a more abstract level, especially if a reduction of the Gothic to its traditional aesthetics with pointed arches and heavy velvet curtains is to be avoided.

In this case, two main characteristics of the Gothic can be identified: an obsession with the past, often accompanied by a particular temporality, and the setting in claustrophobic places (which can also include a physical confinement, but primarily refers to an oppressive atmosphere). The past is typically a dark and traumatic one. It holds a tight grip on the characters and determines their present emotions, psyches, and actions. The oppressive past and the claustrophobic spaces reinforce each other, writes Chris Baldick (2009, p. xix), creating "an impression of sickening descent into disintegration". In the most succinct and simple definition of the Gothic he provides, Baldick (2009, p. xx) summarizes: "Gothic fiction is characteristically obsessed with old buildings as sites of human decay."

The appearance of monsters is often mentioned as a third characteristic, but it proves to be problematic especially with regard to postmodern and contemporary Gothic cinema, because in the twenty-first century vampires and werewolves become friends, lovers and family members. But even classic Gothic cinema already breaks down binary categories of "good" and "evil" when it draws so-called monsters as ambivalent figures, for example, as victims of individual as well as societal abuse in James Whale's *Frankenstein* (1931). Like Frankenstein's creature, other monsters of Gothic cinema are often resurrected from the dead. The return – whether of the (supposedly) deceased, of trauma, or of sinister events – is another central motif of Gothic cinema, conditioned by its obsession with the past. The Uncanny as a motif can also be traced back to recurrency – in this case, the return of the repressed. Gothic's self-referentiality and, in part, its affinity for media – especially recording media that store images, text, and sound – also grow out of its reference to the past. In the following, the most important characteristics of the Gothic will be discussed before the next chapter turns to its history in film.

2.1 The Past

The most striking element is the Gothic's reference to the past. This can already be found in the history of the genre and of the term "Gothic" itself, as it originally referred to the Goths, an East Germanic population group that played a role in the fall of the Roman Empire and in the formation of medieval Europe. While this reference served in the Renaissance to establish a tradition of opposition to the Roman Empire, which was constructed as barbaric and unchristian, relatively little was known about the historical Goths at the time (see Punter 1996, vol. 1, p. 4; on the historiography of the Gothic, see Silver 2014). In eighteenth-century England, "Gothic" became a catch-all term for everything that was medieval on the one hand and opposed to the Roman on the other (see, e.g., Botting 2012; Sowerby 2012, p. 26). "Gothic" here generalized "the Middle Ages" into a culture constructed primarily as barbaric and crude, in contrast to the classical culture of Roman antiquity understood as cultured, elegant, and refined. This is also one of the meanings of the term listed in the *Oxford English Dictionary* (2020): "Barbarous, rude, uncouth, unpolished, in bad taste. Of temper: savage." Initially, then, connoted negatively with a lack of civilizing progress, the meaning of the term "Gothic" changed in English poetry in the second half of the eighteenth century. The savagery and primitiveness associated with the Gothic was now reinterpreted as positive and energetic – and as something English culture lacked (Punter 1996, vol. 1, p. 5 f.). This reevaluation of Gothic culture connoted it as resilient, democratic, and Christian – in contrast to the pagan decadence of the Roman Imperial period (Townshend 2014, p. 27).

"Gothic," then, has always referenced partly fictional history access to which is limited and that serves the self-determination of one's own culture by being constructed either as its counterpart or as an idealized predecessor, with positive connotations predominating in English culture since the late eighteenth century. This reference to the past is found in the Gothic novel, among other things, as (fictional) intertextuality: Horace Walpole's *The Castle of Otranto* (1764) purports to be a reprint of a medieval tale found in the north of England in the library of a traditional Catholic family. Only with the second edition did Walpole reveal himself as the author of the novel that was thus marked as contemporary (see Townshend 2014, p. 12 f.). Moreover, the subtitle added therein, "A Gothic Story," identified *The Castle of Otranto* not only as the first work of the genre, but also – in the conceptual tradition described above – as one that addresses the superstition and brutality of the Middle Ages. Such fictional self-historicizations have pervaded the Gothic ever since, from Ann Radcliffe's *A Sicilian Romance* (1790) to Umberto Eco's *Il nome della rosa* (1980).

Another common form of establishing an explicit historical reference is the designation as a look back on historical events through a framing in the now, as it occurs, for example, in Ken Russel's *Gothic* (1986). This feature film fictionalizes the events at the Villa Diodati by the Lake Geneva in 1816, to which two defining works of Gothic fiction can be traced back: John Polidori's *The Vampyre* (1816) and Mary Shelley's *Frankenstein* (1818) (see Sect 3.3). In *Gothic,* the events during this sojourn steeped in history are framed by shots of tourists visiting the villa in the present day.[1] Another example is Christopher Priest's novel *The Prestige* (1995), whose main action is set in the late nineteenth century and which is recounted as a look back starting in a narrative strand set in the present. Here, the descendants of the two rival Victorian-era magicians reconstruct their life stories through their diaries. At the end, however, a character from this past emerges in the now and thus torpedoes both the fictional status of the past, seemingly fantastic events and the concept of a closed past per se. In the Gothic, the past is not gone by, but permeates the present and intervenes in it.

The Gothic brings the past into the present and shows that the two are inextricably interwoven, interrupting, contextualizing and perspectivizing each other. The past here is dramatic, dark and violent, determining all actions and characters in the present, like a heavy weight that they carry with them and cannot shed. "The past chokes the present," writes Catherine Spooner (2006, p. 18 f.), "prevents progress and the march toward personal or social enlightenment." Accompanied by a sense of loss as well as an "antiquarian" fascination, the Gothic paints the past as a threat that can break into the present at any time – in the shape of secrets, curses, or recurring supposed or actual deaths (typically in the form of ghosts). This threat distinguishes the Gothic, for example, from historical fiction, which also revolves around the past (Aldana Reyes 2020, p. 18).

---

[1] This, too, is of course a fictionalization. In fact, the villa is (and was in 1986, when the film was shot) privately owned and is not open for visits.

2.2   Media

Often overlooked is the fact that the Gothic's obsession with the past consistently leads to an affinity with media – after all, they store and preserve the past, and in the process create their own temporality. In addition, characters in the Gothic often cannot access their emotional world or articulate their needs, which is why this inner world is also often mediated through media rather than presenting itself as personal and immediate. If the works of the Gothic do not (in the tradition of *The Castle of Otranto*) pass themselves off as medieval manuscripts and thus take their own mediality as an occasion to reinforce their reference to the past, then it is media within the narratives – texts, photographs, film or sound recordings – through which the fictional past is revealed. Accordingly, we often encounter the investigative characters of the Gothic in libraries or archives, where they find objects, writings, and memories, either purposefully or by chance. Often these alter the course of the story by adding important elements, questioning the identities of characters, or rearranging their constellations. In Gothic, media become intervening, independent actors that sometimes seem to appear on their own. Gothic's reference to the past is thus conveyed not only through historical settings, but also through incursions of the past into the present – whether figuratively, in the form of ghosts that intervene in the everyday lives of the living, or, more generally, in the form of the past that characters cannot shake off. Time lines loop and overlap themselves in the Gothic.

Beyond the level of temporality, the Gothic is interested in media insofar as they enable perceptions that would not be possible without them. Since the nineteenth century, optical media such as microscopy or X-ray photography have enabled the perception of objects never before seen or imagined – be they armies of bacteria in drinking water or the interior of the human body, which previously could only be seen if its integrity was destroyed. Such glimpses raised the question of what other worlds might be hidden beyond the material limits of human perception, and spurred corresponding fantasies.

Technical media also expanded the possibilities of movement and communication. While telegraphy – the communication medium of the nineteenth century *par excellence* – accelerated the exchange of written messages many times over compared to the exchange of letters, telephony for the first time made it possible to communicate in real-time despite geographical distance. However, the presence of disembodied voices of physically absent persons was perceived as uncanny and invasive from the very beginning. The telephone was also the first medium to open up a virtual space into which the interlocutors enter for the duration of the call. "Whoever makes a telephone call," writes Arno Meteling (2006, p. 298; translation: KR), goes with an unprotected sense to a place that cannot be seen and is therefore unpredictable. [...] Besides the fright of the strange voice or the unidentifiable noise at the other end of the telephone line, there is also the polyphony and cacophony of the background noise in the channel itself.

The telephone also introduced the electronic noise – a real acoustic phenomenon that has no equivalent outside the medium itself (see Enns 2005, p. 15 f.): After picking up the receiver and before a connection was established, nothing else could be heard on the line but the medium itself, which manifested itself acoustically in crackling, rustling, and hissing. Already since the invention of the telephone, attempts were made to identify signals in the noise, the origin of which was often assumed to be in other spheres of existence (see, for example, the autobiography of Alexander Graham Bell's assistant, Thomas Watson from 1926, p. 81 f.). If the telephone enabled hitherto unthinkable real-time communication with the physically absent across geographical distances, why should it not also be able to establish connections across states of being? Technical media have always been suspected of being able to act as spiritualist mediums as well (see Sconce 2000, especially pp. 7–11). Famous in this context is an announcement (never tranformed into reality as far as we know) by Thomas Alva Edison to construct a device that could make phone calls to the world of the dead (Forbes 1920).

Other media also seemed to have a special relationship with the realm of the dead (on media in horror films, see Meteling 2006). If the phonograph preserved voices beyond the death of their owners, photography and film preserve optical doubles. "It is said that all photographs [...] are like spirit photographs;" writes Christopher Frayling (2013, p. 5), "by extension, all motion pictures become ghost stories". If photographs, for example in conjunction with microscopy and X-rays, can record something in our immediate environment that human eyes cannot see, why should they not register other spheres that escape our perception? Spirit photography, popular around 1900, represents an effort to make ghosts visible using optical media technology. It is based on the assumption, popularized by spiritualism, that the deceased continue to dwell among us, but are invisible to our eyes unless they are enticed by (personal) mediums to manifest themselves. But why shouldn't technical media be able to take on this role? In Gothic films, such suspicions are made manifest, for example when the protagonist in *The Asphyx* (1983) tries to photographically capture escaping souls at the moment of death, or when the camera in *Shutter* (2004) registers ghosts next to the photographed living. If *The Asphyx* refers to practices of spirit photography, *The Haunting* (1999), *Paranormal Activity* (2007) or *The Conjuring* (2013) refer to attempts to document hauntings with the help of technical recording media that continue to this day (on ghosts and media, see Meteling 2006, pp. 277–309).

In its early days, film was also associated with a parallel world of ghosts. The Russian writer Maxim Gorky described cinema as a "Kingdom of Shadows" that was "reminiscent of nightmares, of curses, of evil sorcerers" (Pacatus 1995, p. 13 f.). Other contemporaries also described going to the movies as an uncanny experience and the Cinematograph as a medium that resurrected the dead (e.g., Badreux 1896; cited in Solomon 2012, p. 12). Gothic cinema thus proves to have always been self-referential on a medial level as well, since cinema itself produces a partially fantastic parallel world in which fictions can be experienced (see Bronfen 2014, p. 108). Film recordings preserve ghostly doubles who are condemned to the eternal repetition of their actions. The uncanniness of these doubles in their virtual parallel world accompanies media consumption subliminally, but becomes explicit in Gothic and horror films.

If the telephone had opened up the first virtual space, radio technology in the early twentieth century implied a saturation of the seemingly empty space around us with invisible signals that could be registered by media sensitive to them. Again, the question soon arose whether technical media and personal mediums might not be equally susceptible to these signals. Electromagnetic radio waves served as a model for the transmission of thoughts. The first registration and visualization of brain activity using electroencephalography in the 1920s also spurred attempts to build, conversely, devices that could control brain activity or even thoughts by means of electrical impulses. At the same time, scientists and radio pioneers of that time saw a relationship between radio waves and "thought waves" and consequently tried to construct receiving devices for the invisible thoughts imagined as electromagnetic. Convinced that only the right frequency had to be found, radio pioneers such as Manfred von Ardenne or Oliver Lodge undertook such experiments (see Hagen 2002, pp. 232–235 and 2009).

While telegraphy served as a model for spiritualists to illustrate their communication with the realm of the dead, and telephony was primarily analogized with schizophrenia – the pathological hearing of disembodied voices – radio transmission primarily provoked associations with telepathy (on the connection between media and the Uncanny, see Sconce 2000). While projects such as Edison's *spirit phone* were positively charged with hope, fiction still illustrates their dark sides today, for example, when telephones establish unwanted contact with beings from other worlds. Thus the protagonist (Richard Gere) in *The Mothman Prophecies* (2002) receives calls from a mysterious supernatural being that predicts catastrophes. The phone that continues to ring after its cable has been ripped out of the wall that we see in this film echoes a famous sequence from *A Nightmare on Elm Street* (1984), where a disconnected phone puts through a call from dead serial killer Freddy Krueger (Robert Englund). At the same time, the supernatural connection here erases the medial separation of body and voice when the telephone receiver transforms into the mouth of the killer, whose tongue lasciviously licks the lips of the protagonist (Heather Langenkamp) (see Rein 2012, pp. 87–101). Here, the telephone establishes contact with the physically absent not only in other places, but also in other spheres of existence. It thus confirms the suspicion, particularly virulent in the late nineteenth century, that technical media could also be spiritualistic mediums. Not only do they therefore often appear in contexts in which specific attempts are made to contact the deceased, such as in the films *The Changeling* (1980), *Insidious* (2010) or *The Conjuring* (2013). They also spontaneously reveal their supernatural abilities in moments of dys- or rather hyper-function in sequences like the ones described above.

In numerous other examples, Gothic cinema makes explicit the uncanny implications of media that have accompanied them since their early days. While photography, phonography, telephony, and film were clearly more suspect in Victorian times than they are today, media have retained their uncanny potential in Gothic and horror films to this day. On the one hand, non-technical media can also be uncanny, for example, when old books summon demons. On the other hand, the repertoire of media technology is constantly updated by the addition of contemporary media: Since the 1980s, technical media from television to computers to smartphones have not only increasingly invaded our homes and everyday lives, but also Gothic cinema. In the late twentieth and early twenty-first centuries, ghosts inhabit technical media instead of ancient houses: the most famous examples are probably Tobe Hooper's *Poltergeist* (1982), in which ghosts make contact with the living through the television set and Hideo Nakata's *Ring* (1998). Here, watching a videotape dooms one to death after a period of 7 days. As we learn at the end, the spirit of the murdered girl whose ghost created this video then manifests itself physically and literally crawls out of the TV set (see Fig. 4.10) connected to the supernatural VHS tape. In 1981, in Sam Raimi's *The Evil Dead* a tape recording conjured up demons. In Gothic cinema, then, media not only preserve people beyond their deaths. The doppelgangers they produce also develop a life of their own and can escape from these media into reality.

Ghosts also spread through radio waves or the Internet, for example in *White Noise* (2005) or *Pulse* (2006). In the Japanese *Chakushin ari* (2003, US remake *One Missed Call* 2008), characters receive calls or voicemails on their cell phones that they themselves make in the near future, at the time of their unexpected deaths. In *Unfriended* (2014), the ghost of a high school student who committed suicide as a result of an incident of cyber-bullying invades a group chat on Skype a year after her death, murdering her tormentors one by one or forcing them to commit suicide. The film also has the peculiarity that it is conveyed exclusively through the computer screens of the respective characters that show the video chats and social media platforms, which they use. Here, the film aesthetic itself is updated along with the thematized media. In the age of teen suicides resulting from social media bullying and hacking attacks on government servers, the Internet also becomes a site of the Gothic and a source of threat (see Alexander 2013). The anthology *Digital Horror*, edited by Linnie Blake and Xavier Aldana Reyes, is dedicated to twenty-first century media horror under the conditions of digitization of film production and of the everyday lives of consumers. With the ubiquity of digital media technologies, the possibilities of networking and surveillance come into focus, just as paranoia comes to a head in terms of simulation and hyperreality (Blake and Aldana Reyes 2016, p. 3).

Beyond the occurrence of specific media in Gothic cinema, Misha Kavka (2002, p. 228) identifies in it a specific media component that aims at a spiritualist rather than a technical concept of media:

> Rather than understanding film in this instance as a technical medium for representing an independent social, historical, or personal reality, film in the Gothic mode must be understood in the other sense of "medium," the sense given to us precisely by a literary history of ghost stories, séances, and paranormal activities. Gothic film should thus not be thought of as a medium of representation, but as a medium through which things are allowed to pass, from the past into the present, from death into life, from the beyond to here and back again.

Here, too, it is a matter of amalgamating the functions of technical media with those of spiritualistic mediums. Instead of understanding Gothic cinema as a visualization of cultural and individual anxieties and pathologies, Kavka (2002, p. 228) argues for imagining it as a spiritualist medium in a séance, passively delivering messages from other worlds. These articulate themselves less in the form of specific characters or narratives, but rather reach us on a subliminal level, mediated through the visual code of the Gothic. The media-specific possibilities of audiovisual media have proven to be particularly suitable for processing collective fears related to the unrepresentable. Thus, film is the most effective medium of the Gothic to date, having developed a conventionalized, iconographic language to convey its ambivalence (see Kavka 2002, p. 228).

2.3   Spaces

Gothic cinema is not only subject to a particular temporality, but also takes place in specific spaces. One of its central elements therefore is the house. If in the traditional version it is a large, dark, (partly) ruinous, haunted house, since the 1960s, it has transformed without losing its prominence. For example, the Overlook Hotel in

Stanley Kubrick's *The Shining* (1980, based on Stephen King's 1977 novel) is recognizable as a haunted house, where past and present intertwine and Jack Torrance (Jack Nicholson) interacts with figures from times past. Be it the Overlook Hotel, the haunted house in *The Haunting of Hill House* (2018), Dracula's castle, or the planet where the spaceship Nostromo lands in *Alien* (1979) – the spaces of Gothic film are remote and therefore as difficult to reach as they are to leave. Here protagonists find themselves isolated and trapped in an atmosphere of moral, psychological and physical decay. Be it castles, ruins, abandoned monasteries or mansions – the places of the Gothic are labyrinthine, strange and disorienting. They contain secret passages, hidden chambers, locked doors, and dangers lurking in the dark that often reveal themselves to the characters as slowly and gradually (or not at all) as they do to the recipients.

Mountain and moor landscapes or forests also appear frequently as settings. And they too are claustrophobic and disorienting in Gothic films. Autumn and winter are the preferred seasons, which is why swaths of fog, curtains of rain, or snowstorms characterize the landscapes (see Aldana Reyes 2020, p. 19). For example, the fog on the family estate in *The Others* (2001) is so dense that the protagonist (Nicole Kidman) cannot leave it (00:52). Meteorological phenomena in Gothic cinema, like light and darkness and their interplay in the shadows, reflect the mental state of the characters or have their own agency. In Tim Burton's *Sleepy Hollow* (1999), the mists form into hands and extinguish with their fingers the flames of torches meant to illuminate the edge of the forest (00:19). Burton's artificial design also shapes nature, such as the iconic twisted tree in *Sleepy Hollow,* which serves as a gateway to hell. It recalls the highly stylized studio landscapes in the history of Gothic cinema from German expressionist film to Universal Horror to the films of Mario Bava and Terence Fisher.

Since the novels of Charles Dickens, Gothic has also taken place in the sparsely lit cobbled streets of the European metropolis. Here, the city is labyrinthine, claustrophobic, dominated by darkness and shadows, squalid and sick (see Warwick 2007, p. 34). It provides a space in which, for example, the misdemeanors of a Mr. Hyde or a Dorian Gray go unnoticed and their executors stay anonymous, and at the same time it reflects their moral depravity when it metaphorically stands in for troubled states of mind (see Wasson 2013, p. 136). Fog-shrouded London at the time of Jack the Ripper's murders is an archetypal setting of the Urban Gothic film from Hitchcock's *The Lodger* (1927) to the German Edgar Wallace films of the 1960s to David Lynch's *The Elephant Man* (1980). Urban Gothic is more interested in human monsters than supernatural ones. It is related to crime fiction and refuses to separate criminals from the setting that creates and nurtures them (see Cassuto 2018, p. 166). At times, the anonymity of the big city blurs the line between human and supernatural monsters, for example in *Underworld* (2003), where vampires establish their own hidden subculture among humans. Decaying urban landscapes are particularly staged in the form of the ruinous city abandoned after the collapse of civilization in the post-apocalyptic (zombie) film.

In the 1980s, horror moves to the periphery of cities in Gothic and horror films, subverting the supposed middle-class safety and familiality of the suburbs. The traditionally historically charged sites of the Gothic are now replaced by the virtually history-less, suburban uniformity of terraced houses. Instead of coming from the outside, from distant places, the threat now comes from the immediate surroundings – from the community or family, if not from one's own personal crisis. "Horror here inevitably begins at home, or at least very close to it," writes Bernice Murphy (2009, p. 2) in *The Suburban Gothic in American Popular Culture*, "and in that sense the sub-genre continues the uneasy fascination with the connection between living environment and psychology [...]". Functioning as an externalization of the protagonists' psyche, suburbia becomes the site of gruesome, inexplicable, or supernatural events, to which the characters of the Suburban Gothic usually react with denial: "The most characteristic response to uncanny events is to close the curtains and keep quiet about it" (Murphy 2009, p. 3). In the Suburban Gothic, hauntings or dark pasts are primarily something that must be concealed from the neighbors in order to maintain a semblance of conformist normality.

It remains to be said that the places and spaces of Gothic cinema are diverse. From natural and weather phenomena in the service of dark forces, to labyrinthine, claustrophobic castles or the swamps of Louisiana, to urban alleys or the town houses of suburbia, what they have in common, however, is that they are disorienting and are only revealed in fragments. Sometimes they seem to change or grow over the course of the films as new spaces open up. The spaces of Gothic cinema prove to be both an externalization of the mentally unstable state of the characters and an attack on it.

2.4   Monsters

The prominent appearance of monsters is often considered an element that distinguishes horror and Gothic. However, their appearance is by no means limited to these genres, which is why, for example, Xavier Aldana Reyes (2020, p. 15) warns against counting monsters among the features of Gothic cinema. We also encounter monsters and supernatural beings in science fiction, fairy tales, or fantasy, in short, in fantastic films in general. That beings or humans coded as monsters play a central role in the Gothic, however, is beyond question. Especially in film, thanks to the Universal Horror Cycle, monsters have been foregrounded since the 1930s.

At the time of the literary Gothic Revival, Charles Darwin's concept of the mutability of different species and their possible transitions into each other, among other things, fueled fantasies of negative evolution in the sense of degeneration, such as for example H. G. Wells' *The Island of Dr. Moreau* (1896). Roger Luckhurst also attributes Gothic and horror's predilection for transformations, degeneration, and slime to the fact that, after Darwin, the human form had to be understood as metamorphic to a previously unimagined extent: "In late Victorian Gothic fiction," he writes, "this unnerving malleability of human beings and the anxiety about the survival of an animalistic core explains the twin obsessions of the horror mode with degeneration and slime." (Luckhurst 2016, p. 122). These include, for example, the slime prominent in the works of H. P. Lovecraft, which has since become an integral part of the aesthetics of splatter, horror, and science fiction films, or the animalistic traits of Mr. Hyde, which migrated into comics reimagined as The Hulk under the terms of the early 1960s: If in 1886, against the backdrop of the development of organic chemistry in the second half of the nineteenth century, Dr. Henry Jekyll temporarily becomes Edward Hyde as part of a self-experiment with chemicals, Dr. Bruce Banner's transformation into Hulk in 1962, after the experiences of World War II, is triggered by an accident with a bomb that releases gamma radiation. Today, we encounter a version of Hulk in the mainstream in the *Avengers* film series, which is one of the most expensive as well as financially successful blockbuster productions of the recent years.

This exemplifies the transformation of monsters as well as their transmedia proliferation. They are unstable and hybrid. In the course of the nineteenth century alone, as Alexandra Warwick has demonstrated using the example of the vampire, an increasing ability to metamorphose can be observed: John Polidori's "The Vampyre" appears in 1818 as a seductive dandy à la Lord Byron. Some 30 years later, James Malcolm Rymer describes his *Varney the Vampire* (1847) as physically repulsive but consistent in form. J. Sheridan Le Fanu's Carmilla appears in 1872 as either a young woman, a cat-like creature, a ghost, or a black mist. Finally, Bram Stoker's paradigmatic vampire Dracula, another 25 years later, is not only fully metamorphic but also infectious, that is, able to trigger physical transformations in the bodies of others (Warwick 2007, p. 35). This observation could be continued to the present day, when almost every film and series presents its own vampirology and mythology, endowing its monsters with new attributes and abilities.

In particular, the canonical monsters that Victorian England produced and that also inscribed themselves (audio)visually into the cultural imaginary with the Universal Horror Cycle, symbolize the conflict between opposites such as inside and outside, male and female, body and mind, own and foreign, bourgeoisie and aristocracy, and so on. The classic monsters of Gothic cinema blend opposing

signifiers in deviant bodies (Halberstam 1995, pp. 1, 3). For example, Dracula is
sexually ambivalent because, on the one hand, he penetrates female and male bodies alike with his phallic teeth in a masculinely coded function but also because,
when Mina Harker drinks his blood, he himself becomes a bleeding character,
which has female connotations. Jekyll and Hyde – two characters of different
social standing and habitus, with opposing moral views – share one body, while
Frankenstein's creature is literally composed of parts of different people. In the
Hammer production *Dr. Jekyll and Sister Hyde* (1971), the sexual component of
the two souls residing within one breast is as spelled out as the transphobia is
implicit: here, after consuming his elixir, Jekyll becomes a woman whom he passes
off to the neighbors as his sister. This transgressive, sexually unbridled "sister"
ultimately attempts to seize control of the shared body and to displace the male
part. Thus, in 1971, Stevenson's struggle between barbarism and civilization
becomes Jekyll's struggle against his feminine side. It ends – apparently due to the
incompatibility of the two – in death, with Jekyll and Hyde perishing at the moment
of transformation, so that the corpse literally becomes the amalgam of both characters. Only in death is the polar conflict resolved and both sides externalize simultaneously in the hybrid body.

A common reading understands monsters in Gothic as metaphors. "Gothic fiction," writes Jack Halberstam (1995, p. 2) in *Skin Shows,* "is a technology of subjectivity, one which produces the deviant subjectivities opposite which the normal,
the healthy, and pure can be known.". They thus serve, at least in traditional Gothic,
as a negative foil against which the normative, the morally acceptable, and the
socially respected emerge. The thesis that monsters embody the Other as a conceptual category around which our anxieties about "normality" revolve, which became
particularly prominent in horror film studies of the late 1980s and 1990s, needs an
update in the form of greater differentiation. Xavier Alada Reyes (2020, p. 23)
points out that it is no longer tenable in an era when monsters are often associated
with queerness in popular culture and increasingly presented as sympathetic.
Insofar as it can be assumed that queerness is shaking off its connotation with deviant and prohibited sexuality in Western societies, even monsters coded as queer can
no longer be read as incompatible with social norms, as was still possible 25 years
ago when Halberstam published the text cited above. Rather, we need to take into
account that the discourse around queerness should not be about de-discriminating
normatively deviant identities and desires but, conversely, about demanding a jus-
tification for the demands for normality (see Aldana Reyes 2020, p. 23). Against
this background, then, it seems outdated to understand twenty-first century monsters as the radically Other.

If on the one hand supernatural monsters are increasingly humanized, on the other hand monsters in Gothic cinema also appear in human form. A gendered example can be found in Female Gothic, in which we typically encounter a male villain embodying the oppression of patriarchy, who, in the tradition of Bluebeard, often turns out to be a woman-killer. Like Montoni in Ann Radcliffe's classic Gothic novel, *The Mysteries of Udolpho,* he is often driven by financial motivation. Traumatization, psychological terror, and emotional abuse in the Gothic, however, also emanate from women – the female counterpart of this type of character is the tyrannical mother, as we see her (conveyed through her son) in Hitchcock's *Psycho* (1960). To cite a more recent example: in *Crimson Peak* (2015), Lucille takes on the role of tyrant in relation to her brother Thomas, and to some extent also to his new wife Edith. It should be warned, however, against conceiving of serial killers as markers of Gothic film. This, in turn, would dilute the concept to such an extent that it would become obsolete. Rather, such characters show, Aldana Reyes (2020, p. 24) argues, that Gothic often features mentally unstable or confused, violent, and tyrannical figures, as well as those guided by paranoia, obsession, madness, and delusion.

2.5 Reccurency

Another central motif of Gothic film is recurrency in various forms. Here, the past catches up with the present – in the shape of curses, ghosts, or of a need to deal with a suppressed, repressed, or unknown, uncanny past. Related to this are two other characteristics of the Gothic: self-referentiality and intertextuality. They are a consequence of the fact that the Gothic's reference to the past also concerns its own past. In film, this genre-historical repetition leads, among other things, to a strong aesthetic and motivic conventionalization: if, for example, German Expressionist film was influenced, among other things, by the visuality of Dark Romanticism, its aesthetics and *mise-en-scène* were in turn imported – in part directly via contributors such as Karl Freund or Peter Lorre – across the Atlantic, into the Universal Horror Cycle. In the 1930s, the latter put in place a palette of monsters, images, and narrative strategies that later films took up, quoted, and modified.

If these references are partly ironic, the referenced works themselves sometimes slip into the ironic mode as well. For example, in view of the grotesque characters in James Whale's *Old Dark House* (1932) or Bela Lugosi's accent-heavy, highly theatrical performance in Tod Browning's *Dracula* (1931) inevitably raises the question of whether it is not itself parodistic. Clearly marked as such, it returns – mixed with a parody of *Bram Stoker's Dracula* (1992) – in Mel Brooks' *Dracula:*

Dead and Loving It (1995). Not at all parodistic, but still an excellent example of Gothic cinema's self-reference, is Guillermo del Toro's *Crimson Peak*. A feast of references in terms of aesthetics, motifs, characters, locations and story, the film rolls out the entire arsenal of the Gothic and manages not only to harmoniously juxtapose aesthetic borrowings from 100 years of film history, but also to give this amalgam an individual imprint. In films like this, self-referentiality and intertextuality create an additional, enriching level that refers connoisseurs to other artifacts without diminishing the enjoyment for those recipients who do not recognise the references.

The self-referentiality of the Gothic is associated with its preference for revenants of all kinds: It not only repetitively thematizes the return of the dead (or those believed dead) in the form of ghosts, vampires, zombies. Repressed traits and events also return when characters are forced to uncover an uncanny past or confront their traumas and fears. Moreover, Gothic itself is a revenant, as Catherine Spooner (2006, p. 10) has shown:

> Fittingly, considering the genre's preoccupation with all kinds of revenants and returns from the dead, Gothic has throughout its history taken the form of a series of revivals: the period of medieval architecture to which the eighteenth- and nineteenth-century Gothic revivalists harked back, for example, was no more 'original' than they were themselves, being named after a northern European tribal people of the dark ages. There is no 'original' Gothic; it is always already a revival of something else.

While this tendency can already be observed in the classic Gothic novel, self-referentiality and intertextuality take on other dimensions in the late twentieth and early twenty-first century:

> Gothic has from the beginning been a very knowing and self-aware genre – it was artificially constructed by a camp antiquarian, Horace Walpole, and parodies appeared almost as soon as the first novels – but post-Freud, Marx and feminism, it has gained a sexual and political self-consciousness unavailable to the earliest Gothic novelists. More than two centuries of Gothic revivals have also enabled layers of irony beyond anything that Horace Walpole could have imagined, [...]. (Spooner 2006, p. 23)

On a meta-level, Elisabeth Bronfen has also described Gothic as a genre dominated by recurrence: not only do the dead return to walk among the living here, Gothic cinema itself is also haunted by media that precede it, such as literature, (magic) theater, or photography. Bronfen sees this repetition as similar to a psychoanalytic processing: in a modernity marked by irreconcilable opposites, Gothic creates a "protective fiction", she writes, by enclosing conflicts in cinematic repetition (Bronfen 2014, p. 112). On the one hand, it thus offers the satisfaction of mythic solutions to intractable problems, but on the other, it perpetuates our being-haunted by real and fictional horrors (ibid.). Thus, the consumption of the Gothic meets the need to address the inherent controversies of the modern subject, which are dealt with here in a controlled setting. At the same time, the Gothic repeats them endlessly, preventing their resolution, which also explains the persistence of the Gothic itself.

Return lies at the core of the psychoanalytic conception of the Uncanny, which is constitutive of the Gothic. At the time when Dracula, Jekyll and Hyde, Dorian Gray, and Sherlock Holmes moved through foggy gas-lit alleys, establishing the Gothic imagery, the historical manifestation of which is embodied by Jack the Ripper, Sigmund Freud was busy analyzing and articulating phenomena that transcend the conscious and the rational (see Warwick 2007, p. 36). Victorian Gothic and psychoanalysis, Alexandra Warwick writes, are equally concerned with the influence of the past on the present, with the question of what is dead, what survives, and how things can be revived (ibid.). Crucially, Freud's psychoanalysis represents an idea of an inner life, parts of which are fundamentally inaccessible to the individuals themselves. The unknown and unfathomable is located in the deepest sections of the self, from where it controls our thoughts and actions without us being aware of it or being able to control this influence.

Freud's concept of the Uncanny in particular has been widely received in horror and Gothic studies. The starting point of Freud's reflections is the home, *the* place of the Gothic *par excellence*. He first derives the term "uncanny", "*unheimlich*" in the German original, which literally means "unhomely" from its opposite "*heimlich*", which can mean "secretly" but is also an obsolete word for what today is "*heimisch*", i.e. "homely". The Uncanny is thus on the one hand the counterpart of the familiar, the homely; on the other hand, as Freud notes on the basis of several dictionary entries, "heimlich" itself already denotes its own opposite. It means not only "homely" but also "secret" in the sense of "concealed, kept from sight" (Freud 1955, p. 223). Freud defines the Uncanny as "that class of the frightening which leads back to what is known of old and long familiar" (p. 221), to something once familiar that has been repressed and upon its return seems at once strange and familiar. This "repetition of the same thing" creates a "feeling of helplessness and uncanniness," especially when it appears to be "something fateful and inescapable, when otherwise we would have spoken only of 'chance'" (p. 236 f.).

Among the triggers of this feeling Freud counts, in addition to such an inkling of concealed forces being at work, the uncertainty about the a body or a thing being dead or alive, doppelgangers, death, "[a]pparent death and the reanimation of the dead," (p. 246) and "silence, solitude and darkness" (p. 252) – an enumeration that could equally have central motifs of the Gothic in mind. Simon Bacon (2018, p. 3) points out that in the context of Gothic, it is fruitful to conceive of the Uncanny not "as an individual affect but as a social one, as well". Similar to Freud's extension of the concept of individual trauma to society in the form of collective traumatization, it would then be reasonable to assume that there is also a collective repressed, for example of an ideological nature, that haunts a group or culture (Bacon 2018, p. 3). This collective repressed is articulated in its historical and cultural mutability in the Gothic.

Another concept of psychoanalytic cultural theorety central to understanding Gothic cinema is the Abject. Julia Kristeva developed her theory of the Abject in an essay first published in French in 1980 and in an English translation in 1982: *The Powers of Horror. An Essay on Abjection (Pouvoirs de l'horreur. Essai sur l'abjection)*. She defines it as neither subject nor object, repulsive and attractive at the same time. From the Latin *abjecere* for "to throw away, to abandon, to repel," the Abject is something that has been rejected but from which one does not completely separate oneself. It is neither I, nor the Other, but it's also not nothing – "a 'something' that I do not recognize as a thing" (Kristeva 1982, p. 2). A typical reaction to the abject, for example, is disgust, which leads to an inevitable, archaic bodily reaction in the shape of the gag reflex (ibid.). As an example of the Abject, Kristeva cites, among other things, the corpse, which is neither thing nor person, and which she calls "death infecting life" (p. 4). "It is thus not lack of cleanliness or health that causes abjection," she writes further, "but what disturbs identity, system, order. What does not respect borders, positions, rules. The in-between, the ambiguous, the composite" (ibid.). The Abject is therefore not ambivalent, it is liminal. Since it disregards laws and rules, it is related to perversion. It is part of all religious structures, in monotheistic religions, for example, in the form of exclusions or taboos (pp. 9, 15, 17). In horror and Gothic film theory, the concept is often invoked to understand the impact of aesthetics, mood, and characters. For example, the vampire as a living dead can be described as an escalation of the liminal state of the corpse. If, on the one hand, vampires are usually portrayed as attractive, promiscuous, seductive, and mysterious, they simultaneously represent an animalistic, archaic threat. Body fluids and excretions are also as much a part of the concept of the culturally constructed Abject as they are of the imagery of Gothic and horror films (see Creed 2001, p. 73).

2.6 Ambiguity

With the return of the repressed or the Abject, Misha Kavka (2002, p. 211) also associates the abolition of unambiguousness in the Gothic: it reminds us that the boundary between life and death is no more fixed than that between past and present or between masculinity and femininity. Central to the Gothic, then, is also an ambiguity regarding the separation of existential spheres (see Kavka 2002, p. 217), which is to be understood as a processing of central conflicts of modernity. If this epoch is associated with a stronger categorization, order, and demarcation in the history of knowledge, then the Gothic, in contrast, undermines binarities and blurs differentiations. Jerrold E. Hogle also argues that the Gothic addresses the conflict that arises because the construct of the "modern subject" still carries remnants of pre-modernity:

> It is by being extremely and eclectically fictional in a Janus-faced way, we would argue, that forms of the Gothic have become essential to the articulation of such a contentious modernity. The regressive *and* progressive nature of the Gothic has been *and remains* necessary to deal with the social unconscious of modern humanity in all its extreme contradictions bound by its looking backward and forward so much of the time, even today. […] the Gothic is endemic to the modern. After all, the ever-extending tentacles of modern enterprise are always haunted by the doubts, conflicts, and blurring of normative boundaries that the Gothic articulates in every format assumes because, at its best, it is really about the profoundly conflicted core of modernity itself. (Hogle 2014, p. 7; emphasis in the original)

Ambiguity is thus at the heart of the Gothic. If beings such as ghosts or other revenants combine incompatible qualities, the human protagonists in the Gothic also struggle to resolve contradictions. While Victor Frankenstein, for example, failed to reconcile scientific progress with personal and ethical responsibility, other protagonists struggle to bring into accordance traditional and modern worldviews, personal desires and social respectability, or their psychic inner lives with the outside world. Female characters in particular often find themselves trapped in archaic, patriarchal structures while simultaneously feeling a need for greater freedom, equality, and self-realization. If such conflicts are negotiated in Gothic cinema through narrative and *mise-en-scène*, then on an aesthetic level, the traditionally historicist aesthetic of the Gothic and a simultaneous grounding in the now often becomes as much a challenge as balancing the romantic exaggeration typical for the fantastic with a modern realistic minimalism. In his introduction to the *Cambridge Companion to the Modern Gothic,* Jerrold E. Hogle (2014, p. 5) writes:

Since the Gothic is a mixture of quite different elements and inherently unstable any-way, some fictions are only partial forms of it, employing several but not all of the above elements alongside very different conventions. Others attempt a full-blown Gothic recalibrated to the cultural fears of their own times by including all these fea-tures in some form, invoking the thoroughly Gothic, as opposed to the semi- or near-Gothic, for the many layers it offers of symbolic, as well as emotional, suggestive-ness.

Gothic fiction tells of impossible and fantastic events or beings in a world similar to our own. However, these very events and beings are incompatible with the laws of our world. Therefore, if we want to give equal importance to all the events described, we have to decide whether we are dealing with a fictional world that resembles ours, but in which supernatural events take place, or whether our percep-tion deceives us. The first variant leads to the disturbing question of whether this possibility also exists in our world, since it resembles the depicted one in every other respect. The second variant means that the reliability of either our own per-ception, that of the persons portrayed, or that of the narrating character is to be questioned. The latter, however, both reveal that the entire narration is unreliable. This is a consequence of the fact that the Gothic tends to foreground emotionally unstable characters who find themselves in situations of social and geographical isolation, which further exacerbates their subjectively colored, distorted percep-tions of reality.

Likewise, in the Gothic, dream, reality, imagination, and madness are often in-distinguishable. In film, the boundaries between them are purposefully blurred – from Robert Wiene's *The Cabinet of Dr. Caligari* (1920) and Carl Theodor Dreyer's *Vampyr* (1932) to Stanley Kubrick's *The Shining* (1980) or Wes Craven's *A Nightmare on Elm Street* (1984) to David Lynch's *Lost Highway* (1997) or Darren Aronofsky's *Black* Swan (2010). Therefore, the status of seemingly supernatural events between paranoia, hallucinations and reality is often unclear (see e.g. Campbell 2013). Without labeling every paranoid narrative as Gothic, paranoia can be identified as a key element, which is why David Punter (1996, vol. 1, p. 183) refers to Gothic as "paranoiac fiction". The viewers (or readers) are thereby turned into accomplices, as they have no other perspective on events than the unreliable narrative of a mentally unstable, confused, or disoriented character.

In addition, the Gothic preferably unfolds its actions in isolated locations. Here, the main characters find themselves surrounded by untrustworthy people and wit-ness events that are beyond their comprehension. David Punter has pointed out that this individual alienation from everyday norms is an element on which, for exam-ple, Shakespeare's tragedies such as *Hamlet, Othello* or *King Lear* are based on. What distinguishes Gothic from such works, however, is that it unfolds a comprehensive symbolic language of isolation that threatens all criteria for judging the characters: "[I]t is never clear to what extent those circumstances are genuinely imposed on the characters by outside forces and to what extent they are projections of paranoia and vulnerability […]" (Punter 1996, vol. 1, p. 68). The unreliable characters of the Gothic, moreover, insofar as they function as identification figures, bring with them the question of the reliability of our own perception. This question is troubling because we rely on our perception and judgment to navigate the world on a day-to-day basis. Therein lies the unsettling potential of Gothic cinema.

To escape this queasy, uncomfortable feeling of ambivalence, as early as the 1800s tendencies appeared to rationalize fantastic elements in Gothic novels after the fact, for example in the works of Ann Radcliffe, Matthew Lewis, and later Edgar Allen Poe and Jules Verne. "In a sense, both authors are playing a confidence trick on the reader," Punter (1996, vol. 1, p. 67) writes about Radcliffe and Lewis, "by using all the resources in their power to convince us of the reality of phantoms and then sneering at belief". Radcliffe's rationalizations, moreover, are not entirely convincing, which only reinforces the ambiguity created by seemingly explaining something without being consistent. Such rationalizations – the *explained supernatural* – have little effect, writes Punter (1996, vol. 1, p. 10): "even if the ghosts are eventually explained away, this does not mean that their actual presence within the text can be forgotten". Fantastic elements of the Gothic, such as ghosts or other apparitions, are thus concretizations and vehicles of an obsession with delusion, imagination, and illusion. Even if supposed haunting phenomena turn out to be rationally explicable, this does not cancel out the effect of the Gothic. The ambiguity about whether or not this explanation is also to be questioned remains. One of the decisive characteristics of the Gothic is therefore a fundamental uncertainty due to ambivalence: The Gothic challenges rational world views and makes us question our sensory perception as well as our conception of space and time, since these also come under the influence of the Gothic.

References

Literature

Aldana Reyes, Xavier. 2020. *Gothic cinema*. London: Routledge.
Alexander, Bryan. 2013. Gothic in cyberspace. In *The Gothic world*, ed. Glennis Byron and Dale Townshend, 143–155. London: Routledge.
Bacon, Simon. 2018. Introduction. In *The Gothic: A reader*, ed. Simon Bacon, 1–6. Oxford: Peter Lang.

Badreux, Jean. 1896. L'immortalité conquise. *Le Monde*, 29 June.

Baldick, Chris. 2009. Introduction. In *The Oxford book of Gothic Tales*, ed. Chris Baldick, 3rd ed., xi–xxiii. Oxford: Oxford University Press.

Blake, Linnie, and Xavier Aldana Reyes. 2016. Introduction. In *Digital horror: Haunted technologies, network panic and the found footage phenomenon*, ed. Linnie Blake and Xavier Aldana Reyes, 1–13. London: Tauris.

Botting, Fred. 1996. Preface: The Gothic. In *The Gothic*, ed. Fred Botting, 1–21. London: Routledge.

———. 2012. In Gothic darkly: Heterotopia, history, culture. In *A new companion to the Gothic*, ed. David Punter, 13–24. Malden: Wiley-Blackwell.

Bronfen, Elisabeth. 2014. Cinema of the Gothic extreme. In *The Cambridge companion to the modern Gothic*, ed. Jerrold E. Hogle, 107–122. Cambridge: Cambridge University Press.

Campbell, Ramsey. 2013. Waking nightmares. In *Gothic: The dark heart of film*, ed. James Bell, 70–76. London: BFI.

Cassuto, Leonardo. 2018. Urban American Gothic. In *The Cambridge companion to American Gothic*, ed. Jeffrey Andrew Weinstock, 156–168. Cambridge: Cambridge University Press.

Creed, Barbara. 2001. Horror and the monstrous-feminine. An imaginary abjection. In *Horror, the film reader*, ed. Mark Jancovich, 67–76. London: Routledge.

Enns, Anthony. 2005. Voices of the dead. Transmission/translation/transgression. *Culture, Theory & Critique* 46: 11–27.

Forbes, B.C. 1920. Edison working on how to communicate with the next world. *The American Magazine* (October 1920): 10–11, 82, 85.

Frayling, Christopher. 2013. Foreword. In *Gothic: The dark heart of film*, ed. James Bell, 5–7. London: BFI.

Freud, Sigmund. 1955. The 'Uncanny'. In *The Standard Edition of the Complete Psychological Works of Sigmund Freud*. Transl. and ed. James Strachey, in collaboration with Anna Freud, assisted by Alix Strachey and Alan Tyson. Vol. XVII (1917–1919), 219–252. London: The Hogarth Press (first published in 1919).

Gothic, adjective and noun. 2020. In *Oxford English Dictionary Online*. Oxford: Oxford University Press. https://www.oed.com/. Accessed on: 10 Oct. 2020.

Hagen, Wolfgang. 2002. Die entwendete Elektrizität. Zur medialen Genealogie des „modernen Spiritismus". In *Grenzgänge zwischen Wahn und Wissen. Zur Koevolution von Experiment und Paranoia 1850–1910*, ed. Torsten Hahn, Jutta Person, and Nicolas Pethes, 215–239. Frankfurt on the Main: Campus.

———. 2009. Manfred von Ardennes „Gedanken hören". In *Trancemedien und Neue Medien um 1900. Ein anderer Blick auf die Moderne*, ed. Marcus Hahn and Erhard Schüttpelz, 341–348. Bielefeld: Transcript.

Halberstam, J. 1995. *Skin shows: Gothic horror and the Technology of Monsters*. Durham: Duke University Press.

Hogle, Jerrold E. 2014. Introduction: Modernity and the proliferation of the Gothic. In *The Cambridge companion to the modern Gothic*, ed. Jerrold E. Hogle, 3–19. Cambridge: Cambridge University Press.

Kavka, Misha. 2002. The Gothic on screen. In *The Cambridge companion to Gothic fiction*, ed. Jerrold E. Hogle, 209–228. Cambridge: Cambridge University Press.

Kristeva, Julia. 1982. *Powers of horror: An essay on abjection*, Transl. Leon S. Roudiez. New York: Columbia University Press.

Luckhurst, Roger. 2016. Transitions: From Victorian Gothic to modern horror, 1880–1932. In *Horror: A Literary History*, ed. Xavier Aldana Reyes, 102–129. London: The British Library.

Meteling, Arno. 2006. *Monster. Zu Körperlichkeit und Medialität im modernen Horrorfilm.* Bielefeld: transcript.

Murphy, Bernice M. 2009. *The suburban Gothic in American popular culture.* New York: Palgrave Macmillan.

Pacatus, I. M. [i. e. Maxim Gorki]. 1995. Flüchtige Notizen, transl. Jörg Bochow. In *KINtop, 4: Anfänge des dokumentarischen Films*, ed. Frank Kessler, Sabine Lenk, and Martin Loiperdinger, 13–16. Basel: Stroemfeld/Roter Stern.

Punter, David. 1996. *The literature of terror. A history of Gothic fictions from 1765 to the present day.* Vol. 1. *The Gothic tradition.* 2nd ed. London: Longman.

Rein, Katharina. 2012. *Gestörter film: Wes Cravens A Nightmare on Elm Street.* Darmstadt: Büchner.

Sconce, Jeffrey. 2000. *Haunted media: Electronic presence from telegraphy to television.* Durham: Duke University Press.

Silver, Sean. 2014. The politics of Gothic historiography, 1660–1800. In *The Gothic world*, ed. Glennis Byron and Dale Townshend, 3–14. London: Routledge.

Sowerby, Robin. 2012. 2. The goths in history and pre-gothic Gothic. In *A new companion to the Gothic*, ed. David Punter, 25–37. Malden: Wiley-Blackwell.

Spooner, Catherine. 2006. *Contemporary Gothic.* London: Reaktion Books.

Townshend, Dale. 2014. Terror and wonder: The Gothic imagination. In *Terror and wonder: The Gothic imagination*, ed. Dale Townshend, 10–37. London: The British Library.

Warwick, Alexandra. 2007. Victorian Gothic. In *The Routledge companion to Gothic*, ed. Catherine Spooner and Emma McEvoy, 29–37. London: Routledge.

Wasson, Sara. 2013. Gothic cities and suburbs, 1880–Present. In *The Gothic world*, ed. Glennis Byron and Dale Townshend, 132–142. London: Routledge.

Watson, Thomas A. 1926. *Exploring life. The autobiography of Thomas A. Watson.* New York: D. Appleton & Co.

Film

A Nightmare on Elm Street. USA 1984. Directed by Wes Craven. New Line Cinema et al.

Alien, UK/USA 1979. Directed by Ridley Scott. Brandywine Productions.

Black Swan, USA 2010. Directed by Darren Aronofsky. Fox Searchlight Pictures et al.

Bram Stoker's Dracula. USA 1992. Directed by Francis Ford Coppola. American Zoetrope.

Chakushin ari, int. title: One Missed Call. Japan 2003. Directed by Takashi Miike. Kadokawa-Daiei Eiga K.K./Toho Company.

Crimson Peak. Canada/USA/Mexico 2015. Directed by Guillermo del Toro. Double Dare You/Legendary Entertainment.

Das Cabinet des Dr. Caligari. Weimar Republic 1920. Directed by Robert Wiene. Decla-Filmgesellschaft Berlin.

Dr. Jekyll and Sister Hyde. UK 1971. Directed by Peter Sasdy. Hammer Films.

Dracula. USA 1931. Directed by Tod Browning. Universal Pictures.

Dracula: Dead and Loving It. USA 1995. Directed by Mel Brooks. Gaumont et al.

Elephant Man. USA/UK 1980. Directed by David Lynch. Brooksfilms.

Insidious. USA/Canada/UK 2010. Directed by James Wan. FimDistrict et al.

Lost Highway. France/USA 1997. Directed by David Lynch. CiBy 200 et al.

One Missed Call. USA et al. 2008. Directed by Eric Valette. Alcon Entertainment et al.

Paranormal Activity. USA 2007. Directed by Oren Peli. Solana Films/Blumhouse Productions.

Poltergeist. USA 1982. Directed by Tobe Hooper. Metro-Goldwyn-Mayer/SLM Production Group.

Psycho. USA 1960. Directed by Alfred Hitchcock. Shamley Productions.

Pulse. USA 2006. Directed by Jim Sonzero. The Weinstein Company et al.

Ring. Japan 1998. Directed by Hideo Nakata. Basara Pictures et al.

Shutter. Thailand 2004. Directed by Banjong Pisanthanakun and Parkpoom Wongpoom. GMM Pictures Co./Phenomena Motion Pictures.

Sleepy Hollow. USA/Germany 1999. Directed by Tim Burton. Paramount Pictures et al.

The Asphyx. UK 1983. Directed by Peter Newbrook. Glendale Films.

The Changeling. Canada 1980. Directed by Peter Medak. Chessman Park Productions.

The Conjuring. USA 2013. Directed by James Wan. New Line Cinema et al.

The Evil Dead. USA 1981. Directed by Sam Raimi. Renaissance Pictures.

The Haunting. USA 1999. Directed by Jan de Bont. DreamWorks/Roth-Arnold Productions.

The Haunting of Hill House. TV series. USA 2018. Created by Mike Flanagan. FlanaganFilm et al.

The Lodger: A Story of the London Fog. UK 1927. Directed by Alfred Hitchcock. Gainsborough Pictures/Piccadilly Pictures.

The Mothman Prophecies. USA 2002. Directed by Mark Pellington. Lakeshore Entertainment.

The Others. Spain et al. 2001. Directed by Alejandro Amenábar. Cruise/Wagner Productions et al.

The Ring. USA 2002. Directed by Gore Verbinski. DreamWorks et al.

The Shining. UK/USA 1980. Directed by Stanley Kubrick. Warner Bros. et al.

Underworld. USA et al. 2003. Directed by Len Wiseman. Lakeshore Entertainment et al.

Unfriended. USA/Russia 2014. Directed by Leo Gabriadze. Bazelevs Production/Blumhouse Productions.

Vampyr. Weimar Republic 1932. Directed by Carl Theodor Dreyer. Tobis Filmkunst.

White Noise. UK/Canada/USA 2005. Directed by Geoffrey Sax. Universal Pictures et al.

Part II

Historical Overview: Gothic Cinema
1896–2000

Gothic Cinema Before 1960

3.1 Early Film and Illusionism

Gothic cinema is as old as cinema itself: Already the pioneering fantastic silent films established some of its motifs and aesthetics. The oldest film to feature elements of the Gothic is Georges Méliès' *Le manoir du diable* from 1896, where we see vaults, bats, skeletons, witches' cauldrons and brooms, apparitions wrapped in white sheets, and a devil forced to retreat by means of a crucifix. The transformation of a bat into an anthropomorphic figure in flight (00:00, 00:01, see Fig. 3.1) can be traced throughout the twentieth-century vampire film in variations. *Le manoir du diable* also marks the first appearance of an assistant to an antagonist whose main characteristics include a physical impairment – the villain's disabled assistant later returns, for example, in Universal's *Frankenstein* (1931) or in parodic form in Mel Brooks' *Young Frankenstein* (1974) (see Morgart 2013, p. 377).

Unfortunately lost is one of the earliest horror films, Méliès' *Cléopâtre* from 1899, in which the main character (Georges Méliès) dismembers and burns a mummy, after which it is resurrected (portrayed by Jehanne d'Alcy) in the rising smoke. The brevity of these early films did not allow for an elaborate plot or character development. To classify them as representatives of Gothic cinema only on the basis of motivic references would therefore be premature. However, it cannot be dismissed that they used the means of cinematography to create images that Gothic cinema later took up and canonized. "With his penchant for fairies, demons, and other marvels, for both journeys into unknown lands and chilling adventures in haunted houses," Elisabeth Bronfen (2014, p. 107) writes, "Méliès instigated the relation that film was to have with the Gothic, given the emphasis of both on and experience of the world beyond rational comprehension." Films such as *La lune à*

Fig. 3.1 Georges Méliès and the devil in the shape of a giant bat in *Le manoir du diable* (France 1896), 00:01. (YouTube. https://youtu.be/OBArxsdF2rs, Accessed: 07 Dec. 2020)

un mètre (1898), *Le cake-walk infernal, Le chaudron infernal* (both 1903), or *Les quatre cents coups du diable* (1905), too, feature elements of the Gothic and horror film, such as vaults and caves or devils and monsters. The latter film is a comedic adaptation of the legend of Faust and includes a ride across the sky in which a carriage is pulled by a skeleton horse. This exemplifies the fact that Méliès' fantastic films should not be considered adaptations of Gothic novels. Rather, his characters and motifs are taken from fairy tales (for example *Cendrillon,* 1899 or *Barbebleue,* 1901) and folklore (for example, the Faust legend also referenced in *Damnation du docteur Faust* 1904 or *Faust et Marguerite* 1897).

Méliès' work also reveals the affinity of the fantastic with special effects. The influence of stage illusionism on early fantastic film should therefore not be underestimated: before, during, and after his work as a filmmaker, Méliès was – and this aspect of his oeuvre has long been neglected by film historians – a distinguished magician and director of one of the most influential magic theaters of his time, the Théâtre Robert-Houdin in Paris (on magic and early cinema, see Rein 2017).

Following the tradition of the stage magic of the second half of the nineteenth century in his fantastic films, Méliès strung together his latest effects by means of a narrative. His typical carnivalesque aesthetic, including the iconic imps, was more of an import from the stage magic of his time than from Gothic literature (see in detail Rein 2020, pp. 241–276). Thus, what can be retrospectively categorized as an aesthetic of the Gothic in early cinema did not originate from a fascination with a (pseudo)Middle Ages as in the case of Gothic fiction, but rather entered early fantastic film via the tradition of stage illusionism (see also Aldana Reyes 2020, p. 46).

From the beginning, then, in addition to literary influences, the tradition of nineteenth-century stage illusionism, for example, must also be taken into account. Looking back to folkloric traditions such as the Faust legend, their iconography includes, for example, devils, demons, ghosts, and skeletons. Modern performance magic imported its techniques of "invocation of spirits" in part from practices of modern spiritualism, which developed simultaneously, from about 1845 onward (on spiritualism and performance magic, see Rein 2020, pp. 278–288). The imagery displayed on stages as well as on the iconic, colorful magic posters of the time (see Fig. 3.2) stands in the tradition of an illusion that flourished especially around 1800 at the same time as the Gothic novel – the phantasmagoria. This ghostly multimedia spectacle was in turn directly influenced by the motifs and iconography of the Gothic novel. That this new, morbid, and effects-laden form of magic lantern performance also conversely left its mark on literature is attested to by its direct occurrence in Gothic literature and Gothic fiction (see in detail Andriopoulos 2013). To cite just two examples of this interrelation: While, on the one hand, Étienne-Gaspard Robert, called Robertson, the most well-known of the phantasmagoria projectionists around 1800, referenced Matthew Lewis' Gothic novel *The Monk* (1796) in his presentations, on the other hand, Friedrich Schiller described a phantasmagoria show in his novel *The Ghost Seer* (1787–1789).

Spectators attending Roberton's performances from 1799 onward were first guided through the abandoned Capuchin monastery on whose grounds the demonstrations took place (on phantasmagoria, see Castle 1988; Heard 2006; Mannoni 2000; Robertson 1831). Their path led through a cemetery and past a ruinous church, through a corridor decorated with fantastic paintings, first to the *cabinet de physique*, a small exhibition of curiosities, optical illusions, and scientific devices. The phantasmagoria itself took place in a room draped in black cloth and sparsely lit by a memory light. Here, ghosts, mythical creatures and demons were projected onto a semi-transparent screen, without the latter or the projection apparatus being visible to the audience. For this reason, the apparitions seemed to float in the middle of the room. Robertson combined his elaborate projection technique with

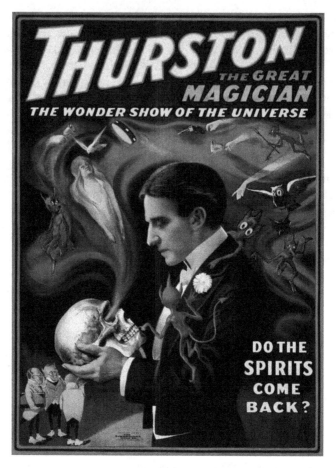

Fig. 3.2 *Thurston the Great Magician. The Wonder Show of the Universe,* color lithograph. (Cincinnati, New York: Strobridge Litho. Co., ca. 1915) (Library of Congress Prints and Photographs Division, Magic poster collection)

haptic and acoustic effects: the performances were set to music by the eerie sounds of the glass harmonica, a musical instrument invented by Benjamin Franklin that was banned in some cities because it supposedly drove listeners mad (Mannoni 2000, p. 151).[1] Terry Castle (1988, p. 34) calls Robertson's performances "a Gothic

---

[1] The glass harmonica it is still associated with ghostly apparitions in *Mr. Holmes* (2015) – here a spiritualist plays it during her séances.

extravaganza, complete with fashionably Radcliffean décor," due to their setting in a "ruinous monastery, motifs involving ghosts, monks, witches, and skeletons, and morbid mood."

Through stage illusionism, then, the motifs of the phantasmagoria found their way directly into the oeuvre of Georges Méliès and his contemporaries such as Segundo de Chomón and Ferdinand Zecca. The latter two directed, for example, *Le spectre rouge* in 1907, a film also heavily inspired by the stage magic of their time. Among other borrowings from performance magic and side shows, it features a variation on the "Aga" levitation illusion – with the difference that the illusion is accomplished by means of a film trick rather than a stage trick, and that the magician appears as the titular red spectre (see Fig. 3.5). He is a Gothic villain *par excellence:* a horned, living skeleton with a dark cloak and magical powers.

If in early cinema film tricks shaped the aesthetics of a number of works that can be retrospectively categorized as precursors to the Gothic, then in the twentieth century – as in other genres – the advent of sound and color film in particular, and later of the handheld camera, proved to be as incisive as the dominance of digital special effects in the twenty-first century. Although around 1900, we are still far from a Gothic cinema identifiable as such, the early fantastic film mixed motifs, themes, and characters with an experimental cinematography and established components of what would later become Gothic cinema (see Aldana Reyes 2020, p. 61 f.). The first direct adaptations of Gothic fiction can be found in the early twentieth century: Robert Louis Stevenson's *Strange Case of Dr. Jekyll & Mr. Hyde*, for example, was adapted for the screen twice in 1908 as well as in 1909, then again in 1910, in 1912, 1913, 1914, and three times in 1920 – all before Rouben Marmoulian's famous 1931 adaptation. The 1920 version directed by John S. Robertson, starring John Barrymore, in particular, left its mark on Gothic film: it features, for example, a close-up shot of Jekyll's hand as it transforms into Hyde's – in a dissolve we see the human hand turning into one with abnormally long fingers. This shot undoubtedly inspired later transformation scenes like the one in *The Wolf Man* (1941) or the very influential metamorphosis in *An American Werewolf in London* (1981) (see Morgart 2013, p. 378).

3.2 German Expressionism

The aesthetic and narrative structure of the cinematic Gothic gained complexity in the fantastic films of German Expressionism. "The Germany of the Weimar period," Marcus Stiglegger (2018, p. 53) writes, "was a place of the unleashing of instincts, a time between the catastrophe of the mustard-gas-infested trenches and

the looming banners of National Socialism. The films of those years bore witness
to this climate". Now, instead of visual spectacle, psychologically richer narratives
come to the fore (see Aldana Reyes 2020, p. 75), whose displacement is external-
ized in set designs that are geometrically oblique and characterized by hard shadows and chiaroscuro. While it is not uncontroversial among Gothic scholars to
what extent the films of German Expressionism belong to the canon (see Morgart
2013, p. 380; see Kavka 2002, p. 214 f.), if we were to assume that they do, then
films such as *The Student of Prague* (1913), *The Golem: How He Came into the
World* (1920), *The Cabinet of Dr. Caligari* (1920) and – the only undisputed
example – *Nosferatu, a Symphony of Horror* (1922) would be counted among the
representatives of Gothic cinema. One of the arguments against viewing German
Expressionist fantastic films as Gothic is their reference to the literature and art of
Dark Romanticism, which had much in common with the Gothic novel, but was
nevertheless distinct in its German manifestation. While the films may have been
inspired by this visual tradition, it did not translate one-to-one into the new
medium. "Goya's *Caprichos* with their depictions of torture, mutilation, rape, cannibalism or madness," Claudia Dillmann (2012, pp. 284 f.) writes, "would not have
been possible in the realistically depicting medium of film. [...] such motifs would
have attracted the attention of the censors and would still be subject to an age
restriction in the cinema today."

Clearly, the pictorial compositions of German Expressionist film are strongly
influenced by the paintings of Caspar David Friedrich, Henry Fuseli, or Arnold
Böcklin (see Dillmann 2012, pp. 285 ff.). Instead of importing the imagery of Dark
Romanticism directly into film, however, these films explored how an aesthetic of
oppression and fear could be created in the moving image through supernatural
themes. They externalised the irrational, emotional inner lives of the characters in
the form of abstract, disorienting spaces, thus not only developing a striking aesthetic, but also placing the psychology of the characters at the center of narratives
that were now becoming much longer. While on the one hand rooted in the tradition of Romanticism, on the other hand these works were created in a time of cultural and political upheaval, marked in Germany as much by the First World War as
by the subsequently founded, unstable Weimar Republic. The new abstraction that
visual art acquired during this period was now, thanks to technical changes in film
production in the early twentieth century, able to spill over into the new medium:
shooting in studios (rather than outside, in sunlight) allowed for the use of elaborate, abstract backdrops, and artificial lighting indoors allowed for the purposeful
placement of spotlights. The black-and-white aesthetic favored chiaroscuro contrasts and shadow play.

Among the arguments for seeing the fantastic German Expressionist films as representatives Gothic cinema is that they drew inspiration equally from artistic and literary motifs of the German *Schauerromantik* as well as the classic Gothic novel, and also the works of the Gothic Revival: The fact that Friedrich Wilhelm Murnau's *Nosferatu* was an unlicensed adaptation of Bram Stoker's *Dracula* resulted in the famous legal dispute with Stoker's widow Florence Balcombe. *Nosferatu* established a canonical cinematic aesthetic of the monstrous whose influences extend far beyond the vampire film. The rat-like appearance of the vampire Count Orlok (Max Schreck) and especially his long fingers with pointed fingernails (see Fig. 3.3) run through the history of Gothic cinema and still echo in the teenage slasher films of the 1980s, where they make a return, for example, in the form of Fred Krueger's (Robert Englund) bladed glove in *A Nightmare on Elm Street* (1984). Orlok's looks also found their way directly into various films: from the Stephen King adaptation *Salem's Lot* (1979) to Tim Burton's Gothic comedy *Dark Shadows* (2012), references to *Nosferatu* are legion. His accentuated shadow

Fig. 3.3 Max Schreck in *Nosferatu, a Symphony of Horror* (Weimar Republic 1922), 00:56. (Blu-Ray Disc, Kino Lorber Films, USA 2013)

has also been taken up by a number of films: in addition to *Dracula* adaptations from that of Tod Browning in 1931 to Francis Ford Coppola's in 1992 to Mel Brook's parody in 1995, these include various films that are themselves authoritative, such as *The Phantom of the Opera* (1925), Hitchcock's *Psycho* (1960) or the already mentioned *A Nightmare on Elm Street.*

This example already shows the influence of German Expressionist film on Gothic cinema, which can hardly be overestimated. Its aesthetics of abstract asymmetries, acute angles and hard shadows (which were sometimes painted on the walls of the set) had a lasting impact on the aesthetics of Gothic cinema in the mainstream as well as in auteur cinema. In German Expressionism, we also encounter the first elaborate cinematic versions of the characters that populate later Gothic cinema: doppelgangers, artificial humans, vampires, sleepwalkers, madmen, and paranoiacs. Here, moreover, the focus was directed for the first time to the inner life of the characters, which, under the conditions of silent film, found its externalization in strongly expressive acting as well as in dramatic set designs, image composition and especially in lighting. This becomes particularly clear in *The Cabinet of Dr. Caligari,* whose abstract architecture is less intended to be a representation of reality than it is oriented towards Expressionist theatrical settings and to be understood as an articulation of the delusional inner lives of the characters. "Tortured spaces," Xavier Aldana Reyes (2020, p. 91) attests, "especially the dramatic, angular architecture of the Gothic building, could now reflect traumatized and obsessive psyches". What also becomes clear in these films is the possibility provided by studio work of putting every single element of the film into service of the narrative: "While sound movies did attempt to retain the visuals of Gothic silents," James Neibaur (2020, p. 19) writes, "silent cinema, by necessity, presented these elements with more depth and greater care".

3.3   The Universal Horror Cycle

The aesthetics of the fantastic German Expressionist film found their way directly into the films of the so-called Universal Horror Cycle in the USA. Here, its possibilities of creating an oppressive atmosphere of the Uncanny merged with the motifs of horror that had been established in early cinema. The label "Universal Horror Cycle" refers to a number of horror films produced by Universal Studios between the years 1923 and 1958. In view of cultural history, the most significant of these films are to be contextualized within the Great Depression, whose anxieties they reflect. In terms of film history, this period coincides with the transition from silent films to talkies, which is also evident in the films, for example, when

Frankenstein's creature learns to speak in *Bride of Frankenstein* (1935), which was released four years after *Frankenstein,* wherein the creature cannot speak. At the heart of these films stand the so-called Universal Classic Monsters, whose iconography has become so entrenched in popular culture that it continues to shape our imagination to this day, even more so than the literary originals.

Universal's first horror film, the 1931 *Dracula*, directed by Tod Browning, was also the first horror sound film. In *Hollywood Gothic*, David J. Skal (1990) showed that Bela Lugosi's portrayal of the famous count in Universal's adaptation broke with the image of the vampire as an eloquent dandy modeled on Lord Byron, as it had become established and consolidated on theatre stages of the time. It is this image of the clean-shaven Dracula (as opposed to Stoker's novel, where he sports a long mustache), with his black hair and formal attire, that has had a lasting impact on the vampiric iconography. Lugosi, who was born in Hungary, played him in a language he was not fluent in – and thanks to sound film technology, which was still young at the time, his distinctive accent accompanies his slightly alienating, eccentric performance. Still attached to the theatricality of silent film, *Dracula* appears as a hybrid that still had to learn to deal with the conditions of sound film production. "Unlike Karloff, who had all the range of a modern actor," David Pirie (2013, p. 130) attests, "Lugosi was frozen in a striking bravura posture, the living tableau of a silent stage actor trapped in modern sound movies". Especially to the eyes of today's viewers, his acting seems theatrical and strikingly slow when, for instance, Dracula bends over his victims' necks as if in slow motion with his mouth silently open. "*Dracula* is as forward-looking as it is steeped in the past," Aldana Reyes (2020, p. 105) writes, "halfway between the silent film and the talkie, both theatrical and cinematic".

Influenced by German Expressionism, this film not only brought to the screen the enormous castle with dark shadows and artificial lighting that would later be reiterated in countless films, it also established the image of the vampire that dominated the twentieth century. Lugosi himself achieved cult status, evidenced not only by Bauhaus' Goth rock anthem "Bela Lugosi's Dead", but also, for example, by his appearance (played by Martin Landau) in Tim Burton's *Ed Wood* (1994). *Dracula* also established a pattern that served as a blueprint for Universal's subsequent films: the monster, as a creature existing outside the norm, is seen as a threat to the social, patriarchal order and consequently must be eliminated in order to restore bourgeois or capitalist ideology (see Smith 2020, p. 27).

Dracula enjoyed outstanding success and inaugurated the Universal Horror Cycle. The film also firmly anchored the monster at its center. In Stoker's novel, it is a group – rather than a single protagonist – that fights an antagonist. This creates a lack of a protagonist, which, especially in the film, led to the loss of a focal point and made it difficult to follow the plot. The obvious solution, Alison Peirse (2018, pp. 180 ff.) writes, was to turn the count himself into the protagonist (especially since Jonathan Harker is relegated to the background here and it is Renfield who travels to Transylvania in the beginning). So the main character in Universal Horror is the monster. This transforms the story into one that tells of the monster's love (in Dracula's case, for two women) and tragic death. The monster becomes an identification figure as viewers are given an audiovisual space in which to empathize with the dark desires of a vampire (see Peirse 2018, p. 180 ff.).

Looking at the conditions of film production and marketing, already the label "Universal Horror Cycle" makes clear that horror now became a business strategy that followed profit-oriented, economic considerations (see Aldana Reyes 2020, p. 99 f.). This was accompanied by a production model based on formulaic plots that recur with slight variations in various sequels, spin-offs, and crossovers – a successful concept that today more than ever characterizes Hollywood's billion-dollar blockbuster production. While today it applies especially to the superhero franchises of Marvel and DC, in the wake of their success, Universal's monsters, too, have recently been resurrected. Universal's concept of creating an equivalent to the DC Universe or the Marvel Cinematic Universe with the so-called Dark Universe was dropped, however, after the kickoff film *The Mummy* (2017), a reboot of a 1930s film which was to be the first in a series, failed to bring the desired success. The second planned film, a remake of *Bride of Frankenstein* starring Angelina Jolie and Javier Bardem as the two artificial humans, was announced for 2019 but never went into production. Universal is, however, still reviving some of its classic monsters in individual films: *Dracula Untold* of 2014 was followed by a 2020 remake of *The Invisible Man.*

The films of the original Universal Horror Cycle – just like the British Hammer films and Roger Corman's Poe Cycle did later – not only cultivated their own franchise but at the same time also their recurring stars. Make-up and transformation artist Lon Chaney, who played Quasimodo in the first Universal horror film in 1923, the prestigious adaptation of Victor Hugo's *Notre-Dame de Paris* under the title *The Hunchback of Notre Dame*, became a star two years later with *The Phantom of the Opera* and subsequently one of the iconic faces of the Universal Classic Monsters. The Phantom also provided the prototype of a Gothic protagonist who inhabits the shadows of cold, abandoned walls, be it the catacombs of a neo-Gothic opera building or a castle (see Aldana Reyes 2020, p. 101). Lon Chaney's son Creighton continued the Chaney franchise. He made a career as Lon Chaney Jr., under his famous father's name – and like him, under a lot of makeup. His face is hidden, among other masks, behind the hairy visage of the iconic werewolf who made his first appearance in *The Wolf Man* in 1941.

Arguably the most defining face of the Universal Horror Cycle was Boris Karloff in the role of Frankenstein's creature, which he embodied not only in the 1931 adaptation, but also in countless sequels and crossovers. A year after *Frankenstein,* which was heavily influenced by Paul Wegener's *The Golem: How He Came into the World,* Karloff also starred in Universal's aforementioned *The Mummy.* The fact that this film was directed by Karl Freund in 1932 once again highlights the transatlantic influence of German Expressionist cinema. Freund, after having worked, for example, on *The Golem* (1915), had become widely known as Fritz Lang's cinematographer, with whom he collaborated on such films as *Metropolis* (1927). In 1929, he emigrated to the U.S., where he worked for Universal on *Dracula* and on *Murders in the Rue Morgue* (1932, also starring Bela Lugosi) before directing several films himself: *The Mummy* was followed by *Mad Love* (1935) with Peter Lorre, another actor who had emigrated from the Weimar Republic and brought the influence of German Expressionism to the United States.

Example: Bride of Frankenstein (1935)
In the following, I would like to examine James Whale's *Bride of Frankenstein* from the Universal Horror Cycle as an example. The very beginning of the film illustrates the high self-referentiality of Gothic cinema, referring not only to its history, but also to the history of the creation of the novel *Frankenstein* and of its film adaptation by Universal. *Bride of Frankenstein* begins at the Villa Diodati on Lake Geneva, where three relevant works of Gothic fiction originated on a night of literary-historical significance in 1816. Here, at the invitation of Lord George G. N. Byron, a group of young intellectuals gathered: Mary Godwin, the daughter of feminist and writer Mary Wollstonecraft; Claire Clairmont, her half-sister and Byron's former lover; writer Percy Bysshe Shelley, who later became Mary's husband; and physician and writer John Polidori. Due to the global climatic effects of a volcanic eruption in Indonesia the previous year, the company was forced to stay indoors most of the time. Here, in addition to consuming laudanum, they passed the time by reading and conversing, among others taking interest in occult topics. After reading ghost stories initially, they then began to come up with their own. Percy Shelley's and Lord Byron's stories remained fragmentary, John Polidori's short story, published three years later under the title "The Vampyre" is considered the first modern vampire tale in world literature, and Mary Shelley developed her story into a novel titled *Frankenstein, or The Modern Prometheus,* which was published in 1818 and became not only a milestone of Gothic fiction but also one of the most influential British novels, marking the beginning of the liaison of Gothic and science fiction.

It is to this place and time of literary-historical significance, then, that we are transported at the beginning of *Bride of Frankenstein*. While Lord Byron encourages Mary to publish the story she has conceived at the Villa Diodati, he recapitulates it, accompanied by scenes from Universal's adaptation of *Frankenstein* which has been released four years earlier (00:04 f.). This sequence can be understood as a precursor to the retrospective we have become accustomed to seeing in television series. There it is usually introduced with "previously on ..." and summarizes those events of the preceding episodes that are necessary for understanding the current one. This not only refreshes the viewers' memory, but also establishes a context for the upcoming story. This is precisely the purpose of the opening sequence of *Bride of Frankenstein*. It is not a frame story that opens a flashback, as we often find in Gothic cinema (such as in *Gothic*). As the film does not return to this plotline at the end, the frame remains open. Rather, this sequence serves to tie the film back to its literary source. On the one hand, this legitimizes it; on the other hand, it circumvents censorship (see Smith 2020, p. 22). When Percy Shelley and Lord Byron express their regret at the abrupt end of Mary Shelley's story (which, in the look back presented here, coincides with the ending of James Whale's *Frankenstein*), she continues the story, thus leading over to film's main plot (00:05).

This picks up where we last saw Frankenstein (Colin Clive) and his creature (Boris Karloff) (in *Frankenstein* from 1931): at the mill that was set on fire by an angry mob, collapsed, and buried Frankenstein's creature. Already in the first three minutes of the plot the main theme is established: the border between life and death and its crossing in both directions. The bystanders are worried whether the "monster" is dead. When one of the men descends into the ruins of the mill, it turns out that Frankenstein's creature is still alive inside. Thinking Frankenstein dead at first, they take his supposed corpse to his bride, where it comes back to life a few minutes later.

Overall, the film is more strongly influenced by ethical and philosophical considerations than its predecessor *Frankenstein*. Frankenstein's creator fantasies are countered by his fiancée (Valerie Hobson) with accusations of blasphemy and hubris (00:13), whereupon he realizes his mistakes and initially wants to refrain from further research. Just at this moment, his former teacher, Dr. Pretorius (Ernest Thesiger), shows up and proposes a partnership (00:14–00:18). Taking a different approach, Pretorius himself has created small artificial humans that he keeps in jars (00:21–00:24, see Fig. 3.4). These stand not only in the tradition of the Faust legend, which contains one of the most well-known imaginings of the alchemistic concept of homunculi, artificial, magical assistants. They also reference a piece of film history, recalling a sequence from the aforementioned *Le spectre rouge* (1907): Among the tricks and curiosities the demon presents here is a series of small artifi-

Fig. 3.4 Ernest Thesiger as Pretorius with his artificial humans in *Bride of Frankenstein* (USA 1935), 00:21. (DVD, Universal Pictures, Germany 2010)

cial people in jars standing on a table (00:04 f., see Fig. 3.5). Accordingly, Frankenstein comments on Pretorius' creations with, "But this isn't science. It's more like black magic!" (00:23). Even for Frankenstein, the miniature people in jars have less to do with science than with alchemy, magic, and demons, with which they were also associated by de Chomón and Zecca.

Pretorius envisions the cooperative creation of a life-size artificial woman to join Frankenstein's first creature in founding a new "race." Thus, a plot point left out of Universal's first *Frankenstein* film is made up for and elaborated on in the sequel: The one in which the creature demands that Frankenstein create a mate for him. In the novel, Frankenstein begins this undertaking, but destroys the woman before she comes to life. In *Bride of Frankenstein*, it is now the scientist's former, Mephistophelian mentor who wants to persuade him to create an artificial woman and who also makes this idea palatable to the creature. With the creature's help, Pretorius is able to thwart Frankenstein's initial refusal by blackmail – of all things, by depriving him of what he is supposed to give to the creature: his bride, whom the "monster" kidnaps at Pretorius' behest.

Once the artificial "bride" (Elsa Lanchester) is completed, Frankenstein acknowledges this with a variation on the iconic phrase from the previous film:

Fig. 3.5 Still from *Le spectre rouge* (France 1907), 00:04. (YouTube. https://youtu.be/ AwHsyCDWRTo, Accessed: December 07, 2020)

"She's alive! Alive!" (01:06). The bandages from which the two scientists subsequently free her not only reference another Universal Classic Monster: the Mummy. They also serve to build tension: the unveiling of the bride as an erotic motif holds out the prospect of a revelation of what is hidden beneath the "clothing." It is, as Misha Kavka (2002, p. 217) notes, a romantic trope, "an unveiling that does not fully reveal". The revelation occurs after a cut, when she is presented with her characteristic hairstyle and dressed in a garment reminiscent of the white sheet of a ghost costume (see Fig. 3.6). However, once she has been unwrapped like a gift, the "bride" refuses to play the role the three men have preordained for her. When she is introduced to her intended partner, she is frightened, screams, and runs away (01:08 f.). Instead of initiating a Pygmalion-inspired re-education scenario à la Henry Higgins, Frankenstein's "monster" decides without further ado to put an end to the repeated goings-on of the men playing god. Frankenstein, from whom no further creations are to be expected anyway, is sent away with his fiancée. Pretorius, the woman who has just been resurrected and himself the creature condemns to death with the statement "We belong dead". Looking tearfully at his unwilling consort, he flips a switch that causes an explosion and makes the building collapse (01:10). Having just crossed the boundary of life and death for the second time

Fig. 3.6   Colin Clive (cropped) as Frankenstein, Elsa Lanchester as "Bride" and Ernest Thesiger as Dr. Pretorius in *Bride of Frankenstein*, 01:07. (DVD, Universal Pictures, Germany 2010)

according to the will of two men, the unwilling bride is immediately transported back across it by another male character.

Bride of Frankenstein exemplifies how Gothic cinema negotiates corporeality and body images as well as the self-perception and perception by others of monstrosity. Frankenstein's (first) creature, here endowed with a rudimentary faculty of speech despite Boris Karloff's protests, turns out to be self-reflective and aware of its own origins: to Pretorius' question whether it knows who Frankenstein is and who it is itself, the creature knows how to answer: "Yes, I know. Made me from dead." (00:48) and immediately adds an empirically gained personal judgment: "I love dead. Hate living." Also evident in Shelley's novel, as well as its adaptations and continuations in popular culture, is the potential of the Gothic to (at least implicitly) address queer characters, conflicts, and issues. Beyond the indication that director James Whale was openly homosexual and that both Colin Clive and Ernest Thesiger, the actors playing Frankenstein and Pretorius, were also said to have been either bi- or homo-

sexual, the queer undertone already evident in the novel has been discussed extensively in existing research (see, e.g., Haggerty 2016).

Frankenstein's concern with creating humans without the participation of
women alone is misogynistic and latently homoerotic at its core. That this work
continually prevents him from marrying his fiancée – whose primary function in
Shelley's *Frankenstein* seems to be to intensify the rivalry between the two main
male characters (scientist and creature) – can be interpreted as the escape of a closeted homosexual who prefers to devote himself to experiments on male bodies
rather than to his fiancée. In *Bride of Frankenstein*, moreover, the ominous former
mentor Pretorius is introduced, whose portrayal Vito Russo (1987, p. 50) has
described as "sissified," i.e., imitating what was perceived as a stereotypical habitus of a homosexual man. He shows up in the middle of the night, asks Frankenstein's
fiancée for privacy and thus to leave the room, and then disappears with the scientist (00:15–00:25). Not only does he stop Frankenstein from devoting his attention
to his fiancée, and instead persuades him to join him in the creation of new humans
under exclusion of women. Pretorius later even blackmails Frankenstein by taking
his fiancée away from him – until he has fulfilled his own needs.

Elizabeth Young (1991, p. 403 f.) has pointed out that the complex gender
dynamics in *Bride of Frankenstein* repeatedly take on a triangular form between
two men and one woman: Mary and Percy Shelley and Lord Byron at the beginning; Frankenstein, his fiancée, and Pretorius in the main section; later, the two
scientists and their female creation; and at the end, the "bride," the "monster," and
Pretorius dying in the ruins. The female characters primarily serve to initially moti-
vate the actions of the male ones and then fade into the background as soon as two
men are engaged with each other (Young 1991, p. 406 f.). The fact that Elsa
Lanchester plays not only the artificial woman but also Mary Shelley at the beginning of the film makes it clear that the latter also appears as an instrumental second-
ary character in a relationship between two men. Although she is acknowledged as
the author of the work, she is only included as a third party in the dialogue (about
her and her work) between Shelley and Byron (Young 1991, p. 407 f.). Flanked by
the two men, she appears in her angelic white dress (see Fig. 3.7), which in this
context appears as a sophisticated variant of the "bride's" dress, and meets their
request to continue the narrative. In the final minutes of the film, instead of closing
this frame story, the same actress reappears as the "bride," thus reinforcing the
parallels between the two characters.

George Haggerty reads Frankenstein's connections to the men close to him as
homosexual, obsessive relationships marked by jealousy. Already in the novel, his

Fig. 3.7 Douglas Walton as Percy B. Shelley, Elsa Lanchester as Mary Shelley, and Gavin Gordon as Lord Byron in *Bride of Frankenstein*, 00:04. (DVD, Universal Pictures, Germany 2010)

fiancée appears as a minor character – it is an arranged marriage to Frankenstein's cousin that follows social norms rather than passion. Here, the creature first murders male characters close to Frankenstein – his little brother and his best friend – and only then his fiancée. The relationship between creator and creature, in turn, is emotional, aggressive, and obsessive, characterized by a high degree of mutual vulnerability and by intentional injuries that in turn respond to slights. Haggerty (2016, p. 118) recognizes this as reminiscent of an experience of multi-layered rejection that he sees as particularly affecting homosexual men: "this calls to mind the struggles of a young gay man, monstrous to himself in so many ways, confronting the man who has perhaps first seduced him but now refuses to support or even acknowledge him". Also, the sequence in which Frankenstein's creature lodges with the blind hermit, which occurs in the novel as well as in *Bride of Frankenstein*, can be interpreted as a homosexual, marriage-like cohabitation. Haggerty (2016, p. 126) attests:

Frankenstein is queer, then, in its very conception. The isolation of the scientist, the un-sexual creativity, the solitude and misery all create a queer uncanny out of which the queer construction of the malevolent creature assumes all the contours of the abject and isolated queer subject, who although the victim of society and public ridicule, is really in the end his own worst enemy. [...], the queer undoes all sociability, and for that he must be isolated and expunged.

The gender relations in *Bride of Frankenstein*, however, are as conventional as they are subversive: The aforementioned triangular constellations are at the same time in a state of permanent flux; instead of competitive male rivalry, a latent homo-eroticism moves in; the misogynistic undertones are subverted by moments of female empowerment (see Young 1991, p. 403 f.). The "monster's" ultimate demonstration of power over the woman whose second "life" it ends is to be read not only as a reaction to her rejection and the resulting insult, but also as a concession of her power. It proves to be a desperate attempt to restore male power – here, moreover, reinforced by the creator discourse as a divine gift – that the rebellious "bride" has brought crashing down by a simple scream.

Young (1991, p. 404) also proposes a reading of the "monster" as "a marker of racial difference". She interprets *Bride of Frankenstein* against the backdrop of the cultural and historical context of the United States and Hollywood film production during the Great Depression and in the context of discourses surrounding gender roles, rape, homosexuality, and lynchings. Other themes, including those of the literary original, such as female authorship, motherhood, corporeality and monstrosity, or imperialism, have been discussed in the existing research but cannot be addressed here for reasons of space.

What can be said is that this example shows how Universal's monster films translated literary Gothic into film and at the same time took up and processed minority discourses. The imagery that emerged was inscribed in the collective imagination and created reference points for later adaptations, satire, and persiflage. Especially the laboratory scene from *Bride of Frankenstein,* in which the artificial woman comes to life, as well as her appearance, have become an integral part of popular culture: the white robe and the striking hairstyle, reminiscent of Nefertiti's bust, but with the raised perm and the two white lightning bolts on the sides suggesting an electric shock, have been copied countless times between film, performance, art and carnival costumes.

If early film had begun to visualize the Gothic and the European, especially German silent feature film subsequently found ways to visually stage its effects in elaborate form, the films of the Universal Horror Cycle provided blueprints for monsters and narratives that continue to be varied and expanded today (see Aldana Reyes 2020, p. 119 f.). By the 1950s at the latest, they were also taken up internationally in the film production of countries not typically associated with the Gothic: Turkey, for example, produced *Drakula Istanbul'da* (1953), while Mexico put out a whole series of Universal Horror Cycle-inspired films in the 1950s and 1960s, such as *El vampiro* (1957), *La bruja* (1954) or *El barón del terror* (1962). The appearance of monsters such as Frankenstein's creature, the murderous mummy or the werewolf, which have solidified even beyond film and television, originate from the Universal Horror Cycle. This formalization, however, also led to stereotyping on the part of both production and reception, especially to the extent that Gothic and horror films are often limited (especially as seen from a critical point of view) to the depiction of various monsters. Beyond the mass aesthetic and motivic canonization of Gothic cinema, the Universal Horror Cycle, whose influence on later films can hardly be overestimated, also gave the starting signal for a horror film industry. Not only did its films demonstrate that Gothic and horror cinema could be financially viable, but also that their historical material could be transposed into their respective contemporary contexts (Aldana Reyes 2020, p. 107).

3.4 Female Gothic

While Universal's monsters, drawing on literary models especially from the Gothic Revival period, at the height of their popularity in the 1930s expressed an imagined threat from outside, in the Gothic of the 1940s, there was also a shift in focus to the domestic sphere. While cultural anxieties about political and economic threats in the period before and during the Second World War played a role for the former, the films examined in this section must be seen against the backdrop of shifts in gender roles in the postwar period (see Kavka 2002, p. 224).

The so-called Old Dark House Mysteries of the 1930s and 1940s go back to a theatrical genre that was popular in the early twentieth century, which typically told of a young woman confronted by a seemingly supernatural entity that – in the tradition of the *explained supernatural* of the Gothic novel – turns out to be human in the course of the story. This genre takes its name from the place where these plays and their later film adaptations are set: old (Victorian) mansions, full of trapdoors, sliding walls, and secret passages leading to hidden chambers (see Aldana Reyes 2020, p. 128). The cinematic sets were atmospherically lit in the manner of the chiaroscuro of German Expressionist cinema. A continuity of personnel can be observed here as well; for example, in 1947 Fritz Lang directed a representative of the Female Gothic: *Secret Beyond the Door*. Director and set designer Paul Leni, who had been a key figure in German Expressionism, adapted John Willard's 1927 play *Cat and the Canary* for Universal Studios, creating one of the most influential

Old Dark House Mysteries. The atmosphere of Old Dark House Mysteries is one of darkness, rain, and thunderstorms. The films' affective repertoire includes fear and suspense. In the tradition of the melodrama, the events often revolve around voices from the past; and in that of Grand Guignol theatre, violence often alternates with humorous sequences in the Old Dark House Mysteries, but unlike in Grand Guignol, it is not shown explicitly, but is usually shifted off screen. Here, too, we encounter the *explained supernatural*: everything that seems not of this world at first, is retrospectively unmasked as quite mundane – and often as a maneuver to seize an attractive inheritance.

Cecil B. DeMille's and Oscar Apfel's *The Ghost Breaker* (1914, followed by a remake eight years later), an adaptation of a 1909 melodramatic farce of the same name, which is set in a Spanish castle and revolves around a revenge scenario, is considered to be the first Old Dark House Mystery shot for the big screen. The Old Dark House Mystery interweaves elements of the classic Gothic novel with romantic and comic ones. As the name implies, the focus here is on houses, which appear as places endowed with a life of their own, with which the characters interact. Here, then, not only is the house reinforced as the central motif of Gothic cinema, but its characteristics are elaborated upon, taking on shapes, which, for instance, would later find their iconic consolidation in Hitchcock's *Psycho* (1960).

The label "Female Gothic" subsumes a number of films made in the 1940s, at a time when the role of women was being redefined as a result of the two world wars of the twentieth century. In them, the motifs of the nineteenth-century haunted house narrative are amalgamated with the cultural and historical reorganization of gender relations in the postwar period. Put simply, Female Gothic cinema revolves around hauntings of women by women, that is, rivals, doppelgangers, or mothers. These can be other characters, but also apparitions, projections of the women's own fears (especially regarding female sexuality and role models), or delusions. Whether these phenomena are real or imagined, the protagonists of Female Gothic are both their victims and investigators. What is decisive is the blurring of the boundary between the supernatural and the psychological. Female Gothic negotiates the conflict between a socially sanctioned, domestic normality that has female connotations and goes hand in hand with a monogamous sexuality aimed at procreation, and an excessive, more liberated and sometimes deviant kind of sexuality and self-determined development that has been traditionally associated with men (see Kavka 2002, p. 219 f.). This already shows that Female Gothic is more interested in psychology than its predecessors were, and thus proves to be a precursor of later manifestations of the psychologically more complex Gothic cinema.

A resurgence of the Female Gothic can be observed in the early 1960s in Film Noir. In terms of genre history, its representatives can be categorized partly as Old

Dark House Mysteries, partly as melodramas, and especially as Films Noir (on the Female Gothic, see, for example, Aldana Reyes 2020, pp. 137–147; Fleenor 1983; Wallace and Smith 2009; Wallace 2013; on Gothic and Film Noir, see McRoy 2020). Unlike Film Noir, whose protagonists are male, here, the main characters are female. The themes (investigations, paranoia, and sexuality) and the aesthetics of Film Noir are negotiated here in a domestic setting instead of in a metropolitan environment and are sometimes enriched with supernatural elements (see Kavka 2002, p. 219 f.). For example, in *The Uninvited* (1944), we are confronted with two ghosts that represent stereotypical female Gothic characters – Madonna and Femme fatale – who fight over the motherhood of the protagonist.

In Jacques Tourneur's *Cat People* (1942), the protagonist's sexual passion, perceived as destructive and dangerous, manifests itself in the form of her transformation into a panther. This motif, quasi the female counterpart to the werewolf, is not only encountered again 40 years later in the remake, but also, for example, in the HBO series *True Blood* (2008–2014). Kavka (2002, p. 222) identifies the protagonist of Tourneur's *Cat People*, Irina Dubrovna Reed (Simone Simon), as an example of the "frigid heroine" of the Female Gothic and an inversion of the male character Dracula: she comes from a Serbian village with a tradition of witchcraft. Unlike the male dandy, however, who accepts and savors transgression, she fears it. In keeping with the patriotism of the time, Irina wants to become a good American and refuses to even kiss her U.S.-American husband until she can curb her sexual desires, which she perceives as transgressive. The panther becomes an alter ego for her to project her anxiety, lack of self-control, and related self-loathing onto (ibid.).

Example: Rebecca (1940)

Considered to be the most significant representative of the Female Gothic, Alfred Hitchcock's first Hollywood film, *Rebecca,* is an adaptation of Daphne du Maurier's novel of the same name published two years earlier, which is in turn recognizable as a variation on Charlotte Brontë's Gothic novel *Jane Eyre* (1847). The 2020 remake attests that the material has not lost its relevance in the past 80 years. That it was co-produced and broadcast by Netflix highlights the dominance of online streaming services in contemporary Gothic cinema, which will be discussed in more detail in Part Three.

Already the opening sequence of Hitchcock's *Rebecca* sets up typical elements of Gothic cinema: the opening credits appear against shots of landscapes drenched in fog. After a glimpse of the full moon obscured by clouds, the camera glides through a heavy, ornate iron gate and through the estate's overgrown, fog-covered garden, toward the dark manor (00:01 ff., see Fig. 3.8). The camera seems to scan this ruin, which is illuminated by moonlight, before a flashback to the past begins,

Fig. 3.8 Manderley in *Rebecca* (USA 1940), 00:02. (Blu-Ray Disc, Great Movies, Germany 2015)

in which the house was still intact and inhabited. Already here it becomes clear that the film is not only concerned with the past of the characters, but primarily with the past of this house, because "the house," Hitchcock said in conversation with François Truffaut, "was one of the three key characters of the picture" (Truffaut 1985, p. 129). Consistently, the main action in *Rebecca* only begins when the two main characters move into the house and it ends with its destruction. The film is divided into two parts, the first of which can be described as a Gothic marriage drama and ends with the housekeeper Mrs. Danvers (Judith Anderson) trying to get the protagonist (Joan Fontaine) to commit suicide (01:21 ff.). The second part resembles a detective story that revolves around Rebecca's death.

At the beginning of the film, the rich widower Maxim de Winter (Laurence Olivier) meets a woman on vacation whom he spontaneously marries. She moves in with him at his manor Manderley, but feels distinctly uncomfortable there from the start. In typical Gothic fashion, "the location of the house is never specified in a geographical sense; it's completely isolated. […] In *Rebecca*," said Hitchcock, "the mansion is so far from anything that you don't even know what town it's near."

(Truffaut 1985, p. 129). Intentionally or not, implicitly or explicitly, the servants and other characters who stay at Manderley suggest to the new bride that it is expected of her to step into the shoes of Maxim's first, deceased wife Rebecca and, further, that she is unable to do so. The housekeeper in particular, a great admirer of the late Rebecca (and, by implication, possibly her secret lover), truly terrorizes her. She even explicitly accuses the new wife, who remains nameless, of illegitimately wanting to take Rebecca's place, in the presumptuous illusion of being able to hold a candle to her – also with regard to Maxim's feelings, who, she says, would never love her (01:21 f.). Not surprisingly, the new wife herself projects the expectation of having to become the second Rebecca onto her husband (which turns out to be false in the end).

The fact that the entire film is determined by the past is already made clear by the title: the character who controls the plot and determines the behavior and emotions of all the other characters is the late Rebecca. If in the first part there is a lot of talk about how much everyone who knew her admired Rebecca, who is often referred to as *the* Mrs. de Winter, the second part also revolves around her, namely the investigation of her death and the accusation of murder against Maxim. Free of ghostly apparitions, Rebecca's phantomatic presence dominates the film – "she is neither perfectly present nor absolutely absent," writes Neil Badmington (2011, p. 70), "neither wholly alive nor definitely dead." Without our ever learning what she even looked like, Rebecca is omnipresent in Manderley. She haunts it in the form of incessant mentions by other characters as well as material objects: Her initials are found on her office paraphernalia (00:39), on a blanket in her boathouse (00:49), on the pillowcase in her bedroom (01:11), and even on a handkerchief Maxim hands to his new wife to dry her tears (00:51). Although she has been dead for over a year, the possibility of Rebecca's return always seems to be there, such as when the new Mrs. de Winter meets the confused Ben (Leonard Carey), who seems to use Rebecca's former boathouse and keeps asking for reassurance that she will not return (00:49 and 01:24 f.). At Manderley, Rebecca's dog lies outside the doors of her rooms as if waiting for her return. The housekeeper preserves Rebecca's chambers in the state in which she left them, as if she expected her to come back at any moment. In an eerie scene, she leads the new Mrs. de Winter through the deceased's rooms, telling her about Rebecca, presenting her clothes – even admiring her underwear – and indicating to comb the new Mrs. de Winter's hair with Rebecca's brush (01:09 ff.).

Here, the absentee Rebecca is not only a phantom, but also an uncanny doppelganger. Both wives share the name Mrs. de Winter – the new wife, unlike Rebecca, has no first name. She can only identify herself as her successor, caught in a haunting loop of repetition (see Munford 2016, p. 124). In some sequences, the impression arises that Rebecca wants to manifest herself in the guise of the new Mrs. de Winter, for example when she orders a dress from a magazine that she finds in the deceased's possession (00:55 f.) or when the housekeeper persuades her to wear a historical costume for the masquerade ball that, as it turns out, Rebecca wore a year earlier (01:16–01:21). Even Maxim declares that Rebecca's shadow has stood between the couple all along, affirming that "Rebecca has won" (01:28). Whether worshipped or demonized, Rebecca's dominant presence is the unpleasant past that intrudes on the characters' present and controls them as if they had no agency of their own.

Rebecca Munford (2016, p. 123) has pointed out that both Mrs. de Winters are spectralized in the film: Rebecca's presence becomes concrete through material objects and her clothing: "Touched by bodies that are no longer present, unowned clothing has a peculiarly spectral quality, offering a tangible reminder of the otherwise intangible, absent body." At the same time, the new Mrs. de Winter becomes a phantom, initially limiting her identity to appearing like a shadow of the late Rebecca as she sneaks shyly and uncertainly through the house, where she feels small and insignificant: "Ethereal, insubstantial and nameless, she too haunts Manderley like a living ghost" (Munford 2016, p. 124). In this, she is overwhelmed not only by Rebecca's ghostly presence, but also by the enormous house itself, in which she feels disoriented, out of place, and helpless (Badmington 2011, p. 68) and in which she also appears visually disproportionately small (see Fig. 3.9). If she initially answers the phone at her desk like a secretary and explains that Mrs. de Winter has passed away and is therefore unavailable (00:39 f.), the "new Mrs. de Winter" empowers herself over the course of the film and grows into the role. She asserts herself to the household staff, who by "Mrs. de Winter" vehemently refer to Rebecca, by declaring to the tyrannical Mrs. Danvers, "*I* am Mrs. de Winter now" (01:14). Especially when she learns from her husband that he did not adore Rebecca, but hated her (01:31), she takes on the role of the lady of the house and of a successful wife.

The protagonist thus stands in the tradition of Emily St. Aubert from Ann Radcliffe's classic Gothic novel *The Mysteries of Udolpho* (1794) as much as she emerges as an independent explorer – as a precursor to the Final Girl that Carol Clover (1987, pp. 201 ff.) identified in the slasher film more than 40 years later. While the female protagonist in *Rebecca* fits into a more traditional image of women, there are also examples of the Female Gothic in which women unmask and outwit male killers, such as in *The Spiral Staircase* (1946).

As in *Rebecca,* the repressed and recurring past in the Female Gothic often manifests itself in the form of a deceased, mysterious ex-wife. The character devel-

Fig. 3.9 Joan Fontaine as Mrs. de Winter virtually disappears into the house, while even Edward Fielding as the butler is more present in it, *Rebecca*, 00:37. (Blu-Ray Disc, Great Movies, Germany 2015)

opment of the female protagonist is tied to her exploring this past, confronting it, and growing through it. Thus, for example, *Crimson Peak* can also be understood as a contemporary manifestation of the Female Gothic, since the protagonist finds herself in a very similar situation (see Chap. 9). "Beyond the […] equations between home and prison, male power and patriarchy, fragility and (female) madness," Xavier Aldana Reyes (2020, p. 144) writes, "the Female Gothic renders patriarchy a barbaric throwback, a Gothic intrusion which manifests architectonically and behaviorally". While the Female Gothic films of the 1940s, especially with regard to the fight for gender equality, are of course bound to their cultural-historical context of the 1940s, they also contributed to freeing Gothic from the dust of (pseudo)medieval architecture and paved the way for a stronger emancipation in the decades to come.

References

Literature

Aldana Reyes, Xavier. 2020. *Gothic cinema*. London: Routledge.

Andriopoulos, Stefan. 2013. Ghostly apparitions. In *German idealism, the Gothic novel, and optical media*. Cambridge: MIT Press.

Badmington, Neil. 2011. *Hitchcock's magic*. Cardiff: University of Wales Press.

Bronfen, Elisabeth. 2014. Cinema of the Gothic extreme. In *The Cambridge companion to the modern Gothic*, ed. Jerrold E. Hogle, 107–122. Cambridge: Cambridge University Press.

Brontë, Charlotte. 2012. *Jane Eyre*. London: Penguin. (first published in 1847).

Castle, Terry. 1988. Phantasmagoria. Spectral technology and the metaphorics of modern reverie. *Critical Inquiry* 15 (1): 26–61.

Clover, Carol. 1987. Her body, himself: Gender in the slasher film. *Representations* 20: 187–228.

Dillmann, Claudia. 2012. Lebende Bilder. Schwarze Romantik im Film. In *Schwarze Romantik – Von Goya bis Max Ernst* [on occasion of the exhibition at the Städel-Museum, Frankfurt on the Main, 16 September 2012 to 20 January 2013], ed. Felix Krämer, 284–92. Ostfildern: Hatje Cantz.

Fleenor, Juliann E., ed. 1983. *The Female Gothic*. Montréal: Eden Press.

Haggerty, George. 2016. What is Queer about Frankenstein? In *The Cambridge companion to Frankenstein*, ed. Andrew Smith, 116–127. Cambridge: Cambridge University Press.

Heard, Mervyn. 2006. *Phantasmagoria. The secret life of the magic lantern*. Hastings: The Projection Box.

Kavka, Misha. 2002. The Gothic on screen. In *The Cambridge companion to Gothic fiction*, ed. Jerrold E. Hogle, 209–228. Cambridge: Cambridge University Press.

Lewis, Matthew. 1998. In *The monk*, ed. Christopher MacLachlan. London: Penguin. (first published in 1796).

Mannoni, Laurent. 2000. *The great art of light and shadow. Archaeology of the cinema*, Transl. Richard Crangle. Exeter: University of Exeter Press.

McRoy, James. 2020. Film Noir and the Gothic. In *Gothic film: An Edinburgh companion*, ed. Richard J. Hand and Jay McRoy, 37–57. Edinburgh: Edinburgh University Press.

Morgart, James. 2013. Gothic horror film from *The Haunted Castle* (1896) to *Psycho* (1960). In *The Gothic world*, ed. Glennis Byron and Dale Townshend, 376–387. London: Routledge.

Munford, Rebecca. 2016. Spectral femininity. In *Women and the Gothic: An Edinburgh companion*, ed. Avril Horner and Sue Zlosnik, 120–134. Edinburgh: Edinburgh University Press.

Neibaur, James L. 2020. Gothic cinema during the silent era. In *Gothic film: An Edinburgh companion*, ed. Richard J. Hand and Jay McRoy, 11–20. Edinburgh: Edinburgh University Press.

Peirse, Alison. 2018. Dracula on Film 1931–1959. In *The Cambridge companion to Dracula*, ed. Roger Luckhurst, 179–191. Cambridge: Cambridge University Press.

Pirie, David. 2013. Princes of darkness. In *Gothic: The dark heart of film*, ed. James Bell, 126–132. London: BFI.

Radcliffe, Ann. 1794. *The mysteries of Udolpho*. Girlebooks E-Book.

Rein, Katharina. 2017. Magicians and early cinema. In *A history of cinema without names/2*, ed. Diego Cavallotti, Simone Dotto, and Leonardo Quaresima. Milan: Mimesis.

———. 2020. *Techniken der Täuschung. Eine Kultur- und Mediengeschichte der Bühnenzauberkunst im späten neunzehnten Jahrhundert*. Marburg: Büchner.

Robertson, Étienne Gaspard. 1831. *Mémoires recréatifs, scientifiques et anecdotiques d'un physicien-aéronaute. Tomme 1: La Fantasmagorie*. Paris: self-published.

Russo, Vito. 1987. *The celluloid closet: Homosexuality in the movies*. New York: Harper & Row.

Schiller, Friedrich. 1922. *Der Geisterseher: Aus den Papieren des Grafen O ****, ed. Hanns Heinz Ewers. Munich: Müller. (first published in 1787–1789).

Shelley, Mary. 1999. *Frankenstein, or the modern Prometeus*. London: Worsworth. (first published in 1818).

Skal, David J. 1990. *Hollywood Gothic: The tangled web of Dracula from novel to stage to screen*. New York: Norton.

Smith, Andrew W. 2020. "So why shouldn't I write of monsters?": Defining monstrosity in Universal's horror films. In *Gothic film: An Edinburgh companion*, ed. Richard J. Hand and Jay McRoy, 21–36. Edinburgh: Edinburgh University Press.

Stiglegger, Marcus. 2018. German Angst? Zur historischen und aktuellen Bedeutung fantastischer Genres im deutschen Kino. In *Fantastisches in dunklen Sälen: Science-Fiction, Horror und Fantasy im jungen deutschen Film*, ed. Christian Alexius and Sarah Beicht, 37–64. Marburg: Schüren.

Truffaut, François. 1985. *Hitchcock*. Rev. ed. New York et al.: Simon & Schuster.

Wallace, Diana. 2013. *Female Gothic histories: Gender, history and the Gothic*. Cardiff: University of Wales Press.

Wallace, Diana, and Andrew W. Smith, eds. 2009. *The female Gothic: New directions*. New York: Palgrave Macmillan.

Young, Elizabeth. 1991. Here comes the Bride: Wedding gender and race in "Bride of Frankenstein". *Feminist Studies* 17 (3): 403–437. https://doi.org/10.2307/317828.

Film

A Nightmare on Elm Street. USA 1984. Directed by Wes Craven. New Line Cinema.

An American Werewolf in London. USA 1981. Directed by John Landis. PolyGram Pictures/ Lycanthrope Films/American Werewolf.

Barbe-bleue. France 1901. Georges Méliès. Star Film.

Bram Stoker's Dracula. USA 1992. Directed by Francis Ford Coppola. American Zoetrope.

Bride of Frankenstein. USA 1935. Directed by James Whale. Universal Pictures.

Cat People. USA 1942. Directed by Jacques Tourneur. RKO Radio Pictures.

Cendrillon. France 1899. Georges Méliès. Star Film.

Cléopâtre. France 1899. Georges Méliès. Star Film.

Damnation du docteur Faust. France 1904. Georges Méliès. Star Film.

Dark Shadows. USA/Australia/UK 2012. Directed by Tim Burton. Warner Bros. et al.

Das Cabinet des Dr. Caligari. Weimar Republic 1920. Directed by Robert Wiene. Decla Film-Gesellschaft.
Der Golem. German Reich 1915. Directed by Henrik Galeen and Paul Wegener. Deutsche Bioscop GmbH.
Der Golem, wie er in die Welt kam. Weimar Republic 1920. Directed by Paul Wegener and Carl Boese. Projektions-AG Union.
Der Student von Prag. German Reich 1913. Directed by Paul Wegener and Stellan Rye. Deutsche Bioscop GmbH.
Dr. Jekyll and Mr. Hyde. USA 1931. Directed by Rouben Marmoulian. Paramount Pictures.
Dracula Untold. USA/UK/Ireland 2014. Directed by Gary Shore. Universal Pictures.
Dracula: Dead and Loving It. USA 1995. Directed by Mel Brooks. Gaumont/Castle Rock Entertainmend/Brooksfilms.
Drakula Istanbul'da. Turkey 1953. Directed by Mehmet Muhtar. And Film.
Ed Wood. USA 1994. Directed by Tim Burton. Touchstone Pictures.
El barón del terror. Mexico 1962. Directed by Chano Urueta. Cinematográfica ABSA.
El vampiro. Mexiko 1957. Directed by Fernando Méndez. Cinematográfica ABSA.
Faust et Marguerite. France 1897. Georges Méliès. Star Film.
Frankenstein. USA 1931. Directed by James Whale. Universal Pictures.
Gothic. UK 1986. Directed by Ken Russell. Virgin Vision.
La bruja. Mexico 1954. Directed by Chano Urueta. Internacional Cinematográfica.
La lune à un mètre. France 1898. Georges Méliès. Star Film.
Le cake-walk infernal. France 1903. Georges Méliès. Star Film.
Le chaudron infernal. France 1903. Georges Méliès. Star Film.
Le manoir du diable. France 1896. Georges Méliès. Star Film.
Le spectre rouge. France 1907. Directed by Segundo de Chomón and Ferdinand Zecca. Pathé Frères.
Les quatre cents coups du diable. France 1905. Georges Méliès. Star Film.
Mad Love. USA 1935. Directed by Karl Freund. Metro-Goldwyn-Mayer.
Metropolis. Weimar Republic 1927. Directed by Fritz Lang. UFA.
Murders in the Rue Morgue. USA 1932. Directed by Robert Florey. Universal Pictures.
Nosferatu, eine Symphonie des Grauens. Weimar Republic 1922. Directed by Friedrich Wilhelm Murnau. Jofa-Atelier Berlin-Johannisthal/Prana-Film GmbH.
Psycho. USA 1960. Directed by Alfred Hitchcock. Shamley Productions.
Rebecca. UK/USA 2020. Directed by Ben Wheatley. Netflix/Working Title Films.
Rebecca. USA 1940. Directed by Alfred Hitchcock. Selznick International Pictures.
Salem's Lot. TV miniseries. USA 1979. Warner Bros. Television.
Secret Beyond the Door. USA 1947. Directed by Fritz Lang. Diana Production [i.e. Walter Wanger Productions].
The Cat and the Canary. USA 1927. Directed by Paul Leni. Universal Pictures.
The Ghost Breaker. USA 1922. Directed by Alfred E. Green. Famous Players-Lasky Corporation.
The Ghost Breaker. USA 1914. Directed by Cecil B. DeMille and Oscar Apfel. Jesse L. Lasky Feature Play Company.
The Hunchback of Notre Dame. USA 1923. Directed by Wallace Worsley. Universal Pictures.
The Invisible Man. USA 1933. Directed by James Whale. Universal Pictures.

The Invisible Man. USA/Australia 2020. Directed by Leigh Whannell. Universal Pictures et al.

The Mummy. USA 2017. Directed by Alex Kurtzman. Universal Pictures et al.

The Mummy. USA 1932. Directed by Karl Freund. Universal Pictures.

The Phantom of the Opera. USA 1925. Directed by Rupert Julian. Universal Pictures.

The Spiral Staircase. USA 1946. Directed by Robert Siodmak. RKO Radio Pictures/Dore Schary Productions/Vanguard Films.

The Uninvited. USA 1944. Directed by Lewis Allen. Paramount Pictures.

The Wolf Man. USA 1941. Directed by George Waggner. Universal Pictures.

True Blood. TV series. USA 2008–2014. Created by Alan Ball. Your Face Goes Here Entertainment/Home Box Office.

Young Frankenstein. USA 1974. Directed by Mel Brooks. Gruskoff et al.

Gothic Cinema After 1960

4

4.1 Gothic in Transition

Already in the postwar period, the canon established by the Universal Studios began to break up. On the one hand, it was challenged by a number of filmmakers working outside of the film series and labels established by major production companies, who explored the possibilities of Gothic cinema in ambitious films and took up elements from Film Noir or crime fiction, for example. On the other hand, under the influence of the paranoia of the McCarthy-era, a number of science fiction horror films emerged, some of them low- to no-budget productions that were typically screened as double or triple features in U.S.-American drive-in theaters. Based on their atmosphere, some of these films can be classified as Gothic cinema. For example *The Man from Planet X* (1951) opens with a foggy landscape, wolves howling, and a view of a lonely mansion on a mountain. Decisive, however, is the paranoid atmosphere in which the Uncanny is omnipresent but does not manifest itself as a tangible enemy. The most relevant example is probably *Invasion of the Body Snatchers* (1956), in which an unknown force from outer space invades Earth by hatching doppelgangers in oversized cocoons that kill their human models and take their place, then proceed to duplicate and replace more humans. As a prominent metaphor for political and ideological infiltration, much of the impact of *Invasion of the Body Snatchers* comes from the fact that from a certain point in the film onwards, the trustworthiness of any and all characters must be questioned because it is no longer clear who is actually still one's husband, mother, or longtime friend and who has already been replaced by a murderous alien double that has slipped out of a cocoon.

According to Adam C. Hart (2020, p. 58), the science fiction wave of the 1950s, and especially its drift into low-budget realms, provoked a nostalgic look back at the Universal horror films and a desire for classic Gothic aesthetics. Responding to this at the right moment were Terence Fisher's *The Curse of Frankenstein* (1957) and *Dracula* (1958), which ushered in the revival of the traditional Victorian Gothic in film by the British Hammer Film Productions. The 1960s also witnessed the first wave of mainstreaming of Gothic and horror, when, among other things, family-friendly variations emerged – mediated by television, which not only increasingly invaded private households, but also opened up a new terrain for Gothic cinema. This decade of film history began in 1960 with the release of three milestones of Gothic cinema: Mario Bava's *La Maschera del demonio,* Roger Corman's *House of Usher* and Alfred Hitchcock's *Psycho.*

Example: Psycho (1960)

Alfred Hitchcock's *Psycho* can undoubtedly be considered a watershed in the history of Gothic cinema, as well as film in general. The influence of Hitchcock's work experience as Murnau's assistant in Berlin on his own film-making and his preference for Gothic is not only evidenced by the already discussed *Rebecca* (1940) or *Shadow of a Doubt* from 1943, but also, for example, his earlier film *The Lodger* (1927), set during the London Fog in the late nineteenth century and referencing the Jack the Ripper murders. The attribution of *Psycho* to Gothic cinema is not without controversy. While some authors perceive it as a milestone of the Gothic, others do not want it to be understood as a Gothic film at all (but as a horror film). Some even place it at the beginning of the end of Gothic cinema. An argument against considering *Psycho* as a Gothic film is that, if Gothic cinema was monster-centered before, then *Psycho* gave horror the human face of Norman Bates (Anthony Perkins) and rationalized his actions as symptoms of his mental illness. Subsequently, over the next two decades, the focus in Gothic and horror films shifted to human serial killers and contemporary settings, while the traditional Gothic aesthetic took a back seat. Adam Hart (2020, p. 59) points out, however, that this narrative, in maintaining that *Psycho* set a historical caesura in terms of the importance of "monsters" in the Gothic, on the one hand overlooks crucial exceptions. On the other hand, while the traditional aesthetic of the Gothic receded into the background in the 1960s, at the same time there was a stronger orientation towards literary models. However, this replaced supernatural creatures and Gothic crypts with a post-Freudian interest in psychological abysses and their dangers (ibid.).

That *Psycho* negotiates central elements of the Gothic – a strong reference to the past, madness, isolation, incestuous love, trauma, secrets, and murder – within the Gothic aesthetic is beyond question, as is its influence on post-1960 Gothic cinema. *Psycho* replaced the ruinous castle by a no less menacing mansion standing alone on a little hill next to a dead tree (see Fig. 4.1). Its proximity to the Bates Motel, however, anchors the plot firmly in the U.S.-American present. The internal structure of the Bates mansion seems almost like an illustration of psychoanalytic theories: while everyday life takes place on the first floor of the Ego, to which visitors are also admitted, the tyrannical mother, a stereotypical Gothic character, dominates the attic as the personified Superego of Norman Bates. At the end of the film, she is brought down to the basement, where she is found by outsiders and turns out to be a mummy of the mother he murdered long ago, which Bates embodies as a projection of his Superego. In the basement, she is also revealed as the embodiment of the Id – unrestrained in its lust for murder, since it enables Bates to carry out his further murders as "mother" and consequently to attribute them to her.

That creatures of the night inhabit basements and subterranean spaces has become a clichéd topos of Gothic and horror films. Hitchcock's famous introduction of a false protagonist – Marion Crane, prominently cast with Janet Leigh, who is murdered after 15 of 109 minutes – also reverberates in later films (for example, Wes Craven's *The Last House on the Left*, *A Nightmare on Elm Street* and *Scream*). Unmistakable references to what is arguably Hitchcock's most well-known film permeate pop culture to an extent that makes it more likely to come into contact with these quotes and allusions long before the original. Foremost among these is the shower scene, in which a figure with a drawn knife first becomes visible as a

Fig. 4.1   Still from *Psycho* (USA 1960), 01:07. (DVD, Universal Studios, UK 2010)

shadow on the shower curtain before pulling it aside to stab the person taking a shower. It ends with the murdered woman collapsing, a shot of the drain into which her blood is running, and then the iconic close-up shot of her lifeless eye, slowly zooming out in a spiral motion. References to this sequence are so many that they defy enumeration. To name a few heterogeneous examples, they range from Francis Ford Coppola's *The Conversation* (1974) via *Police Academy 3* (1986) to the music video for German punk-pop musician's Farin Urlaub's "Dusche" (2005). In *The Simpsons* alone, there are numerous references to *Psycho;* for example, the episode "Treehouse of Horror XX" (2009) cites the distinctive soundtrack by Bernard Herrmann, who set new standards for suspenseful, disruptive horror film music. Particularly striking is the accompaniment to the murder sequence in the shower with its dissonant string sounds, which Frank Hentschel (2011, p. 14) describes as "destroying musical grammar" on account of it being particularly effective because it "breaks through its otherwise uniform style". With the unusual use of comparatively elitist Neue Musik in a relatively popular film genre, "Herrmann," Hentschel (2011, p. 15) continues, "has designed the almost prototypical stylistic device for the musical representation of horror" (translations: KR).

Critically, it should be noted that *Psycho* also popularized a highly problematic portrayal of transgender characters. While the film does follow Robert Bloch's novel in this respect, its impact on popular culture has been instrumental in spreading the motif. The multiple takes on the shower scene and films inspired by *Psycho* also took on a stereotypical portrayal of psychotic serial killers who dress as women to murder or are identified as transgender persons. The most famous example, which recently came under fire for its 40th anniversary, is Brian De Palma's *Dressed to Kill* (1980). In it (as in other De Palma films), there are numerous references to *Psycho,* including the relatively swift murder of the main female character (Angie Dickinson) and a shower scene. Particularly problematic is the serial killer, who here turns out to be the mentally ill, closeted transgender psychiatrist Robert Elliott (Michael Caine), whose masculine side, such is the film's representation, struggles against the feminine one, which seeks to get gender-affirming health care (01:29 f.). As a woman in a blond wig and sunglasses, Elliott commits murders of women to whom he is attracted as a man because heterosexual desire threatens "the feminine part of his personality". It is beyond question that this portrayal of a transgender identity as dissociative identity disorder and conducive to serial murder is highly problematic. While this film must also be interpreted in its historical context, it is important to note that the legacy of Hitchcock's *Psycho* unfortunately also includes depictions such as this one. Even though the focus in *Psycho* is not on Bates' gender identity but his slipping into the role of his dead mother in the wake

Fig. 4.2 Anthony Perkins in *Psycho,* 01:43. (DVD, Universal Studios, UK 2010)

of a dissociative identity disorder, he nonetheless adopts a female role whenever he is about to commit murder.

In another way, the immediate ending of *Psycho* set the tone for the serial killer and slasher films of the 1980s and 1990s, namely a psychologizing one: After the murders are revealed, Bates has lost himself in his psychosis, refuses verbal communication, and is declared incurable by a psychiatrist. The film concludes with a partial superimposition of his face with a skull (see Fig. 4.2). Thus, *Psycho* dismisses us with the disturbing indication that the Other that is to be feared is not lurking out there in the form of hairy monsters with long teeth, but is always already and necessarily here, deep inside (Morgart 2013, p. 384 f.).

4.2 Television Gothic

In the 1960s, the aesthetics, characters and narratives of Gothic film also invaded the at the time relatively young medium of television. While motion pictures became increasingly graphic in their visualisation, the more strictly regulated television became an experimental field for suggestive modes of representation (Abbott 2018, p. 198). In this medium, Gothic also clearly tends toward family friendliness and humor rather than fear and the Uncanny. Here we encounter a less risqué Gothic aesthetic in black and white, more reminiscent of the Universal films of the 1930s than the more explicit motion pictures of the 1960s. In the wake of this, not only were Universal Classic Monsters featured in television productions, but so were the Universal stars who embodied them. Here, they often appeared in variations on their famous roles from the movies, such as in the episode "Lizard's Leg and Owlet's Wing" (1962) of the series *Route 66,* in which Peter Lorre, Boris Karloff and Lon Chaney Jr. play themselves, slipping into their old horror roles as actors. *The Munsters* (1964–1966), on the other hand, references the classic monsters of the Universal Horror Cycle, who are the series' protagonists as the title suggests. Here, when monsters live together as a family, unaware of their oddity, they are not only reinterpreted as sympathetic and endearing – by presenting a counterweight to the bourgeois, heteronormative television family, the series also challenges concepts of normality. The migration of the Gothic into television, and thus into domestic living rooms, undermined traditional notions of family, gender roles, and patriarchal authority (see Abbott 2018, p. 202).

Another popular television series centering on a family that seems to have stepped straight out of a Universal horror film, but is portrayed as endearing and loving, is *The Addams Family* (1964–1966), which is based on Charles Addams' cartoons that first appeared in the *New Yorker* in the 1930s. The continuing success of *The Addams Family* is evidenced not least by a series of remakes of various kinds: after two fairly well-known U.S.-American feature films, *The Addams Family* (1991) and *Addams Family Values* (1993), there was also a new television series, *The New Addams Family* (1998–1999), whose pilot episode was remade in 1998 as the direct-to-video production *Addams Family Reunion,* starring Tim Curry and Daryl Hannah. This was followed in 2009 by a musical composed by Andrew Lippa called *The Addams Family,* and in 2011 a parodistic porn film, *The Addams Family XXX.* In 2022, the Netflix teenage mystery series *Wednesday,* produced by Tim Burton, who also directed four episodes, and based on the Addams family character of the same name, broke viewer records at its release, attesting to the material's lasting relevance.

Another successful Gothic television series featuring classic monsters and with soap character is *Dark Shadows* (1966–1971). While the series itself drew inspiration from Gothic literature such as *Dracula, Frankenstein* or *Wuthering Heights,* several novels and two feature films were also published during its run, revolving around the main character Barnabas Collins (Jonathan Frid in the original TV series), a hybrid of Stoker's Dracula and the vampire from Fritz Lang's *Nosferatu.* In 1991, a remake of *Dark Shadows* as a TV series followed, and in 2012 a feature film directed by Tim Burton and starring Johnny Depp.

These examples clearly show how the aesthetics of Gothic cinema and its characters and stories, which have since become classics, are translated into typical television formats. The introduction of horror monsters into sitcoms and soaps also shook up established structures and conventions of Gothic cinema. If the films of the Universal Horror Cycle were already serialized, this characteristic was reinforced in the face of potentially endless Gothic television series. With its translation into another medium, Gothic also became increasingly family-friendly. The animated series *Scoobie Doo, Where Are You?* (1969–1976) was the first Gothic series to target children and young adults, and its success can be seen not only in several films made for television, video and cinema release, but also in the re-runs that continue to this day. In contrast to the live-action series mentioned above, *Scoobie Doo* was in color. Although color television had already emerged in the late 1960s, it would take another decade before it became wide-spread. Moreover, the visuality of the Gothic was unquestioningly black and white thanks to its tradition: German Expressionist film, the Universal Horror Cycle, and the Female Gothic. That changed with a series of British films that for the first time explored the Gothic's historicist aesthetic in the splendor of color film.

4.3 Hammer Film Productions

Between 1955 and 1974, Hammer Film Productions Ltd., which had been established in London in 1934, produced a series of films that visually reimagined literary Gothic fiction as well as the monsters of the Universal Horror Cycle. They proved to be a link between an older style strongly oriented toward the Victorian Gothic Revival and the more daring cinematic depictions of sexuality and violence of the following decades. After Hammer's film production ceased in 1979, it too later followed the logic of Gothic cinema's resurgence by coming back to life in the twenty-first century. The "Hammer Films" label was revived in 2010, beginning with *Let Me In* (a remake of the Swedish vampire film *Låt den rätte komma in* from 2008), followed among others by *The Woman in Black* (2012), an adaptation of Susan Hill's novel of the same name, whose first film adaptation from 1989 is considered a classic of Gothic cinema (on the motif of the Woman in Black, see Clarke 2013).

As with Universal, the most notable representatives of Hammer Gothic horror are adaptations of *Dracula* and *Frankenstein*. And like Universal, Hammer serialized these narratives, systematically building not only the studio as a label of horror film production, but also its own stars. The first film in Hammer's *Frankenstein* series, *The Curse of Frankenstein,* was released in 1957, starring Peter Cushing as Frankenstein and Christopher Lee as his creature. In addition to these two actors, who became the primary faces of Hammer Gothic cinema, the label's stars also included Ingrid Pitt and Oliver Reed.

Characteristic of Hammer's Gothic cinema are historicist settings from the late eighteenth and nineteenth centuries, an increase in eroticism compared to its predecessors, and especially the depiction in color. The latter circumstance was partly celebrated, partly criticized at the time (see Hart 2020, p. 61 f.; see also Abbott 2018, p. 195 f.). A break with the tradition of Gothic cinema, color film was initially perceived by some as vulgar and tasteless. With the blood glowing in rich Technicolor red, Hammer also introduced a new degree of explicit depiction of violence that stood out from the conventions according to which violent action had previously taken place predominantly off-screen or at least in black and white. Jack Halberstam (1995, p. 25) therefore locates Hammer's Gothic films in the literary tradition of the Gothic novel as well as at the beginning of the splatter film. John McCarty (1984, pp. 9–22) also identifies them as the starting point of the splatter tradition in film, considering the representation in color as one of its essential elements. Whereas horror and Gothic had until then been tied to the black-and-white aesthetic of their predecessors, Hammer set out to counter this tradition by celebrating the new, rich colors and, with them, literally the possibility of a bloodier visuality. Elsewhere, too, color was used to great effect in Gothic cinema at that time. For example, is Roger Vadim's *Et mourir de plaisir* (1960), an adaptation of Joseph Sheridan Le Fanu's Gothic novella *Carmilla* from 1872. In this film, which was shot in Technicolor, we encounter two sequences in black and white in which single elements – including blood – stand out in red.

In most cases, the Hammer Gothic films are only very loosely based on their literary models. In keeping with the serial format, moreover, the literary-inspired narratives are supplemented by others; for example, *The Curse of Frankenstein,* in which the "Baron Frankenstein" (a title his father is also given in the adaptation by Universal) is stylized into a Dracula-like villain, was followed by six more films featuring Peter Cushing as Frankenstein. Hammer's *Dracula* series (1958–1974), in which Christopher Lee appears as the vampiric count and Peter Cushing as Abraham van Helsing, even encompasses nine films, of which only the first is (also rather loosely) based on Stoker's novel.

Example: Dracula (1958)

Terence Fisher's *Dracula* internationally kicked off a wave of vampire films featuring a historicist Gothic aesthetic. Already the title sequence celebrates the color red and at the same time leaves no doubt that we are to expect traditional Gothic aesthetics: scarlet letters appear in front of a castle decorated with stone figures (see Fig. 4.3) to dramatic music. Set in German type, the writing recalls the roots of the Gothic in the (partly fictitious) Middle Ages. The title sequence ends with a tracking shot toward a stone coffin and a zoom in on blood dripping down onto the plaque inscribed with "Dracula" (00:00 f.). Also bright red in this film are Dracula's bloodshot eyes and the lining of his cape – both of which are still found in the 2020 *Dracula* adaptation produced by the BBC and Netflix (see Chap. 7). As in *Dracula*

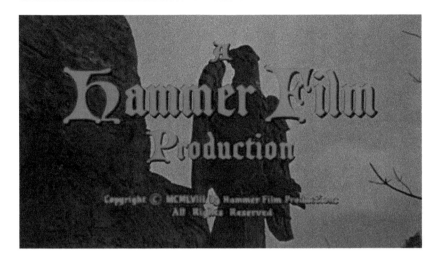

Fig. 4.3 Still from the title sequence of *Dracula* (UK 1958), 00:00. (DVD, Lionsgate Home Entertainment, UK 2013)

of 1931, the crypt is the first place in the vampire's castle to which the film takes us. Instead of the count himself, however, here, we first see his name, which is literally drenched in blood. Already this title sequence, with its dramatic, powerful background music, strong focus on visual symbolism, and screaming red color, makes it clear what kind of film we are to expect (see Peirse 2018, p. 186). It also illustrates that the central theme – the drinking of blood – does not take place off-screen in this film, as it did in the 1931 black-and-white adaptation, but enters the frame in bold color (Abbott 2018, p. 195).

Jonathan Harker's (John van Eyssen) arrival at Dracula's castle is one of the key sequences in any adaptation of Stoker's novel (in Universal's version, it is Renfield who travels to Transylvania and then back to England by ship with Dracula). The first encounter between Dracula and his guest is therefore a sequence that provides particular opportunity to identify differences from earlier adaptations (see Hutchings 2003, p. 47). In Hammer's *Dracula*, Harker not only finds a castle that is rarely seen in such rich color even in later films, he also encounters a charismatic and energetic lord of the castle. Christopher Lee enters the scene wearing the characteristic opera cloak which had been well-established in the iconography of the vampire film by Universal's *Dracula* (and which had already found its way into the aesthetic of Gothic cinema 6 years earlier in Universal's *Phantom of the Opera*). His portrayal of the vampire *par excellence*, however, breaks decidedly with that

Fig. 4.4 Bela Lugosi as
Dracula (USA 1930), 00:13.
(DVD, Universal Pictures,
Switzerland 2004)

by Bela Lugosi, which – aided by the placement of light on his eyes (see Fig. 4.4) – brought the strange and grotesque to the fore.

Hammer's Dracula is not only surprisingly young and agile, but also polite and charming as he greets Harker in perfect British English (00:07). "Dracula is not the white haired old man of the novel," writes Alison Peirse (2018, p. 187), "the pestilent beast in *Nosferatu,* or the creaking, otherworldly foreign Count embodied by Lugosi. This confident, charming, relatively young man is engaging, enticing even." Later in the film, we also experience him as fearsome, merciless, and animalistic: contrasting this first encounter, he later appears with bloodshot eyes and a bloody mouth (00:15), as well as moving bat-like at the end of the film as he scurries about his estate, hunted by Arthur Holmwood (Michael Gough) and van Helsing (Peter Cushing) (01:17). The Hammer film repeatedly emphasizes Dracula's imposing stature and virility as well as his long teeth (which are absent in the Universal film) and their penetration of his victims' necks as a metaphor for sexual penetration. While Max Schreck portrayed the vampire of folklore and mythology in *Nosferatu,* and Bela Lugosi posed with an opera cloak and an accent, Christopher Lee appears as a sexualized English aristocrat (Smith 2020, p. 27).

The sequence immediately following Harker's arrival at the castle also holds a surprise: having been established as the supposed protagonist at the beginning of the film, Harker writes in his diary. In Hammer's adaptation, Stoker's subplot about Dracula's real estate purchase in England has been replaced with a different motivation. The previous sequence has made it clear that Harker is not a lawyer who is to facilitate the purchase of Carfax Abbey, but that he has been hired by Dracula to work as a librarian at his castle. As we now learn, however, Harker is pursuing his own agenda: his first diary entry at Dracula's castle surprisingly ends with the words "with God's help I will forever end his reign of terror" (00:11), revealing him to be a vampire hunter. So, some 60 years after the publication of Stoker's novel, we are no longer dealing with an ignorant Jonathan Harker who unsuspectingly enters the vampire's castle. In Terence Fisher's *Dracula*, Harker, as we later learn, works together with Abraham van Helsing and intentionally seeks out Dracula to kill him. He brings with him the knowledge and equipment necessary to do so, thus proving himself to be the predecessor of later vampire hunters such as Blade, Buffy, and numerous other versions of van Helsing. Here, unlike in Stoker's novel, Harker's diary documents neither his gradual mental and physical deterioration in the castle nor the strange and for him inexplicable incidents he observes there. Rather, he studies the vampire and his companion, and writes about his findings as well as about his plan to murder them.

Consistently, when he awakens with bite wounds on his neck, Harker notes: "it may be that I am doomed to be one of them" (00:18). This shows that he also knows about the spreading of vampirism, which van Helsing compares to drug addiction and a contagious disease in a later sequence (00:36). In this film, van Helsing is clearly the protagonist and Dracula the antagonist. When van Helsing reveals to Arthur Holmwood (who is Mina's husband and Lucy's brother here, not her fiancé – that role falls to Jonathan Harker) that Lucy (Carol Marsh) has fallen victim to Dracula and is now about to become a vampire, the latter begins to try to match his knowledge of vampirism with van Helsing's empirical experience: Can Dracula turn into a wolf? Into a bat? (00:58). The vampire here, then, is a creature commonly known from fiction and folklore, even to the British characters. This situation does not correspond to that in Stoker's novel, but to a world in which it has been read and adapted for six decades, i.e. the time when the film was made. This shows how the Hammer films modernized the material of traditional Gothic fiction in an energetic and innovative way, while at the same time preserving its historicist flair in the tradition of Gothic cinema's visual style.

If the Universal Horror Cycle established the iconography, motifs, and monsters of Gothic cinema under the influence of German Expressionism, then the films of the Hammer Film Productions took up these elements and fused them together, diversifying and streamlining Gothic cinema (see Aldana Reyes 2020a, p. 157). Despite their historicist aesthetic, in comparison to the Universal Horror Cycle, these films appear fresh and modern. In addition to their more energetic acting style, the Hammer horror films introduced and popularised the rich color aesthetics of Technicolor and the widescreen format into the Gothic (see Abbott 2018, p. 194). They also blended the aesthetics of their predecessors with sensationalism and a more daring depiction of sex and violence, preparing the transition to contemporary Gothic cinema (see ibid., p. 195). "[T]he significance of [...] Hammer horrors," Adam C. Hart (2020, p. 63) writes, "comes from their importation of older forms into a new milieu. Hammer reached back not just to established, but older, archaic Gothic traditions, and invigorated them with novel cinematic sensationalism". In particular, Hart sees *Curse of Frankenstein*, as a precursor to later films with a distinctly psychological focus such as *Night of the Living Dead*. The Creature (Christopher Lee), who is clearly recognizable as the main character in Universal's *Frankenstein* series, recedes into the background in favor of Victor Frankenstein (Peter Cushing), who, for the first time, is depicted as a sadistic villain.

> *Curse [of Frankenstein]* conceives of horror as observational, as an examination of sick or traumatised psyches to which we have only limited access. That limitation, that mystery, is at the heart of horror after *Curse*. [...] *Curse* offers a traditional monstrous spectacle of Christopher Lee's creature, but hides the mental, moral rot of its true villain within a proper aristocratic, Gothic exterior. (Hart 2020, p. 74)

The resonance of Hammer's Gothic films, however, is also directly evidenced by the fact that their specific visuality, with its depiction of violence and eroticism in color, has been widely imitated in Great Britain and elsewhere. Known for copying Hammer's Gothic style, for example, is Amicus, a film production company founded in the UK in 1961 by the Americans Milton Subotsky and Max Rosenberg. However, what Amicus developed as its own characteristic were anthologies marked by black humor and playing rather gently on the keyboard of terror. Beginning with *Dr. Terror's House of Horrors* (1965), which even featured the two stars of the Hammer horror films, Christopher Lee and Peter Cushing, Amicus released seven anthology films between 1965 and 1974. Unlike most Hammer horror films, these are set in the present. No later than now it became clear that Gothic cinema could emerge from the cobwebbed crypts and also unfold its effect in the viewers' present time (Aldana Reyes 2020a, p. 163).

4.4   Roger Corman's "Poe Cycle"

Hammer Gothic horror's real competition, however, came from across the Atlantic in the form of a series of films directed by Roger Corman. Corman had already made horror films in black and white for American International Pictures in the 1950s, and now enthusiastically picked up the production design of the Hammer films in rich color. Between 1960 and 1965, he adapted traditional U.S.-American Gothic fiction as Technicolor spectacles in historicist settings, primarily promoting Vincent Price as the films' star. Corman's so-called "Poe Cycle" comprises eight loose adaptations of works by Edgar Allan Poe. Like Hammer's Gothic films, they are set in a fictionalized version of Victorian England. Here, familiar faces from the Universal Horror Cycle also return. For example, in *The Raven* (1963) Boris Karloff starred alongside Vincent Price and Peter Lorre, whose last film appearances include Corman's Gothic films, as well as alongside 26-year-old Jack Nicholson, who would rise to fame 6 years later with *Easy Rider.*

Example: House of Usher (1960)
The first and most significant one of Corman's Poe adaptations is *House of Usher,* for which (just like for three other films of the Poe cycle) science fiction writer Richard Matheson wrote the screenplay, based on Poe's 1839 short story "The Fall of the House of Usher." Vincent Price stars as Roderick Usher and Myrna Fahey as his sister Madeline. Already the opening sequence celebrates the bright colorfulness of the film, as multicolored wisps of mist move across the screen, foreshadowing the prominent and symbolic use of color in Corman's Poe Cycle (see Fig. 4.5).

Like in the Hammer Gothic films, red consistently dominates the color palette in *House of Usher* – the Ushers' costumes in particular are dominated by shades of red, such as Roderick's striking red velvet coat or Madeline's matching red velvet dress (see Fig. 4.6). The Ushers' strikingly anachronistic ancestral gallery is also dominated by shades of red. The portraits of his ancestors – as Roderick says, all thieves, murderers, swindlers and other criminals – are paintings by Burt Schonberg, which, with their impressionistic-abstract style, seem like foreign elements in the ornamental Victorian set design, but unfold their alienating effect all the more impressively.

Vincent Price, who appears in all films of the Poe Cycle, became a cult star of horror in the 1960s and 1970s, though unlike Bela Lugosi or Boris Karloff, he was not associated with one specific role. Rather, he embodied a new, characteristic type of Gothic character, described by Misha Kavka (2002, p. 224) as "the intro-

Fig. 4.5 Still from the title sequence of *House of Usher* (USA 1960), 00:00. (Blu-ray Disc, Metro-Goldwyn-Mayer, UK 2013)

Fig. 4.6   Myrna Fahey as Madeline Usher in *House of Usher,* 00:18. (Blu-ray Disc, Metro-Goldwyn-Mayer, UK 2013)

spective, pathological hero whose monstrosity lies within". She therefore situates the Poe Cycle in the tradition of the Female Gothic, which also revolves around the monstrosity of social transgression as a supernatural manifestation of an individual psychopathology (Kavka 2002, p. 224). If, in *Rebecca,* as discussed above, the house Mandeley can be read as a materialization of the deceased Rebecca, who dominates it and all the characters within it, then the titular house of the Usher family proves to be an externalization of the unstable mental state of its inhabitants. As a family residence, it is to be understood as an unhindered projection of the inner life of the master of the house in particular, who sees himself as an isolated aristocrat – a relic from a bygone era – chained to the labyrinthine manor with its winding secret passages, hidden prisons, narrow towers, and steep staircases (see Kavka 2002, p. 224). Combined with Gothic cinema's obsession with aristocratic decadence and incestuous degeneration, the entire *mise-en-scène* in the Usher family home serves to express the mental instability of the last two remaining family members. Along with them, it literally perishes at the end of the film as it surreally breaks apart and sinks into the swamp, making the house of Usher disappear not only in the sense of an architectural structure, but also in the genealogical sense.

Corman's films strike in the same vein as those of Hammer Film Productions or Amicus, but are more artistically ambitious compared to them. Beginning with *House of Usher,* whose surprising success initiated the Poe Cycle, Corman set new standards for Gothic cinema. His atmospheric Poe adaptations subtly shift the focus to psychological horrors rather than costumed monsters like those of Universal. This shift is already evident in Hammer's Gothic films (see Hart 2020, p. 72). As described above, it comes to bear in Hitchcock's *Psycho* in particular, and comes to full fruition in the Gothic and horror films from the 1960s onward, when psychological abysses increasingly intermingle with deviant sexuality and socially critical commentary. "If the hallucinatory dream sequences hatched by Corman and cinematographer Nicolas Roeg stray from the straightforward narrative presentation of [Terence] Fisher and his Hammer cohorts," writes Adam Hart (2020, p. 72 f.), "the film is grounded in a largely Fisher-esque *mise-en-scène* that prioritizes staging and performance over camerawork or editing". Together they created a film stock of Gothic cinema in dazzling color.

Hammer, in particular, broke with the black and white tradition of the Gothic. The films opened up possibilities for reinventing the specific atmosphere of Gothic cinema under the conditions of color film, opening the door for the characteristic color schemes of the later Italian Gothic and especially the *giallo*.[1] A second crucial aspect, as Hart (2020, p. 73) also points out, is that behind the backdrop-like settings and kitschy costumes of Hammer Gothic or Corman's Poe Cycle lies a previously unprecedented cinematic reappraisal of destroyed and devastating psyches. This, along with the cobwebs of the traditional Gothic cinema aesthetic, partially receded into the background in the decades that followed. Although, in the long run, the focus shifted from monsters to humans, it also shifted from villains to victims, which meant that some of the fascination with the abysses of the villains' psyches, that Fisher's *Curse of Frankenstein* or Corman's *The Masque of the Red Death* (1964) explored, was lost (see Hart 2020, p. 73).

4.5 International Gothic

With its British roots and the strong influence of the Universal horror films of the 1930s and 1940s, Gothic is historically a predominantly British and U.S.-American phenomenon. However, Gothic has always also been received and produced in other parts of the world. For example, one of the first cinematic representations of the vampire emerged in Hungary 5 years before Murnau's iconic *Nosferatu* was made: Alexander Korda's *Mágia* from 1917, which was followed by the first *Dracula* adaptation in 1921: *Drakula halála*. These examples already reveal a problem of early Gothic cinema: both films are considered lost, although a Hungarian novel version of the latter from 1924 has survived (see Aldana Reyes

---

[1] In Italian cinema *giallo* refers to the crime or police film in the broadest sense and also includes, for example, Film Noir, gangster films, agent films or thrillers. The specifically Italian form, which is referred to in the German- and English-speaking film discourses as *giallo*, in Italy is called *giallo all'italiana*.

2020a, p. 87 f.). Since the 1950s and 1960s at the latest, there has been a strong production of Gothic cinema in Turkey and Mexico, among other countries. Western influences are often mixed with the modalities of local cultures and film industries, which makes these films particularly interesting objects of study. Addressing global manifestations of Gothic cinema, however, is beyond the scope of this introduction. A few individual examples are highlighted below; there are plenty of existing studies that can be referred to for more detailed investigations. To name just a few, in addition to Katarzyna Ancuta's work on Asian Gothic, Rebecca Duncan's on African Gothic, Enrique Ajuria Ibarra's on Mexican Gothic, Inés Ordiz's on Spanish and Latin American, and Tuğçe Bıçakçı Syed's on the Turkish Gothic.

Especially in the wake of the British and U.S.-American color Gothic films discussed above, Gothic in color flourished internationally in the 1960s. If Gothic in literature was already dominated by British works, a clear British influence is also evident in U.S.-American Universal horror films: the Englishman James Whale, director of the canonical Universal films *Frankenstein, Bride of Frankenstein, The Old Dark House* and *The Invisible Man*, often cast British colleagues such as Boris Karloff, Colin Clive, and Claude Rains in the leading roles of his films, which were based on British literature. In particular, the Gothic films of the Hammer Film Productions, with the distinctive English accents of stars Christopher Lee and Peter Cushing, provided Gothic cinema with a "Britishness" that was subsequently exported to other countries. Terence Fisher's *Dracula* sparked a wave of Gothic film production internationally, often as part of transnational collaborations. Numerous continental European productions hired the stars of the Hammers Gothic films. Christopher Lee, for example, appeared in the Italian-French horror comedy *Tempi duri per i vampiri* (1959) 1 year after his success as Dracula, and in 1972 in the Spanish-British co-production *Pánico en el transsiberiano* together with Peter Cushing. Outside of their homeland British performers also frequently moved through sets that depicted misty British landscapes or cities, in adaptations of British material – whether of literary works or, for example, of fictionalizations of the Jack the Ripper murders (see Forshaw 2013).

In the late 1960s and 1970s, Gothic and horror films also moved away from the big screens of the mainstream and increasingly served niche formats. In the U.S.A., they increasingly migrated to drive-in and grindhouse theaters. Here, numerous low-budget productions were shown that relied on formulaic plots, explicit violence, nudity, and sexuality. A number of artistically ambitious films show that these niche markets, however, also became a field of cinematographic experimentation and offered a space in which Gothic could break away from long-established conventions. We no longer meet the witches and vampires of the 1970s in southeastern

European castles, but in contemporary settings. In the tradition of the Female Gothic, female characters are prominent in the Italian and Spanish Gothic cinema of the 1960s and 1970s. And in typical Gothic fiction fashion, they often represent two polarized stereotypes here: the dangerous, sexualized *femme fatale* and the threatened, infantilized Lolita, although both are now much more permissive under the changed conditions of cinema. Last but not least, especially Sexploitation Gothic stressed the connotation of female vampires with the sexual activeness that had already been established in Sheridan Le Fanu's *Carmilla* in 1872.

Exploitation film, which flourished in the 1960s and 1970s, often formed alliances with Gothic cinema. Produced on a low-budget, Exploitation, simply put, relies primarily on sex and violence, formulaic, efficient production, and fast-paced storylines. It appeals to a younger audience and often imitates other successful productions, blurring the lines between parody, homage, and copy. In the course of this, horror became one of the most prominent genres. Motifs, characters and stories of Gothic cinema were increasingly not only imitated, blended, modified and expanded internationally in the 1960s and 1970s, they also mixed with elements of comedy, parody, science fiction as well as historical and especially erotic film. Under the conditions of a film industry whose restrictions on the depiction of sex and violence were loosened as a result of cultural changes – in 1967, for example, the Motion Pictures Production Code, which governed the self-censorship of feature film production in the United States, was abolished – the sexual subtext of Gothic cinema also came to the surface. Many of the continental European productions were not afraid to include (female) nudity and sexuality in the films. Especially the previously more or less subtle sexual connotations of vampirism now became more explicit.

The surrealistic, dreamlike vampire films of French director Jean Rollin are particularly noteworthy in this regard. With their slow narrative tempo, the often oblique stories, the poetic dialogues these films are artistically ambitious. The main characters are often women scantily clad in transparent dresses who freely indulge in sexual activities in remote castles. Rollin, who later focussed on the production of porn films in the mid-1970s, here already blurred the line to softcore sex films. His directorial debut *Le Viol du Vampire* caused a veritable scandal in Paris in 1968. Elsewhere, too, films that mixed Gothic horror with eroticism and pornography were made – so many in number that they are collectively referred to as "horrotica." In Spain, Jess Franco's films are particularly noteworthy, some of which contain sadomasochistic and later also pornographic elements. His 1971 film *Vampyros Lesbos* popularized lesbian eroticism as a central element in vampire sex films, underpinned by a psychedelic soundtrack. A pertinent example of Gothic sexploitation from Italy is *Malabimba* (1979), which strings together partially explicit sex scenes with the aid of a flimsy narrative. Here, characters become possessed by a castle ghost that has been summoned during a séance and entices them to engage in sexual acts.

4.5.1 Italian Gothic

The first and most significant Gothic film industry outside of Britain and North America developed in Italy around 1960, followed by that of Spain. A pioneering work that combined the motif of serial murder of the later *giallo* with that of vampirism and with the character of the Mad Scientist is Riccardo Freda's *I vampiri* of 1957. Initially, Italian Gothic cinema primarily took up classic monsters such as Frankenstein's creature, Dracula, the Mummy, or the werewolf before gaining more originality. The imitation of Anglo-American Gothic cinema sometimes bore fruit that seems strange from today's perspective. For example, the title character in *L'orribile segreto del Dr. Hichcock* (1962) was named after the British director although there is no connection between the two. The fact that the director and screenwriter are listed in the credits of this film not as Riccardo Freda and Ernesto Gastaldi, but as Robert Hampton and Julyan Perry shows another peculiarity of Italian Gothic cinema of the 1960s: many Italian directors adopted English pseudonyms – Antonio Margheriti called himself Anthony Dawson; instead of Mario Bava, John M. Old appears in the credits of *La frusta e il corpo* (1963), and Sergio Corbucci, who from the mid-1960s became one of the formative characters of the Italian Western alongside Sergio Leone, received credits as Gordon Wilson Jr. (qtd. in Lucas 2013, p. 57). These pseudonyms, however, attest not only to the influence of Anglo-American Gothic cinema on continental European film production, but also to a stronger public interest in U.S.-American and British films as opposed to Italian ones at the time (see Koven 2020, p. 156 f.). Not only did titles and directors at first glance suggest an English production on the Italian market, but most of these films were made for export – partly because the domestic market showed less interest in them. For example *La maschera del demonio,* now considered a milestone of Italian Gothic cinema, was not particularly successful at the Italian box office at the time. It was not until American International Pictures (AIP) bought the rights to the film and distributed it in U.S. grindhouse and drive-in theaters that it reached a larger audience.

Example: La maschera del demonio (1960)
La maschera del demonio, a loose adaptation of Nicolai Gogol's story *Wij* (1835), became one of the most influential continental European films ever made. The lead

role helped British actress Barbara Steele achieve her breakthrough, and she subsequently became an iconic figure of the Italian Gothic. She appears here in a double role, representing both stereotypes of women mentioned above, Lolita and *femme fatale* (as well as echoing Jekyll and Hyde). The sexualized Asa was accused of witchcraft, tortured and murdered 200 years ago, and now comes back to life to exact revenge on her tormentors' descendants, together with the vampire/demon Dracula (Arturo Dominici). A witch-vampire-hybrid, she ends up sucking the blood of her contemporary doppelganger Katia, a member of the family on whom Asa seeks revenge. Like Elisabeth Báthory, the vampire/witch rejuvenates herself as a result and gains new life force. However, her double, the innocent, melancholy descendant of her killer, survives the ordeal and awakens in the final sequence to seal her love for her savior (John Richardson) with a kiss, while outside a mob consigns the newly invigorated vampiress/witch Asa to a fiery death (01:22 ff.).

The film brings together a myriad of topoi of Gothic cinema. Its title echoes Hammer's *Curse of Frankenstein*, which was released in Italy as *La maschera del Frankenstein*. Similar accumulations of motifs of Gothic cinema and iconography can be found in other Italian films, such as Antonio Margheriti's *Danza macabra* (1964), a haunted-house scenario with vampires, which also stars Barbara Steele as the female lead, or Mario Bava's *La frusta e il corpo* (1963). *La maschera del demonio*, however, presents a veritable catalog of Gothic elements. Xavier Aldana Reyes (2020a, p. 187 f.) writes about it:

> The list of Gothic motifs and tropes in *La maschera del demonio*, from family curses to secret passageways, bat-ridden crypts and a ruinous castle, is so extensive as to constitute a veritable compendium. These all add to the overall feeling of dread and apprehension, solidifying around aesthetic vignettes that showcase Bava's incredible eye for depth of space, use of shadows and experience of special effects.

The film is set in nineteenth-century rural Moldavia, a variation on Bram Stoker's Transylvania. The spaces in which the protagonists move are also typical of Gothic cinema: a castle full of hidden secret passages and trapdoors, whose great hall is dominated by a fireplace as well as full-body portraits of Asa and Dracula, the former of which changes when she comes back to life; an abandoned, cobwebbed crypt along with a ruinous graveyard (see Fig. 4.7); a forest and a swamp are also found among the settings. Here there are downpours that obey the witch and fog that seems to accompany Dracula. We even encounter the superstitious coachman from Stoker's *Dracula,* along with scientists who laugh at his fear at first and later fall victim to the dark forces themselves; and finally even a witch-burning mob led by the village clergyman. In *La maschera del demonio* we also see a variation on

Fig. 4.7 Barbara Steele as Katia Vajda in *La maschera del demonio* (IT 1960), 00:14.
(DVD, Arrow Films, UK 2013)

Nosferatu's iconic long fingernails on bony, long hands, though here they appear
much more aesthetically pleasing because they are the hands of the leading actress
(00:41, see Fig. 4.8).

Looking beyond the zeal for imitation, it becomes apparent that Bava's Gothic
films are distinguished from those of Universal or Hammer by a much more mobile
camera, a more expressive cinematography strongly reminiscent of the German
Expressionist film, but also by a more daring depiction of violence and gore.
Particularly in his color films and especially through his striking use of lighting,
Bava's sets appear uniquely macabre and display a dreamlike quality (Lucas 2013,
p. 57). "Bava stages symbolic spaces," Marcus Stiglegger (2008, p. 420; translation: KR) writes, "to which light and shadow accents lend enormous depth, but
which at the same time become multi-layeredly legible as inner landscapes of
fear – as literal angst-spaces."

While *La maschera del demonio* is classically kept in black and white, reveal-
ing an atmospheric setting of light and shadow in the style of Expressionist film,
other iconic works of Italian Gothic cinema shine in garish, surreal colors. Antonio
Margheriti, for example, made a color remake of his black-and-white film *Danza
Macabra* under the title *Nella stretta morsa del ragno* (1971), in which Klaus
Kinski appears as Edgar Allan Poe. Also directed by Mario Bava, 1965's *Terrore*

Fig. 4.8 Barbara Steele as the witch Asa in *La maschera del demonio*, 00:41. (DVD, Arrow Films, UK 2013)

nello spazio is a curious science fiction cross-over in which a group of space travelers, following a distress signal, land on a planet inhabited by disembodied parasites. Reminiscent of *Invasion of the Body Snatchers*, the parasites take over the bodies of the space travelers and turn them into vampires, again echoing traditional Gothic motifs. Prominent references to this film, up to the citation of a complete sequence, are found 14 years later in a milestone of Gothic science fiction horror, Ridley Scott's *Alien*, which tells a similar story, but sheds the blatant pulp aesthetic of Bava's film. In *Terrore nello spazio* Bava notably illuminates the scenery on the alien planet in garish colors and striking complementary contrasts (see Fig. 4.9). If the use of color in Italian Gothic cinema was also initially an imitation of the Hammer Gothic film, directors like Bava thus raised the atmospheric use of color to another level. Marcus Stiglegger (2008, p. 422; translation: KR) writes in this regard:

> Mario Bava's Gothic phase, which lasted from *La maschera del demonio* to *Gli orrori del castello di Norimberga*, strictly speaking even up to *La Venere d'Ille* (1979), once again illustrates the director's original ambition as a painter, a quality he developed with the style cultivated in color film and still used in his contemporary material.

This colorful aesthetic found its most iconic, surreal expression in Dario Argento's films of the late 1970s and 1980s. Heavily influenced by Gothic cinema is espe-

Fig. 4.9   Barry Sullivan as Capt. Mark Markary in *Terrore nello spazio* (Italy 1965), 00:28. (YouTube. https://youtu.be/Wlux-btra2k, Accessed: 09 December 2020)

cially his trilogy *Le Tre madri,* consisting of *Suspiria* (1977), *Inferno* (1980) and *La Terza madre* (2007). While Argento is primarily celebrated as the father of the *giallo*, his striking use of colorful lighting in films like *Suspiria* reverberates in Gothic cinema to this day, for example in Guillermo del Toro's *Crimson Peak* (see Chap. 9).

4.5.2   Edgar Wallace in Germany

An interesting example of a German variant of the Gothic are the West German adaptations of a series of detective novels by the British author Edgar Wallace. Recently, Wieland Schwanebeck examined the films as transcultural artifacts in an essay. In it, he shows that it is clearly inadequate to understand the film series, which was produced between 1959 and 1972, as a Germanized adaptation of English literature and traces other transnational influences, such as the Italian *giallo* (Schwanebeck 2020). The crime series clearly feature recognizable elements of the Gothic: it is preferably set in bad weather, in foggy London (as a back projection of archival footage) or in no less foggy landscapes; favorite themes and motifs include murder, sexuality, and paranoia. The films also include slightly whimsical takes on traditional Gothic cinema, such as the titular, red-cape-clad, murderous *Monk with the Whip* (1967), who chases women in the brightly-colored style of the Italian *giallo*. Shot in color from 1966 onward, the later Edgar Wallace films also reveal influences of sexploitation, Alfred Hitchcock's films, and the James Bond films, while the literary models increasingly faded into the background and were reduced to a label from 1964 onward (Schwanebeck 2020).

The Edgar Wallace films, which were particularly influential on West German television, continue to have an impact to this day, not least due to repeated television broadcasts and parodies such as famous comedian's Otto Waalkes *Otto – Die Serie* (1995), in which he re-dubbed sequences from the films, or the successful comedy feature film *Der WiXXer* (2004), which was followed by the sequel *Neues vom Wixxer* in 2007. The latter can be contextualized in the course of an upswing of genre cinema in Germany after 2000, which Marcus Stiglegger (2018b, p. 51) attests especially to the crime film, thriller, and horror film.

4.5.3 American and Southern Gothic

Gothic cinema has long been transnationalized, easily interweaving as much with local myths and legends as with specific sociocultural and political issues. This section takes a look at American and Southern Gothic, by which I refer not simply to Gothic films produced in the United States (as, for example, in Davison 2018). Rather, this term here refers to a manifestation of Gothic cinema that does not adapt European Gothic fiction, but rather grows genuinely out of the specific cultural context of the United States and is distinctly different from the output of other regions. Because of its marginalized position, Gothic provided a space to articulate uncomfortable themes and nonconformist ideas from its beginning. American Gothic, therefore, became a rallying point for anxieties specific to the U.S.A. "American Gothic," Ardel Haefele-Thomas (2018, p. 2) write, "is able to capture all of the complicated layers of various social and cultural concerns like racism and the after-effects of colonialism, genocide, and slavery; sexism and classism in the wake of the early Salem Witch Trials; homophobia and transphobia perpetuated by sodomy laws, anti-cross-dressing laws, and the demonization of people suffering from AIDS."

From the European tradition of the Gothic, the U.S.-American one took on the associations with violence and spirituality that had produced its macabre, fantastical, monster-inhabited imagery. "These sensitivities," according to Josef Benson (2020, p. 195), are "variably combined with the added texture of America's unique and insidious spiritual vision of manifest destiny and frontier masculinity responsible for the victimization of Africans and Native Americans". The preferred genre for addressing these concepts, as well as the associated violence and idealization of self-righteous, gun-wielding men, is the Western. Insofar as elements of the Gothic can be found within it, coupled with a specific reference to the American history of slavery and genocide, as well as an idealization of violence, Westerns such as Sam Peckinpah's *The Wild Bunch* (1969), Sergio Corbucci's *Django* (1966), Quentin Tarantino's *Django Unchained* (2012) and especially Jim Jarmusch's *Dead Man* (1995) can be classified as Gothic Westerns (see Benson 2020, p. 204).

A specific Southern American variant of Gothic also emerged. Southern Gothic traces its origins to the literary works of Edgar Allan Poe, among others, but especially to twentieth-century authors such as Tennessee Williams, Katherine Anne Porter, and William Faulkner. The first cinematic representatives of the Southern Gothic were adaptations of plays like *The Glass Menagerie* (1950) with Jane Wyman and Kirk Douglas. A milestone came in 1955 with *The Night of the Hunter.* Southern Gothic is set in the swampy subtropical landscapes of the southern states inhabited by alligators and other creatures. Instead of the supernatural European spectacle, it confronts us with the historical or imagined horrors of the U.S.-American South. The supernatural and mythic are superfluous in the face of the "hothouse reality of the American subtropics," writes Michael Atkinson (2013, p. 213). Southern Gothic often blends with so-called Backwood Horror (for example, in *The Texas Chain Saw Massacre,* 1974), which often makes the American backcountry the isolated scene of archaic violence (on Backwood Horror, also in relation to the Gothic see, for example, Stiglegger 2018a, pp. 68–83).

If such films are set in the now, it can still be argued that their setting outside civilization takes them back to a barbaric past that is characteristic of Gothic cinema. In the case of the U.S.-American South, this is particularly marked by racism, slavery, poverty, violence, and religious oppression. Further dominant themes are sexual violence and incest, moral decomposition, and, as Atkinson (2013, p. 213) writes, an "all-American, self-reliant gun lust". While Southern Gothic had faded into the background in the 1980s and 1990s, it revived in the twenty-first century with the production of films such as *Winter's Bone* (2010) starring Jennifer Lawrence. Further, Southern Gothic is also increasingly found on online streaming platforms in the form of series such as *True Blood* (2008–2014) or *True Detective* (2014–2019).

4.5.4   Asian Gothic

A rich corpus of Gothic cinema can also be found in Asia. It should be noted, however, that it remains open to question to what extent the transference of the Western concept of the Gothic tradition represents a colonial gesture that subordinates

Asian national, regional and local histories and customs to a Eurocentric view. The designation "Asian Gothic" also implies a pan-Asian culture rather than tracing the very different local cultural tendencies. For example, Katarzyna Ancuta (2012, 2014, pp. 428 ff., 208 f.) has repeatedly pointed out that the term "Asian Gothic" is complex and should be used with caution. She divides works of Asian Gothic – regardless of whether or not they contain supernatural phenomena – into three categories: First, works that imitate Western Gothic conventions, often depicting Asia and Asian cultures as the exotic other. Second, originally Asian works that give local conventions a Gothic touch, so to speak, thereby referring to the Western tradition and modify it by replacing Western motifs and elements with Asian ones. The third and most self-reflexive type is the postcolonial hybrid that addresses dichotomies between West and East, old and new, global and local, etc. (Ancuta 2012, p. 435).

Although Asian authors and filmmakers sometimes consciously reference the Western Gothic tradition, Ancuta also points out, the term "Gothic" does not feature in any Asian language except Japanese. Here the term has been internalized as *goshikku*, however, it refers mainly to pop cultural phenomena rather than to literature and film (Ancuta 2014, p. 209). At the same time, various influences from Asian folklore, mythology, and literature that existed prior to the import of Western Gothic cinema are also unmistakable (Balmain 2013, p. 399 f.). Subsuming these under the label "Gothic" is problematic, as it runs the risk of not only blurring cultural differences but also imposing a Western concept. A reading of Asian works under the auspices of the Western "Gothic" is therefore sometimes rejected in their countries of origin (Ancuta 2014, p. 210).

Moreover, cultural-historical aspects must be considered: if the Western concept of Gothic fiction, like Dark Romanticism, is often associated with the Enlightenment and modernization, these did not occur simultaneously or in the same way in other cultures. Consequently, the traumas thematized in Asian Gothic arise from the specific cultural-historical imprint of each context, which differs from that of the West. Viewing artifacts beyond Western European cultures through a lens of Gothic is nonetheless fruitful, as it helps to perceive certain aspects that would otherwise remain unrecognized (Ng 2008, p. 2 f.). Insofar as Asian Gothic can be seen as a partial import from the West, psychoanalytic theory, for example, which is often used to interpret Western Gothic cinema, can also be applied to it. Jee-woon Kim's South Korean film *Janghwa, Hongryeon* (int. title: *A Tale of Two Sisters,* 2003, US remake *The Uninvited* 2009), for example, paints a bleak psychological scenario revolving around a teenager's dissociative identity disorder within the context of a family drama. It was the first Korean film to be released in U.S.-American theaters and one of the most successful representatives of Asian Gothic with Western audiences – possibly because of its psychological approach, which these are familiar with from Western Gothic cinema. In any case, the film lends itself to psychoanalytical readings and provides an example of how Gothic cinema is predestined to address that which is difficult to put into words. Classic themes of Gothic fiction such as madness, (family) violence, abuse and oppression also can be found here. The film is inspired, as the Korean title reveals, by a folk tale from the time of the Joseon Dynasty called *Janghwa Hongnyeon jeon* (*The Story of Rose and Lotus*), which has been adapted for the screen several times. Because of such influences, Ancuta (2014, p. 222) argues that a meaningful interpretation of Asian Gothic should also draw on Asian folklore, philosophy, theories of subjectivity, or Buddhist concepts – i.e., the contexts against which the works were created and, consequently, should be interpreted.

The regionally and locally variable narratives and mythologies include, for example, an entirely different attitude toward spirits than in Western cultures. Ghosts and demons play an important role in many Asian cultures to this day and are predominantly perceived as benevolent, and encounters with them as commonplace. Here, then, a kind of Other emerges that is incompatible with the Western conception of ghosts (Ancuta 2012, 2014, pp. 430, 211). Therefore, the Western reading of the ghost as a recurring trauma is often misleading in relation to Asian Gothic, especially since Asian spirits sometimes take on forms that seem rather bizarre to Western eyes (Ancuta 2014, p. 211). Again, some of these seem more accessible to Western audiences than others: The most widely known depiction of Asian spirits was brought to us by Hideo Nakata's *Ring* (1998) with its iconic image of an Asian vengeful spirit in the form of a pale young woman with long black hair, crawling out of a television set at the end of the film (see Fig. 4.10). In addition to a 2002 U.S.-American remake, *Ring* also inspired a number of other films revolving around similar vengeful spirits, such as *Ju-On* (2002), in which a curse becomes visible on photographic and film records in the form of a long-haired woman, and which, in addition to a U.S.-American remake (*The Grudge, 2004*) continues to generate sequels to this day. The pale women with long black hair may be Japanese *onryō*, Malaysian *pontianak* or *langsuyar,* Indonesian *kunti-lanak* or Thai *phii tai thang klom*. Ancuta (2014, p. 212) points out that Western audiences, for one thing, often fail to make distinctions between such supernatural creatures and, for another, quickly grew tired of long-haired vengeful spirits after a wave of Asian Gothic in the early twenty-first century, while the vampires or werewolves that have recurred in Western Gothic cinema for over a century do not seem to bore them.

A long tradition of ghost stories can be identified in Japan: Here, the references of today's Asian Gothic films go back a whole millennium. For example, the pro-

Fig. 4.10   Sadako's ghost (Rie Ino'o) comes out of the television set in *Ring* (JP 1998), 01:26. (DVD, Anolis Entertainment/e-m-s, Germany 2003)

totypical female vengeful ghost is the murderous, jealous Rokujō from the *Genji Monogatari* (*The Tale of Prince Genji*, c. 978–1014), the first Japanese psychological novel. Japan's folkloric ghost stories can be traced back in part to Chinese tales, such as the genre of *kaidan-shū*, which often incorporates Buddhist teachings (for an overview of the Japanese Gothic tradition, see Sharp 2013). It flourished during the Edo period (1603–1868), in which also one of its most influential collections appeared, Akinari Ueda's *Ugetsu Monogatari* (*Tales Under the Rain Moon*, 1776), whose stories are partly inspired by older ones. While Gothic cinema played a special role in Japan in the postwar period, there are also several film adaptations of the *Ugetsu Monogatari:* the film of the same name by Kenji Mizoguchi (1953) is based particularly on two stories from the collection and is considered a masterpiece of Japanese cinema. The anthology film *Kaidan* of 1964 adapts tales from Lafcadio Hearn's influential 1904 collection of Japanese ghost stories of the same name. Also made in Japan in the 1960s were Kaneto Shindōs influential horror films such as *Onibaba* (1964) or *Yabu no naka no kuroneko* (1968), in which two women return from the realm of the dead in the shape of cats[2] in order to take revenge on their murderers (on monstrous women in Japanese popular culture see Dumas 2018). The fact that Shindō's first success as a director, *Genbaku no Ko*

---

[2] Ghosts in cat shape have a tradition in Japan (see Davisson 2017).

(1952) dealt with the atomic bombing of Hiroshima, a theme he revisited several times in later works, illustrates the proximity between cultural trauma and Gothic cinema.

Looking at more recent Asian Gothic cinema reveals how the characters, elements, and motifs of such folkloric narratives are interwoven with recent technological developments as ghosts inhabit telephones, television sets, or the Internet: In *Ring*, an adaptation of Kōji Suzuki's 1991 novel of the same name, the vengeful spirit Sadako produces a videotape by willpower, the reception of which leads to death after a period of 7 days. In *Cairo* (2001, US remake *Pulse* 2006), people who got in touch with ghosts via the Internet then begin to stare catatonically at their screens and eventually disappear. In one impressive scene, the protagonist Junko (Kurume Arisaka) steps backwards towards a wall after an encounter with such a ghost and turns into a dark spot that remains on the wall. Thus, while the connection between spirits and mediums in Western Gothic cinema is traditionally made through spiritualist séances, the spirits of Asian Gothic bring forth mediumistic artifacts that include technical media and vice versa.

4.6   Postcolonial Gothic

Due to Asia's long colonial history, many representatives of Asian Gothic can also be classified as Postcolonial Gothic (not least the third, hybrid type of Asian Gothic identified by Katarzyna Ancuta, which places dichotomies at its center). Postcolonial Gothic is characterized by contemporary themes and narratives centered around the transgenerational traumas and individual as well as cultural aftermaths of colonialism, racism, and migration. However, a detailed treatment of this transnational manifestation of the Gothic with its rich literary tradition is beyond the scope of this chapter. Therefore, I would like to refer here to the works of colleagues, in particular Lizabeth Paravisini-Gebert's works on the Postcolonial Gothic of the Caribbean, Ken Gelder's works with a regional focus on Australia, and Rebecca Duncan's works that concentrate on South Africa, while, for instance Alison Rudd's *Demons from the Deep*, Tabish Khair's *The Gothic, Postcolonialism and Otherness*, and Julie Hakim Azzam's dissertation *The Alien Within* each offer cross-regional overviews.

As the world's former largest colonial power, the birthplace of Gothic fiction, Great Britain, is deeply marked by its colonial history. In particular, the two main literary phases of Gothic fiction – respectively roughly in the second halves of the eighteenth and nineteenth centuries – were marked by major changes in Britain's colonial position. The rationalism of the Enlightenment brought with it a conception of the human that demarcated them on the basis of civilizational achievements not only from non-humans but also from other humans. The idea that some humans were "superior" to others served to construct racist theories, which in turn underpinned Western colonialism (see Smith and Hughes 2003, p. 1 f.). Postcolonial Gothic is often closely associated with the term Imperial Gothic, which traces the continuity of these themes back to the British Empire, thus tying them back to the Gothic literature of the eighteenth and nineteenth centuries. Not surprisingly, colonial ideas also found their way into works of the Gothic.

Gothic fiction is concerned with the marginal, the oppressed, the outcast, and the unspoken (see Turcotte and Sugars 2009, p. vii). Among other things, it addresses (as described in Sect. 2.4) the transitions between the human and the nonhuman – whether through the transformation of humans into wolves, panthers or other animals, or through vampires, ghosts, and other monsters. At the same time, Gothic fiction thus explores the question of what it means to be human, which is also directly related to racist and other hierarchies. Postcolonial Gothic is created against the background of cultural and individual traumas resulting from colonial exploitation, violence and genocide, but also deals with contemporary migration and its traumas, and processes direct colonial experiences as well as their effects and after-effects over several generations. Traces of unresolved experiences, of memories of colonial oppression, migration and national consolidation return in Postcolonial Gothic in the form of ghosts and monsters that haunt the respective individuals or cultures (Turcotte and Sugars 2009, p. viif.).

In doing so, Postcolonial Gothic can reflect the perspective of both the colonized and the colonists or migrants who set out for foreign lands out of necessity or with the prospect of a better life. Sometimes these categories are dissolved and their mutual influence and interaction are emphasized (Gelder 2014, p. 202). On the one hand, this exposes colonial strategies of constructions of otherness, but on the other hand, it also reveals the instability of the subject underlying them, which requires a distinction from an Other to be able to form its own identity (see Smith and Hughes 2003, p. 4). Postcolonial Gothic thematizes (disappointed) hopes for redefinition and metaphorical rebirth as well as identitary uprooting, guilt, violence, torn families, and foreign domination or slavery.

Postcolonial Gothic includes, on the one hand, works that refer to colonial, postcolonial, and often racist ideas as well as corresponding (historical) practices, and, on the other hand, works that were created in colonial or postcolonial contexts and span corresponding horizons of experience. On a personal and collective level, it negotiates themes of loss and impossibility: Loss of family, of home, of identitary (up-)rootedness, an impossibility of return, of change, or of becoming one with one's surroundings. Often, it also articulates the feeling of not having a voice and of being under foreign influence (Punter 2000, pp. 11–21). The construction and demonization of the Other as uncanny, monstrous, or terrifying becomes a theme in Postcolonial Gothic in a direct, metaphorical, or codified way, as do narratives and fears around migration, immigration, and foreign domination. Most importantly, Postcolonial Gothic challenges dominant political and social narratives (Turcotte and Sugars 2009, p. xviii). Cinematic examples range from postcolonial re-imaginings of canonical British Gothic novels such as Charlotte Brontë's *Jane Eyre* (1847) in Jacques Tourneur's *I Walked with a Zombie* (1943) or Emily Brontë's *Wuthering Heights* (1847) in Jane Campion's *The Piano* (1993) (see also Gelder 2014, pp. 194, 202) to original postcolonial narratives such as the Australian film *The Hunter* (2011), based on Julia Leigh's 1999 novel of the same name.

4.7   Queer Gothic

Gothic fiction's affinity for minority discourses also gives rise to its own hybridity, as well as its predilection for transgression, which includes sexual practices and identities that deviate from dominant social norms. Its marginal position as a film style, respectively literary genre, in turn, allowed it – especially in Victorian England – to address topics that were considered socially unacceptable and to articulate views that were marginalized by dominant discourses (see Haefele-Thomas 2012, p. 2). Gothic fiction, in this regard among others, proves to be a kind of testing ground for, as George Haggerty (2006, p. 2) writes, "unauthorized" gender and sexuality. If the emergence of the novel celebrated the codification of bourgeois values, Haggerty (2006, p. 10) continues, the Gothic novel documents the horror inherent in the increasingly dictatorial rule of those values. It describes the inner conflicts and anxieties of a dominant culture that demonizes deviance. Perhaps this explains the often ambivalent position of Gothic narratives, which display deviance but ultimately affirm heteronormativity. In this way, Queer Gothic questions traditional gender identities on the one hand, but on the other hand also frequently portrays queerness as the monstrous Other: "Historically, Gothic has been used as a mode to make the queer monstrous," Ardel Haefele-Thomas (2018, p. 116) write. And later: "both overt and covert queer monstrosity [have] often [been] equated with mental illness." (ibid.). Thus, queerness can be portrayed as monstrous and at the same time as sympathetic and identificatory – one does not exclude the other. Xavier Alada Reyes (2020a, p. 23) has pointed out that the increasing representation of monsters in Gothic cinema as sympathetic also entails an affirmation of monsters associated with queerness (see Sect. 2.4).

Beyond sexual orientation and gender identities, for example, E. L. McCallum (2014, p. 77) regards Gothic fiction's fascination with transgression, ambivalence, and borderlands in itself as queer:

> What makes the Gothic queer, in fact, is its investment in the liminal, the in-between, the brink – particularly, although not exclusively, the line between life and death, whether figured as the living dead of vampires, mummies, zombies, or similar supernatural beings, or the trope of living burial. This liminality, however, is especially valuable symbolically because of its dynamic uncertainty, its irresolvability.

Queerness in Gothic cinema is thus not exclusively articulated in the form of non-heteronormative sexuality. It does, however, have a particular affinity to it, especially in the twentieth century, when the Gothic closely interacted with psychoanalytic theory (see Haggerty 2006, p. 5), which in turn had a strong influence on feminist and queer theories. McCallum (2014, p. 71) has also pointed to the mutual influence of sexual politics and Gothic fiction on one another: Not only does the Gothic reflect sociocultural shifts in gender roles and identities, it also stimulates the engagement with cultural concepts of sexual and gender normativity. Gothic cinema, then, offers insights into mutable socio-sexual roles in general. It does so, among other things, through an interest in people who identify as lesbian, gay, bisexual, transgender, or queer, and in the social, cultural, and political landscapes in which they operate (see Haefele-Thomas 2018, p. 116).

According to Brian Robinson (2013, p. 143), queerness is even inscribed in the DNA of Gothic fiction itself: Not only were authors of Gothic literature from Horace Walpole to Mary Shelley, to Bram Stoker, to Oscar Wilde demonstrably or allegedly homo-, bisexual or queer, but their works, too – be it *Frankenstein, Dracula* or *The Picture of Dorian Gray* – deal with forbidden love and with the topos of being different (ibid.). Analogously in film, adaptations of these works were often made with the participation of queer or homosexual filmmakers and actors such as Friedrich Murnau or James Whale, and clearly feature queer subtexts. Some of the performances in these films (especially before the time when the sexual subtexts of the Gothic could become more explicit) can also be read as latently queer – be it Ernest Thesiger in *Bride of Frankenstein,* Vincent Price in Corman's Poe adaptations (both actors were bisexual), or Judith Anderson as Mrs. Danvers in Hitchcock's *Rebecca.* Queer Gothic is thus not so much a subcategory within the Gothic as a special interest that threads its way through its history. Listing typical representatives is therefore difficult, although queer latencies, which tend to be found in the subtexts of Gothic films of the 1930s and 1940s, become more explicit in later films, such as Polanski's *The Fearless Vampire Killers* (1967) or in *Interview with the Vampire* (1994). Finally, the most obvious example of Queer Gothic cinema, rightly celebrated as a cult classic, needs to be mentioned: *The Rocky Horror Picture Show* from 1975, an adaptation of the stage musical *The Rocky Horror Show* by Richard O'Brien (1973), which is inspired, among other things, by James Whale's *Old Dark House*.

4.8   Body Gothic

While sexuality has always been one of the favourite subjects of Gothic cinema, it has also increasingly revolved around questions of body politics and aesthetics. Not least under the influence of New Hollywood, but especially following the abolition of the Motion Picture Production Codes in the U.S.A. in 1967, which set guidelines for self-censorship, an increase in the explicit depiction of sex and violence can also be observed in mainstream film. In addition, Herschell Gordon Lewis, beginning with *Blood Feast* (1963), established a new subgenre of horror film that was later labeled "splatter." At a time when occultist movements were flaring up in the U.S.A. and Anton Szandor LaVey was about to establish the First Church of Satan in California, a series of films centering on devil worship, the incarnation of the Antichrist, and demonic possession were being made. Collectively, such films, including *Rosemary's Baby* (1968), *The Omen* (1976) or *The Exorcist* (1973), are subsumed under the label "Occult Gothic" (see for example on *The Omen:* Stiglegger 2018a, pp. 85–90).

The Exorcist not only contains a number of now iconic special effects, such as the head of the possessed girl Regan (Linda Blair) rotating by 180°, or the green jet of vomit with which she practically attacks the exorcising priest (Max von Sydow). This film also gained a new place on the screens of mainstream cinemas for supernatural horror. It replaced the historicist aesthetic of the Hammer Gothic with a contemporary setting in a fictional reality that resembled the everyday world of the viewers, thus prompting some critics to proclaim that Gothic cinema ended in 1973, the year of *The Exorcist*'s release (see e.g., Newman 2011, pp. 46–49). It is questionable to what extent it is meaningful to meet changes in the Gothic film style with a proclamation of its end. If Gothic in film has evolved beyond the historical (or historicist) settings of eighteenth- and nineteenth-century literature, then this observation should be followed by an adjustment of its theorization, including a redefinition of the conceptualization of Gothic cinema to free it from the cobwebs of Gothic vaults.

Such reflections on the end of the Gothic are grounded in particular on the differentiation between Gothic and horror films on the basis of drastic depictions of violence as mentioned at the beginning of this book (see Sect. 1.3). The moment the historical, opulent aesthetic gives way to a contemporary, simpler one, and violence and sexuality increase in front of the camera (instead of taking place off-screen) – this narratice, simply put, claims – Gothic cinema became vulgarized and therefore indistinguishable from horror film. Consequently, the end of Gothic cinema is proclaimed as soon as it undergoes a drastic change. However, transgressive physicality and sexuality have in fact been among the aesthetic and narrative components of the Gothic since its literary beginnings. The Gothic novel in the eighteenth and nineteenth centuries negotiates body images and discourses as much as it confronts its readers with graphic descriptions of injuries, corpses, or bodily fluids. Although the depiction of violence is usually only marginal here, as Aldana Reyes (2014, pp. 3–9) writes, the bodies of classical Gothic literature already had disturbing qualities through their status as an "in-between", as resisting an unambiguous categorization and thus an existence as normative bodies: They refuse the differentiation between humans and animals (e.g., in H. G. Wells' *The Island of Doctor Moreau*), of living and dead (e.g., in Edgar Allan Poe's *The Facts in the Case of M. Valdemar*) or of male and female (e.g., in Richard Marsh's *The Beetle*). The bodies of Gothic fiction, then, Aldana Reyes (2014, pp. 3–9) concludes, have always been grotesque, deformed, excessive, and transgressive. Depictions of monsters and bodily fluids are often abject, and excessive depictions of violence also have a long tradition, including the theater of the Grand Guignol (see Aldana Reyes 2020b, p. 398, on the Grand Guignol see Gordon 1988).

In contrast, since the late 1970s, films that can be summarized under the label of Body Gothic have focused on the corporeal, the somatic, and the visceral (see Aldana Reyes 2014, p. 17). Here, one's own body becomes a site of unstoppable and sometimes inexplicable changes – be they caused by puberty, illness, surgery, violence or something else. These metamorphoses, as well as the crisis of self-perception that is linked to them, become the primary source of the Uncanny. The claustrophobic space of the Gothic shifts inward, which consequently entails a turning away from castles, vaults, and secret passages.

Since the 1980s, the target group for horror and Gothic (as well as for popular culture in general) has increasingly been adolescents and young adults, whose bodies, due to puberty, become the scene of transformations and an increased hormonal control of behavior. This is another reason for Gothic cinema's rapprochement with contemporary everyday life. The slasher, a subgenre of the horror film, foregrounds the serial mutilation of teenage bodies. While these films are often not considered to be representatives of Gothic cinema, Peter Hutchings (1996), for example, has shown that slasher films such as *Halloween* (1978) or *A Nightmare on Elm Street* (1984) do in fact explore new manifestations of the monstrous in the tradition of Gothic fiction. Not only is their serial structure, including the theme of the return of the (un)dead monster, an import from the Universal Horror Cycle of the 1930s and 1940s, the slasher film also stands in the tradition of the Italian *giallo*, the German Edgar Wallace films or Hitchcock's *Psycho*. "Freddy Krueger, Jason Vorhees and Mike Myers," Xavier Aldana Reyes (2020b, p. 400) writes, "of course operate much like the classic Universal monsters, but their lack of humanity and their brute force shifted the parameters of the horror film and of body horror. [...] With the slasher, body horror went mainstream."

Unlike serial killers like Norman Bates, the faceless, masked, or disfigured murderers in *The Texas Chainsaw Massacre, Halloween, Friday the 13th* or *A Nightmare on Elm Street*, however, represent a more abstract threat whose origins often lie in a past to be uncovered and thus prove characteristic of Gothic cinema. In particular, the *Nightmare on Elm Street* franchise, with its clear focus on the paranoiac indistinguishability of dream, imagination, and reality, can be identified as representative of Gothic cinema. Here, a group of teenagers are hunted in their nightmares by the child molester and murderer Freddy Krueger (Robert Englund), who was killed by their parents, after the justice system failed to convict him. Krueger returns as the personification of this traumatic event from the past in the dream world of the teenage children. As the film progresses, these find it increasingly difficult to distinguish whether they are asleep or awake, whether they are paranoid or not careful enough. As a monster who ultimately questions the differentiation of reality and fantasy, Freddy Krueger is a threat from within *par excellence*. He also exhibits traits of two classic monsters of Gothic fiction: the vampire and the ghost, and thus emerges as a hybrid Gothic monster (see Hutchings 1996, p. 96; on Krueger, see also Rein 2015; on *A Nightmare on Elm Street* in general see Rein 2012).

In the 1980s, Gothic cinema took hold of small towns, suburbs, and owner-occupied housing developments, invading the nuclear family and its immediate social environment, which it presents as destructive rather than nurturing. Surrounded by their parents and siblings, the young protagonists of 1980s teenage Body Gothic are alone and isolated. What is more, parents and other authority figures often contribute to the teens' untimely and violent demise. Instead of offering support and security, they are typically clueless, inflexible and intransigent, not taking their children's worries and needs seriously, getting in the way of their attempts at finding solutions, and thereby unwittingly playing into the hands of the killers. In the slasher film, the home and the family offer no security. On the contrary, the domestic environment is one of isolation and threat.

As the metamorphic body becomes the central place and medium of the Gothic, the fascination with monsters increases. Cinematographically, this shift in attention is accompanied by a new prominence of special effects – be it the transformation into a werewolf in *An American Werewolf in London* (1981), which is echoed in the music video for Michael Jackson's *Thriller* (1983) (also directed by John Landis and with special effects by Rick Baker) or the omnipresence of blood, slime and prosthetics in the body Gothic from *Friday the 13th* (1980) to David Cronenberg's *Videodrome* (1983) to Stuart Gordon's *Re-Animator* (1985). The attention to corporeality, identity, and sexuality in the Body Gothic also opens the view to political or sociocultural criticism. "[T]he Gothic often provides a perfect stage upon which to question normative ideas about gender, sexuality, race, class and religion," writes Xavier Aldana Reyes (2020a, p. 215). He cites *Elephant Man* (1980) as an example in which biographical incidents of the historical figure Joseph Merrick become a vehicle for moral-ethical criticism of his exploitation and the monetization of his illness by others.

In view of cultural history, Gothic cinema's heightened interest in corporeality can – as well as that of the literature of the Gothic Revival in the late nineteenth century – be tied back to developments in science, medicine, and technology: the 1980s saw the emergence of bioengineering, stem cell research and cloning, enormous advances in organ transplantation, and accompanying shifts in the boundary between life and death. The rampant AIDS pandemic raised awareness of the potential consequences of infectious diseases and established a new link between sexuality and death. At the same time, a cult of youthfulness, slimness and body culture emerged, which, in addition to the heyday of aerobics, also caused an increase in diseases such as anorexia or bulimia. In academia, specifically in the field of Cultural Studies, Women's Studies, which had been emerging internationally since the 1970s, enjoyed increasing attention and dissemination and gradually formed into Gender Studies, which established itself as an independent field of study and research. This was joined in the 1980s by Queer Studies and Disability Studies as new fields of research that, among other things, focused on the intertwining of body and identity and critiqued social constructions of the normative body (see Aldana Reyes 2014, pp. 20 f.).

Example: The Fly (1986)

As an example of Body Gothic outside of the teen film, in the following I would like to take a closer look at David Cronenberg's *The Fly*. In the tradition of *Frankenstein*, the film focuses on a scientist who proclaims the creation of a new human being while being irresponsible with his research. Unlike previous Mad Scientists, Seth Brundle (Jeff Goldblum) experiments on himself and does not initially endanger others. However, as his transformation into a human-sized fly progresses, his empathy dwindles, making him increasingly reckless and ultimately an acute threat to those around him, especially his lover Veronica Quaife (Geena

Davis). It is not only because of this that *The Fly* and Brundle's physical degeneration can be interpreted as an allegory of the rampant social and physical effects of AIDS (see, e.g., Mathijs 2003).

Particularly in comparison to the literary original, a 1957 short story by George Langelaan, as well as to the 1958 film adaptation starring Vincent Price, the focus on Brundle's body as a site of metamorphosis is striking in Cronenberg's film. In the earlier works, the scientist's accidental fusion with a fly produces *two* bodies: a monstrous human one with the head and arm of a fly, and the body of a fly with a tiny human head. Under the cultural and scientific historical conditions of the 1980s described above, however, Brundle in Cronenberg's version genetically fuses with the fly at the molecular level and successively transforms from a human into something else over the course of the film: into a new being that is neither human nor fly (see Fig. 4.11). This clearly shows the difference between the Body Gothic of the 1980s and its predecessors: While earlier representations of corporeality and monstrosity in Gothic cinema focused on an externalization of the Other and the distancing from it – if not elimination of it – the Body Gothic of the 1980s emphasizes the inseparability of the monstrous from the "normal," which can fluidly merge into one another.

In the tradition of Kafka's Gregor Samsa, Brundle follows and documents his own transformation very closely – with caution and curiosity as much as with fascination and disgust. The scientist gives a name to the new being he transforms

Fig. 4.11 Jeff Goldblum as Brundlefly in *The Fly* (USA/UK/CA 1986), 01:05. (DVD, Twentieth Century Fox Home Entertainment, Germany 2001)

into, as if he had discovered a new species: Brundlefly. Thus, while the short story and the 1958 adaptation follow the logic of a monstrous Other that is to be eliminated and stylize the monstrous fly as an enemy, Cronenberg's Brundle not only successively becomes this Other himself, he also observes and accepts this change. For him, the monstrous body as the scene of inexplicable change is an object of fear as much as of acceptance and redefinition of himself, which is also associated with hope (Aldana Reyes 2014, p. 59 f.).

Consequently, Brundle's body is not only portrayed as a source of fear and threat and its metamorphosis not exclusively as horrifying, abject, and disgusting. Positive effects of the transformation are also shown, for example Brundlefly needs less and less sleep and develops extraordinary physical abilities such as increased strength or the capability to walk on the ceiling. He optimistically conceives of his metamorphosis as a physical improvement and a liberation from societal body norms. Brundlefly even begins to develop an insectoid philosophy from his specific perspective. As the transformation progresses, however, it becomes apparent that it is not headed towards a superhumanly gifted version of Seth Brundle, but towards something animalistic and threatening that successively escapes his (self-)control. Among the human abilities and qualities that Brundlefly gradually forfeits is his identification with himself (or rather with his former personality). "His protagonists," Arno Meteling (2006, p. 202) writes about David Cronenberg, "are torn and dissolved between the colonizing technique of rational reason and the irrationally rampant and metastasizing body". Last but not least, the scientist and inventor Seth Brundle, during his metamorphosis into Brundlefly, as his body increasingly forms bulges and takes on animalistic features, finds himself in the conflict between rationality and irrationality, which is one of the fundamental ambivalences of Gothic cinema. The central angst of Body Gothic, *The Fly* reveals, consequently no longer revolves around becoming an Other, but around the loss of one's own subjectivity and identity (Aldana Reyes 2014, p. 63).

References

Literature

Abbott, Stacey. 2018. Dracula on film and TV from 1960 to the present. In *The Cambridge companion to Dracula*, ed. Roger Luckhurst, 192–206. New York: Cambridge University Press.

Aldana Reyes, Xavier. 2014. *Body Gothic: Corporeal transgression in contemporary literature and horror film*. Cardiff: University of Wales Press.

————. 2020a. *Gothic cinema*. London: Routledge.

————. 2020b. Abjection and body horror. In *The Palgrave handbook of contemporary Gothic*, ed. Clive Bloom, 393–410. New York: Palgrave Macmillan.

Ancuta, Katarzyna. 2012. Asian Gothic. In *A new companion to the Gothic*, ed. David Punter, 428–441. Malden: Whiley-Blackwell.

————. 2014. Asian Gothic. In *The Cambridge companion to the modern Gothic*, ed. Jerrold E. Hogle, 203–223. Cambridge: Cambridge University Press.

Atkinson, Michael. 2013. Southern Gothic. In *Gothic: The dark heart of film*, ed. James Bell, 121. London: BFI.

Azzam, Julie Hakim. 2008. *The alien within: Postcolonial Gothic and the politics of home* (Dissertation, University of Pittsburgh). D-Scholarship. Institutional Repository at the University of Pittsburgh. https://d-scholarship.pitt.edu/id/eprint/9521. Accessed on: 26 Oct. 2020.

Balmain, Colette. 2013. Southeast Asian Gothic cinema. In *The Gothic world*, ed. Glennis Byron and Dale Townshend, 399–411. London: Routledge.

Benson, Josef. 2020. American Gothic westerns: Tales of racial slavery and genocide. In *Gothic film: An Edinburgh companion*, ed. Richard J. Hand and Jay McRoy, 194–205. Edinburgh: Edinburgh University Press.

Clarke, Roger. 2013. Spectres of the past. In *Gothic: The dark heart of film*, ed. James Bell, 84–92. London: BFI.

Davison, Carol Margaret. 2018. Gothic American film & TV. In *The Cambridge companion to American Gothic*, ed. Jeffrey A. Weinstock, 215–228. Cambridge: Cambridge University Press.

Davisson, Zack. 2017. *Kaibyō: The supernatural cats of Japan*. Seattle: Chin Music Press Inc./Mercuria Press.

Dumas, Raechel. 2018. *The monstrous-feminine in contemporary Japanese popular culture*. New York: Palgrave Macmillan.

Duncan, Rebecca. 2018. *South African Gothic: Anxiety and creative dissent in the post-apartheid imagination and beyond*. Cardiff: University of Wales Press.

Forshaw, Barry. 2013. The British influence. In *Gothic: The dark heart of film*, ed. James Bell, 22 f. London: BFI.

Gelder, Ken. 2014. The postcolonial Gothic. In *The Cambridge companion to the modern Gothic*, ed. Jerrold E. Hogle, 191–207. Cambridge: Cambridge University Press.

Gordon, Mel. 1988. *The Grand Guignol: Theatre of fear and terror*. New York: Amok Press.

Haefele-Thomas, Ardel. 2012. *Queer others in Victorian Gothic: Transgressing monstrosity*. Cardiff: University of Wales Press.

————. 2018. Queer American Gothic. In *The Cambridge companion to American Gothic*, ed. Jeffrey A. Weinstock, 115–127. Cambridge: Cambridge University Press.

Haggerty, George E. 2006. *Queer Gothic*. Urbana: University of Illinois Press.

Halberstam, J. 1995. *Skin shows: Gothic horror and the Technology of Monsters*. Durham: Duke University Press.

Hart, Adam C. 2020. Transitional Gothic: Hammer's Gothic revival and new horror. In *Gothic film: An Edinburgh companion*, ed. Richard J. Hand and Jay McRoy, 58–76. Edinburgh: Edinburgh University Press.

Hentschel, Frank. 2011. *Töne der Angst: Die Musik im Horrorfilm*. Berlin: Bertz + Fischer.

Hutchings, Peter. 1996. Tearing your soul apart: Horror's new monsters. In *Modern Gothic: A reader*, ed. Victor Sage and Allan Lloyd Smith, 89–103. Manchester: Manchester University Press.

———. 2003. *Dracula*. London: I.B. Tauris.

Kavka, Misha. 2002. The Gothic on screen. In *The Cambridge companion to Gothic fiction*, ed. Jerrold E. Hogle, 209–228. Cambridge: Cambridge University Press.

Khair, Tabish. 2009. *The Gothic, Postcolonialism and Otherness: Ghosts from elsewhere*. New York: Palgrave Macmillan.

Koven, Mikel J. 2020. The Italian Gothic film. In *Gothic film: An Edinburgh companion*, ed. Richard J. Hand and Jay McRoy, 155–169. Edinburgh: Edinburgh University Press.

Le Fanu, Joseph Sheridan. 1872. *Carmilla*. WikiSource. https://en.wikisource.org/wiki/Carmilla. Accessed on: 22 Nov. 2020.

Lucas, Tim. 2013. Mario Bava and the Italian Gothic. In *Gothic: The dark heart of film*, ed. James Bell, 56 f. London: BFI.

Mathijs, Ernest. 2003. AIDS references in the critical reception of David Cronenberg: "It may not be such a bad disease after all". *Cinema Journal* 42 (4): 29–45.

McCallum, Ellen L. 2014. The "queer limits" in the modern Gothic. In *The Cambridge companion to the modern Gothic*, ed. Jerrold E. Hogle, 71–86. Cambridge: Cambridge University Press.

McCarty, John. 1984. *Splatter movies: Breaking the last taboo of the screen*. Bromley: Columbus Books.

Meteling, Arno. 2006. *Monster. Zu Körperlichkeit und Medialität im modernen Horrorfilm*. Bielefeld: transcript.

Morgart, James. 2013. Gothic horror film from *The Haunted Castle* (1896) to *Psycho* (1960). In *The Gothic world*, ed. Glennis Byron and Dale Townshend, 376–387. London: Routledge.

Newman, Kim. 2011. *Nightmare movies: Horror on screen since the 1960s*. London: Bloomsbury.

Ng, Andrew Hock Soon. 2008. Introduction: The Gothic visage of Asian narratives. In *Asian Gothic: Essays on literature, film and anime*, ed. Andrew Hock Soon Ng, 1–15. Jefferson: McFarland & Co.

Peirse, Alison. 2018. Dracula on Film 1931–1959. In *The Cambridge companion to Dracula*, ed. Roger Luckhurst, 179–191. Cambridge: Cambridge University Press.

Poe, Edgar Allan. (1839). The fall of the House of Usher. The Poe Museum. https://www.poemuseum.org/the-fall-of-the-house-of-usher. Accessed on: 22 Nov. 2020.

Punter, David. 2000. *Postcolonial imaginings. Fictions of a new world order*. Edinburgh: Edinburgh University Press.

Rein, Katharina. 2012. *Gestörter film: Wes Cravens A Nightmare on Elm Street*. Darmstadt: Büchner.

———. 2015. The proletarian ghost. Freddy Krueger as parasite. In *Beyond the night: Creatures of life, death and the in-between*, ed. Nadine Farghaly, 181–201. Newcastle upon Tyne: Cambridge Scholars Publishing.

Robinson, Brian. 2013. Queer Gothic. In *Gothic: The dark heart of film*, ed. James Bell, 143. London: BFI.

Rudd, Alison. 2010. *Postcolonial Gothic fictions from the Caribbean, Canada, Australia and New Zealand*. Cardiff: University of Wales Press.

Schwanebeck, Wieland. 2020. From German Grusel to giallo: Transculturality in the West-German Edgar Wallace series. *Literature/Film Quarterly* 48/2 "Transcultural adaptation". https://lfq.salisbury.edu/_issues/48_2/from_german_grusel_to_giallo_edgar_wallace_series.html. Accessed on: 20 Nov. 2020.

Sharp, Jasper. 2013. Japanese Gothic. In *Gothic: The dark heart of film*, ed. James Bell, 94 f. London: BFI.

Smith, Andrew W. 2020. "So why shouldn't I write of monsters?": Defining monstrosity in Universal's horror films. In *Gothic film: An Edinburgh companion*, ed. Richard J. Hand and Jay McRoy, 21–36. Edinburgh: Edinburgh University Press.

Smith, Andrew W., and William Hughes. 2003. Introduction: The Enlightenment Gothic and Postcolonialism. In *Empire and the Gothic: The politics of genre*, ed. Andrew Smith and William Hughes, 1–12. Basingstoke: Palgrave Macmillan.

Stiglegger, Marcus. 2008. In den Farben der Nacht. Mario Bava zwischen Gothic Horror und Giallo Thriller. In *Das goldene Zeitalter des italienischen Films*, ed. Thomas Koebner and Irmbert Schenk, 412–426. München: edition text+kritik.

———. 2018a. *Grenzüberschreitungen. Exkursionen in den Abgrund der Filmgeschichte: Der Horrorfilm*. Berlin: Martin Schmitz.

———. 2018b. German Angst? Zur historischen und aktuellen Bedeutung fantastischer Genres im deutschen Kino. In *Fantastisches in dunklen Sälen: Science-Fiction, Horror und Fantasy im jungen deutschen Film*, ed. Christian Alexius and Sarah Beicht, 37–64. Marburg: Schüren.

Syed, Tuğçe Bıçakçı. 2018. *Theorising Turkish Gothic. National identity, ideology and the Gothic*. (PhD dissertation, Lancaster University).

Turcotte, Gerry, and Cynthia C. Sugars. 2009. Introduction: Canadian literature and the postcolonial Gothic. In *Unsettled remains: Canadian literature and the postcolonial Gothic*, ed. Cynthia C. Sugars and Gerry Turcotte, vii–xxvi. Waterloo: Wilfrid Laurier University Press.

Film

A Nightmare on Elm Street. USA 1984. Directed by Wes Craven. New Line Cinema.

Addams Family Reunion. USA 1998. Directed by David Payne. Fox Family Films und Saban Entertainment.

Addams Family Values. USA 1993. Directed by Barry Sonnenfeld. Paramount Pictures.

Blood Feast. USA 1963. Directed by Herschell Gordon Lewis. Friedman-Lewis Productions.

Bride of Frankenstein. USA 1935. Directed by James Whale. Universal Pictures.

Crimson Peak. Canada/USA/Mexico 2015. Directed by Guillermo del Toro. Double Dare You/Legendary Entertainment.

Danza macabra. Italy/France 1964. Directed by Anthony Dawson [i.e. Antonio Margheriti] and Sergio Corbucci. Giovanni Addessi Produzione Cinematografica/Ulysse Productions/ Vulsinia Films.

Dark Shadows. TV series. USA 1966–1971. Created by Dan Curtis. Dan Curtis Productions.

Dark Shadows. TV series. USA 1991. Created by Dan Curtis. Dan Curtis Productions/MGM Television.

Dark Shadows. USA/Australia/UK 2012. Directed by Tim Burton. Warner Bros. et al.

Dead Man. USA/Germany/Japan 1995. Directed by Jim Jarmusch. Pandora Filmproduktion et al.

Der Golem. German Reich 1915. Directed by Henrik Galee and Paul Wegener. Deutsche Bioscop GmbH.

Der Mönch mit der Peitsche. West Germany 1967. Directed by Alfred Vohrer. Rialto Film.

Der WiXXer. Germany 2004. Directed by Tobi Baumann. Rat Pack Filmproduktion.

Django. Italy/Spain 1966. Directed by Sergio Corbucci. B. R. C. Produzione Film-Rome/ Tecisa.

Django Unchained. USA 2012. Directed by Quentin Tarantino. The Weinstein Company/ Columbia Pictures.

Dracula. UK 1958. Directed by Terence Fisher. Hammer Films.

Drakula halála. Hungary/Austria/France 1921. Directed by Károly Lajthay. Corvin Film [lost].

Dressed to Kill. USA 1980. Directed by Brian De Palma. Filmways Pictures/Cinema 77/ Film Group.

Easy Rider. USA 1969. Directed by Dennis Hopper. Pando Company/Raybert Productions.

Et mourir de plaisir. France/Italy 1960. Directed by Roger Vadim. Films EGE/Documento Film.

Farin Urlaub: Dusche. Music video clip. Germany 2005. Directed by Norbert Heitker. QFilmproduktion.

Frankenstein. USA 1931. Directed by James Whale. Universal Pictures.

Friday the 13th. USA 1980. Directed by Sean S. Cunningham. Paramount Pictures/ Georgetown Productions Inc./Sean S. Cunningham Films.

Genbaku no Ko. Japan 1952. Directed by Kaneto Shindō. Kindai Eiga Kyokai/Mingei.

German Angst. Germany 2015. Directed by Jörg Buttgereit, Michal Kosakowski and Andreas Marschall. Kosakowski Films.

Halloween. USA 1978. Directed by John Carpenter. Compass International Pictures.

House of Usher. USA 1960. Directed by Roger Corman. Alta Vista Productions.

I Vampiri. Italiy 1957. Directed by Riccardo Freda. Titanus/Athena Cinematografica.

I Walked with a Zombie. USA 1935. Directed by Jacques Tourneur. RKO Radio Pictures.

Inferno. Italy 1980. Directed by Dario Argento. Produzioni Intersound.

Interview with the Vampire. USA 1994. Directed by Neil Jordan. Geffen Pictures.

Invasion of the Body Snatchers. USA 1956. Directed by Don Siegel. Walter Wanger Pictures.

Janghwa, Hongryeon. South Korea 2003. Directed by Jee-woon Kim. B.O.M. Film Productions Co./Masulpiri Films/iPictures.

Ju-on. Japan 2002. Directed by Takashi Shimizu. Pioneer LDC et al.

Kaidan. Japan 1964. Directed by Masaki Kobayashi. Bungei et al.

Kairo. Japan 2001. Directed by Kiyoshi Kurosawa. Daiei Eiga et al.

L'orribile segreto del Dr. Hichcock. Italy 1962. Directed by Robert Hampton [i.e. Riccardo Freda]. Panda Film.

La frusta e il corpo. Italy/France 1963. Directed by John M. Old [i.e. Mario Bava]. Vox Film et al.

La maschera del demonio. Italy 1960. Directed by Mario Bava. Galatea Film/Jolly Film.

La terza madre. Italy 2007. Directed by Dario Argento. Medusa Film et al.

Låt den rätte komma in. Sweden 2008. Directed by Tomas Alfredson. EFTI et al.

Le Viol du Vampire. France 1968. Directed by Jean Rollin. Les Films ABC.

Let Me In. UK/USA 2010. Directed by Matt Reeves. Overture Films et al.

Mágia. Hungary 1917. Directed by Alexander Korda. Corvin Film.

Malabimba. Italy 1979. Directed by Andrew White [i.e. Andrea Bianchi]. Filmarte.

Michael Jackson: Thriller. Music video clip. USA 1983. Directed by John Landis. Optimum Productions.

Nella stretta morsa del ragno. Italy/France/West Germany 1971. Directed by Anthony M. Dawson [i.e. Antonio Margheriti]. Paris-Cannes Productions/Produzione DC7/Terra-Filmkunst.

Neues vom Wixxer. Germany 2007. Directed by Cyrill Boss and Philipp Stennert. B.A. Produktion/Medienfonds GFP/Rat Pack Filmproduktion.

Nosferatu, eine Symphonie des Grauens. Weimar Republic 1922. Directed by Friedrich Wilhelm Murnau. Jofa-Atelier Berlin-Johannisthal/Prana-Film GmbH.

Onibaba. Japan 1964. Directed by Kaneto Shindō. Kindai Eiga Kyokai/Tokyo Eiga Co. Ltd.

Otto – Die Serie. TV series. Germany 2015. Directed by Otto Waalkes. RTL/Ruessel Video & Audio.

Pánico en el transsiberiano. UK/Spain 1972. Directed by Gene Martin [i. e. Eugenio Martín]. Granada Films/Benmar Productions.

Police Academy 3: Back in Training. Canada/USA 1986. Directed by Jerry Paris. Police Academy Productions/Warner Bros.

Psycho. USA 1960. Directed by Alfred Hitchcock. Shamley Productions.

Pulse. USA/Rumania/South Africa 2006. Directed by Jim Sonzero. The Weinstein Company/Distant Horizon/Neo Art & Logic.

Re-Animator. USA 1985. Directed by Stuart Gordon. Empire Pictures/Re-Animator Productions.

Rebecca. USA 1940. Directed by Alfred Hitchcock. Selznick International Pictures.

Ring. Japan 1998. Directed by Hideo Nakata. Basara Pictures et al.

Rosemary's Baby. USA 1968. Directed by Roman Polanski. William Castle Productions.

Route 66, TV series. USA 1960–1964. Lizard's Leg and Owlet's Wing (season 3, episode 6), broadcast: 26 Oct. 1962 on CBS. Directed by Robert Gist. Lancer-Edling Productions/Screen Gems.

Scoobie Doo, Where Are You!. Animated TV series. USA 1969–1976. Created by Joe Ruby and Ken Spears. Hanna-Barbera Productions/Taft Broadcasting.

Shadow of a Doubt. USA 1943. Directed by Alfred Hitchcock. Universal Pictures.

Suspiria. Italy 1977. Directed by Dario Argento. Seda Spettacoli.

Tempi duri per i vampiri. Italy/France 1959. Directed by Steno [i.e. Stefano Vanzina]. CEI et al.

Terrore nello spazio. Italy/Spain 1965. Directed by Mario Bava. Italian International Film/Castilla Cooperativa Cinematografíca/American International Pictures.

The Addams Family. TV series. USA 1964–1966. Created by David Levy. Filmways Television.

The Addams Family XXX. USA 2011. Directed by Rodney Moore. Sweet Mess Films.

The Addams Family. USA 1991. Directed by Barry Sonnenfeld. Orion Pictures/Paramount Pictures/Scott Rudin Productions.

The Conversation. USA 1974. Directed by Francis Ford Coppola. The Directors Company et al.

The Curse of Frankenstein. UK 1957. Directed by Terence Fisher. Hammer Films.

The Elephant Man. USA/UK 1980. Directed by David Lynch. Brooksfilms.

The Exorcist. USA 1973. Directed by William Friedkin. Warner Bros./Hoya Productions.

The Fearless Vampire Killers. UK/USA 1967. Directed by Roman Polanski. Cadre Films/ Filmways Pictures.

The Fly. USA 1958. Directed by Kurt Neumann. Twentieth Century Fox.

The Fly. USA/UK/Canada 1986. Directed by David Cronenberg. SLM Production Group/ Brooksfilms.

The Glass Menagerie. USA 1950. Directed by Irving Rasper. Charles K. Feldman Group.

The Grudge. USA 2004. Directed by Takashi Shimizu. Columbia Pictures et al.

The Hunter. Australia 2011. Directed by Daniel Nettheim. Porchlight Films et al.

The Invisible Man. USA 1933. Directed by James Whale. Universal Pictures.

The Last House on the Left. USA 1972. Directed by Wes Craven. Sean S. Cunningham Films/The Night Co./Lobster Enterprises.

The Lodger: A Story of the London Fog. UK 1927. Directed by Alfred Hitchcock. Gainsborough Pictures/Piccadilly Pictures.

The Man from Planet X. USA 1951. Directed by Edgar G. Ulmer. Mid Century Film Productions.

The Masque of the Red Death. USA/UK 1964. Directed by Roger Corman. Alta Vista Productions.

The Munsters. TV series. USA 1964–1966. Created by Allan Burns and Chris Hayward. CBS/Kayro-Vue Productions.

The New Addams Family. TV series. USA/Canada 1998–1999. Fox Family Channel et al.

The Night of the Hunter. USA 1955. Directed by Charles Laughton. Paul Gregory Productions.

The Old Dark House. USA 1932. Directed by James Whale. Universal Pictures.

The Omen. UK/USA 1976. Directed by Richard Donner. Twentieth Century-Fox et al.

The Phantom of the Opera. USA 1925. Directed by Rupert Julian. Universal Pictures.

The Piano. New Zealand et al. 1993. Directed by Jane Campion. CiBy 2000 et al.

The Raven. USA 1963. Directed by Roger Corman. Alta Vista Productions.

The Ring. USA 2002. Directed by Gore Verbinski. DreamWorks et al.

The Rocky Horror Picture Show. USA/UK 1975. Directed by Jim Sharman. Twentieth Century Fox/Michael White Productions.

The Simpsons. TV series. USA 1989–. Treehouse of Horror XX (season 21, episode 4), first broadcast: 18 Oct. 2009 on Fox Network. Directed by Mike B. Anderson and Matthew Schofield. Gracie Films/20th Century Fox Television.

The Texas Chain Saw Massacre. USA 1974. Directed by Tobe Hooper. Vortex.

The Uninvited. USA 2009. Directed by Charles and Thomas Guard. Dreamworks Pictures et al.

The Wild Bunch. USA 1969. Directed by Sam Peckinpah. Warner Bros./Seven Arts.

The Woman in Black. UK 1989. Directed by Herbert Wise. Central Films et al.

The Woman in Black. UK et al. 2012. Directed by James Watkins. Hammer Films et al.

True Blood. TV series. USA 2008–2014. Created by: Alan Ball. Your Face Goes Here Entertainment/Home Box Office.

True Detective. TV series. USA 2014–2015, 2019. Created by Nic Pizzolatto. Anonymous Content/HBO Entertainment/Passenger.

Ugetsu monogatari. Japan 1953. Directed by Kenji Mizoguchi. Daiei Studios.

Vampyros Lesbos. West Germany/Spain 1971. Directed by Franco Manera [i.e. Jesús Franco]. CCC Telecine et al.

Videodrome. Canada/USA 1983. Directed by David Cronenberg. Filmplan International et al.

Vincent. USA 1982. Directed by Tim Burton. Walt Disney Productions.

Wednesday. TV series. USA 2022. Created by Alfred Gough and Miles Millar. Netflix et al.

Winter's Bone. USA 2010. Directed by Debra Granik. Anonymous Content/Winter's Bone Productions.

Yabu no naka no kuroneko. Japan 1968. Directed by Kaneto Shindō. Toho Company.

Gothic Cinema Around 2000: Old Monsters in a New Guise

5

If the Universal Studios were already producing Gothic films in series almost a century ago, in recent decades, it has been serialized even more: Not only is Gothic increasingly migrating to series formats, but film production is also dominated by sequels, prequels and remakes – old familiar monsters are revived, dusted off and restaged. Characters, elements and aesthetics of the Gothic have increasingly appeared in other film genres than horror since the 1980s. Crossovers with other genres proliferate: *Near Dark* (1987), for example, is a blend of vampire film, the Western, and a road movie. Another example is *The Name of the Rose* (1986), a historicist murder mystery set in a monastery, based on Umberto Eco's novel of the same name. The film is heavily influenced by Gothic aesthetics and can be identified as a hybrid between Gothic, historical drama, and crime film. New possibilities in the field of special effects also brought about changes in film aesthetics, for example when the vampires in *The Lost Boys* (1987) can switch between a human and a monstrous face with distinctly animalistic features, fangs and colored contact lenses. A variation on this so-called Game Face later also distinguished the vampires in *Buffy the Vampire Slayer* (1997–2003), who only become recognizable as such in this temporary metamorphosis. A reduced version of the Game Face still appears in *True Blood*, where vampires are outwardly indistinguishable from humans because they can "retract" their elongated fangs at will.

Around the turn of the millennium, we can observe an accumulation of ghosts in Gothic cinema, in some cases reinterpreting and re-staging canonical narratives. In Chap. 7 the Netflix series *The Haunting of Hill House* (2018), based on Shirley Jackson's 1959 novel of the same name, is examined as an example of this. As described in Sect. 2.2, haunting phenomena in recent decades have been strongly associated with technical media, for example in *Sixth Sense* (1999), in which the

© The Author(s), under exclusive license to Springer Fachmedien Wiesbaden GmbH, part of Springer Nature 2023
K. Rein, *Gothic Cinema*, https://doi.org/10.1007/978-3-658-40721-6_5

boy Vincent (Donnie Wahlberg) is talking to a ghost, whose voice is inaudible to other characters but is registered by a tape recorder (see Meteling 2006, p. 301 f.). In *The Blair Witch Project* (1999), teenagers attempt to capture an alleged witch in the woods on video via a handheld camera. Its famous found footage aesthetic, which spurred a wave of imitations in the early twenty-first century, can also be seen as an update of what has been a tradition in the Gothic novel: the found manuscript narrative (see Sect. 2.1).

Especially since the 1990s, Gothic aesthetics have become increasingly mainstream – not only does the Gothic attract larger audiences, but its elements increasingly diffuse into other genres such as the romantic comedy, or children's and teen films. Tim Burton's films in particular, discussed in the final section of this chapter, have blended the aesthetics of Gothic cinema with those of the Goth subculture, popularizing both for a wide audience.

5.1   New Zombies

Gothic cinema's interest in corporeality caused, among other things, a turn toward the zombie film, whose first representatives walked stiffly across the screen as early as 1932 in *White Zombie*, at the command of the "voodoo master" "Murder" Legendre (Bela Lugosi). While in 1978 the zombie became a symbol of criqtique of capitalism and its dull, thoughtless consumption in George A. Romero's *Dawn of the Dead*, this monster is on the rise in the twenty-first century, in times of climate catastrophe and hypercapitalism. The scenarios of the zombie film, typically associated with cannibalism, with their display of internal organs and decomposing bodies, are predestined for a splatter aesthetic.

In the twenty-first century, zombies, too, are diversifying. Some of them appear sexualized and become protagonists in films that deal with queer sexuality (see, for example, Fürst 2010; Grilli 2010). We also encounter them in other genres, from romantic comedies to slapstick to more thoughtful films that stand less in the tradition of splatter zombie films like *Braindead* (1992) than in that of Romero's socially critical cinema like *Night of the Living Dead* (1968) and its successors. An example is the Canadian *Pontypool* (2008), which also offers an interesting variation on the epidemiological metaphor of zombiism: here, it is as a disease transmitted not through bites and bodily fluids, but through language. While vampirism is also often compared to a contagious disease, zombiism is better suited to the analogy with a virus because of its aimless and indiscriminate dissemination through bites. When, in *Pontypool*, it is the speaking and hearing of certain words or combinations of them that triggers zombification, the epidemiological metaphor is transformed into political criticism. Insofar as Gothic cinema, as outlined in Part I, takes place in claustrophobic spaces, explores the horrors within, and uses ambivalence and the Uncanny as atmospheric tools along with monsters and an atmosphere of diffuse threat, *Pontypool* is an outstanding example of contemporary Zombie Gothic. The film is set mostly in a radio studio, largely cut off from the wintry outside world. Those inside this claustrophobic, isolated space gradually fall into the grip of a deadly threat from the outside about which they have no information. Due to the high infectivity of zombiism via language, even former allies within this enclosed space run the risk of becoming monsters at any time – and even without physical contact with zombies. As an intimate play, the film is comparatively minimalistically staged, slowly narrated, and builds an atmosphere of dreariness and oppressiveness that is characteristic of Gothic cinema.

While the vampire is more and more portrayed as human-like, especially in the recent blending of the vampire film with romance, the zombie, more strongly associated with a visceral aesthetic, maintains its role as the abject other even in comedic settings. It proves better suited as a monster, therefore, to represent strangeness and menace than the vampire, who has recently been increasingly depicted as sympathetic. As Stacey Abbott has pointed out in *Undead Apocalypse* (2016), however, the difference between the vampire and the zombie has been shrinking in the twenty-first century as their characteristics and narratives interact and influence one another to a greater extent.

5.2 New Vampires

Thought of in terms of social class, among the living dead the zombie appears emblematic of the proletarian, while the vampire is recognizable as an aristocrat. If zombies tend to inhabit suburban or urban landscapes of the present or of a dystopian future, vampires traditionally move amid Gothic-style architecture and therefore seem predestined for traditional Gothic cinema. For this reason, however, vampires also have something old-fashioned and dusty about them, especially 126 years after Stoker's paradigmatic vampire novel. While the formal attire of the vampire was already occasionally parodied as costume-like and outmoded in the 1960s, George A. Romero radically brought the vampire into the present for the first time in *Martin* in 1977. Nine years earlier, in *Night of the Living Dead*, he had already modernized the zombie, but in *Martin* he presented a vampire who did not follow the established iconography: Free of supernatural elements, the teenager

Martin (John Amplas) drugs his victims with syringes and slashes their wrists with razor blades to drink their blood. This often overlooked film proves to be as much a link between classical depictions of vampires and the later vampire film tailored to teenagers as it stands between the fantastic vampire film and the renderings of blood-sucking serial killers without supernatural abilities in later films such as *Near Dark* or *Låt den rätte komma in* (see Billson 2013, p. 16).

Dracula's 1897 quest to move from the Transylvanian hinterlands to urban, industrialized London translates into vampires' entry into the subculture, especially in the 1980s. In *The Hunger* (1983), an adaptation of Whitney Strieber's 1981 novel of the same name, Catherine Deneuve and David Bowie embody a pair of glam rock vampires who hang out in New York underground clubs. Thirty years later, we encounter an echo of the immortal glam rock couple in Jim Jarmusch's *Only Lovers Left Alive*. In *The Lost Boys,* a reference to *Peter Pan*, and in *Near Dark*, teenage vampires wear leather jackets and cowboy boots and ride motorcycles and RVs. In the era of post-punk and the Goth subculture, vampires, such as those portrayed in these two films, are charged with a romanticism of rebellion and stylized as cool role models for teenagers.

If the traditional Gothic cinema aesthetic was on the decline in the 1980s, it experienced a brief revival around 1990 in the form of a few prestige productions. The most significant example is *Bram Stoker's Dracula*, directed by Francis Ford Coppola in 1992. On the one hand, as the title promises, this is an adaptation closely based on the novel. On the other hand, Coppola adds a love story, which here becomes the vampire's primary motivation. As the first cinematic adaptation, *Bram Stoker's Dracula* gives the media the prominent role they play in Stoker's novel. The latter is told through diary entries, correspondence, newspaper articles, transcriptions of sound recordings, etc., reflecting the role all these media play in the story. As Friedrich Kittler (1993) has shown, the group of vampire hunters only succeed in destroying Dracula in the end because Mina Harker collects all medially recorded information about him from various sources, bundles it, and distributes it to the team in the form of typewritten copies.

Coppola succeeds not only in conveying the historico-cultural significance of media in the late nineteenth century in the film, but moreover, in creating a striking aesthetic that is both historicist and alien. He also studs his film with references, not only to earlier adaptations of *Dracula* – especially to *Nosferatu*, whose seemingly inhuman long fingers and animalistic features return here in modified form, as well as to those of Tod Browning and Terence Fisher. *Bram Stoker's Dracula* also proves to be a tribute to film history itself – and even more, to the history of optical media. Not only does Coppola add to the media described by Stoker one that was just 2 years old at the time of his novel's initial publication: the cinematograph that Dracula and Mina Harker admire in London (00:51 f.). Here we also find references to silhouette animation, an early form of animated film inspired by shadow play; to early special effects such as multiple exposure or rear projection; and to the entertainment culture of fairground shows, which is closely linked to the early history of film.

The association with the historical, late medieval army commander Vlad III Drăculea – in the tradition of the Gothic's medieval reference – is also prominent in Coppola's film and has since become a standard element of contemporary *Dracula* adaptations. It is particularly noticeable in *Dracula Untold* (2014), which borrows aesthetical elements as well as the tragic love story from *Bram Stoker's Dracula*. Whereas in 1992 Dracula was still clearly endowed with animal characteristics and in one scene even appeared as a kind of werewolf, 12 years later, *Dracula Untold* is exemplary of the humanization of vampires in the twenty-first century. Here, the ruler Dracula altruistically takes the curse of vampirism upon himself and becomes an immortal monster – and thus also a tragic hero – in order to save his people. Aldana Reyes (2020, p. 216) has pointed out that the Gothic here returns to its roots in the chivalric novel through the detour of nationality, family honor, and the horrors of war, and becomes nostalgically charged.

The predominantly human form of vampires, as well as their increasing "taming," helped Gothic cinema invade the mainstream beginning in the 1980s, for example, in the wake of the success of the film adaptation of Anne Rice's *Interview with the Vampire* (1976, film 1994). Rice's works established the (male) vampire figure as romantic, sensitive, brooding, queer, and struggling against his murderous nature – a representation that has become especially prominent in popular culture in the last decades. A crucial representative is Angel in Joss Whedon's cult television series *Buffy the Vampire Slayer,* which has since spawned its own branch of research in the Anglo-American world, the Buffy Studies, which organizes itself in the Whedon Studies Association and shares its research biennially at the *Slayage Conference*. *Buffy* is considered a landmark in television history on the road to Quality TV and an important precursor to the romantic teen vampire film that we encounter again in the *Twilight* franchise (2008–2012) or in *The Vampire Diaries* (2009–2017). Marcus Recht (2011) refers to this vampiric romantic identification figure, whom he identifies as postmodern and partially gender-fluid, as a "sympathetic vampire". Vera Nazarian (2010, p. 124) describes him with an ironic note as "a very special 'vapire romantic hero prototype' package": masculine but with a feminine side, tormented by remorse and trapped in his own personal hell.

5.3   Family-Friendly and Mainstream Gothic

The growing number of manifestations of the Gothic outside traditional parameters of horror cinema can be seen, for example, in the subgenre of "paranormal romance," which gained prominence and visibility especially in the wake of the popularity of Stephenie Meyer's *Twilight* tetralogy (2006–2009) and its film adaptations (2008–2012) (see Aldana Reyes 2020, p. 226). Here, as Fred Botting writes, the "vegetarian" (and chaste until marriage) vampire Edward Cullen (Robert Pattinson) becomes a supernatural variant of the rebellious, teenage biker as embodied by James Dean in 1955's *Rebel Without a Cause*. He has little in common with the repulsive animalistic vampire as we know him from *Nosferatu* or even still from Coppola's 1992 adaptation of *Dracula* (see Botting 2014, p. 200). To be sure, the romantic vampire, eternally brooding and fighting a constant inner battle, stands in the tradition of Lord Ruthven in John Polidori's short story *The Vampyre* (1819) and has previously appeared in *Interview with the Vampire* (1992) or *Buffy the Vampire Slayer* (1997–2003), whose Angel likely served as an inspiration for Edward Cullen. In the twenty-first century, however, the romantic vampire's appearance is also proliferating outside of horror films, in works that target an audience of children and young adults (see Aldana Reyes 2020, pp. 226 f.).

Catherine Spooner, in *Post-Millennial Gothic*, has argued that these films should also be included in the corpus of Gothic cinema because in the twenty-first century it can no longer be reduced to narratives that focus on staging the Uncanny and on evoking fear. These works develop a counter-narrative that engages with identity politics and the politics of representation, revealing the changing role of Gothic cinema (Spooner 2017, p. 17). Spooner also identifies an increasing prominence of the Goth subculture, whose representation in mainstream media has not only increased but also has been connoted more positively in recent decades. In addition, she observes a rise of comedic (especially with a proximity to camp), romantic, and positively charged narratives in twenty-first century Gothic cinema. These are more interested in spectacular aesthetics than profound narratives, and they not only connote deviations from the norm positively but also celebrate them (Spooner 2017, pp. 22–27, 184 ff.).

"No longer confined to a horror subgenre," Annie Billson (2013, p. 10) writes about twenty-first century monsters, "the undead have emerged from the shadows to become teen idols, lifestyle models and children's entertainers". The tendency to target children and teens is even more evident in animated films such as *The Nightmare Before Christmas* (1993) or the Neil Gaiman adaptation *Coraline* (2009, 2002 novel), where Gothic cinema aesthetics are mixed with less menacing elements or musical interludes (see Aldana Reyes 2020, p. 227). The old familiar Gothic monsters are tamed, trivialized, and humanized in twenty-first-century mainstream cinema. Although Mary Shelley's *Frankenstein* (1999) as a canonical text of Gothic fiction already appeals to compassion for the "monster," it is only in recent decades that the latter has been increasingly portrayed explicitly in film as misunderstood, harmless, and lovable. Fred Botting (1996, p. 3) writes in this regard:

> Though the attractions of evil always lurked in the texts, the movement towards sympathy (beginning with Mary Shelley's humane depiction of her monster) underlines a shift in perceptions of Gothic monstrosity from a horrifying sight of that which was most unbearable in a culture to a recognition and embrace of the monster as the image, the inner, often denied aspect, of who we, in a (post)modern western world, truly are: Love all monsters, love your monster as yourself, becomes the new refrain.

In the last decades, the vampire has proven to be the most mutable monster, appearing in every genre imaginable, from action films (*Blade*) to Tex-Mex hybrids (*From Dusk Till Dawn*) to family films (*Hotel Transylvania*), and from feminist (*We Are the Night*) to pornographic films (*Vampire Sex Diaries*).

Vampires have also been part of the repertoire of television programs, films, and series since the 1960s. Long before they have heard of Stoker's novel, children are familiar with vampiric characters from popular culture, advertising, and cereal boxes. Through the teenage years, *Buffy the Vampire Slayer*, *Twilight*, or *The Vampire Diaries* accompany them until adulthood, when more serious artifacts serve the vampire theme and metaphor (see Abbott 2013, p. 236). The vampire was domesticated primarily in television, the medium that gave it access to family living rooms. Compared to other monsters, vampires are able to disguise themselves as humans – especially since they have been stripped of their permanently monstrous appearance since the late 1980s. Their recent humanization, however, is only due to ethically motivated self-control and is therefore always associated with the danger of giving in to their bloodthirsty desires. The vampires have not had their fangs pulled; their proximity to humans has only enmeshed us more closely in their emotionally complex and morally ambivalent world, attests Stacey Abbott (2013, p. 236). This makes the vampires' relapse to bloodthirsty, animalistic violence only more perfidious and shocking (Abbott 2013, p. 236). Spooner also emphasizes that, given the comedic and romantic manifestations of Gothic cinema, we should not overlook its post-2000 diversity. The exploration of individual and collective trauma and angst has by no means receded into the background; rather, a new, celebratory, positive variation has emerged (Spooner 2017, p. 187). The popularity of which since the 1990s is particularly indebted to Tim Burton's mainstream films.

5.4   Tim Burton's Gothic

While elements of Gothic cinema have increasingly diffused into various genres and mainstream cinema, there is often simultaneous talk of the Gothic being diluted. The increasing familiarity with its aesthetics not only causes the films to lose some of their emotional effects, but the conscious reference back to the original (literary) genre also is lost when its characteristics become ubiquitous. Tim Burton in particular is considered a filmmaker whose work made a specific Goth(ic) aesthetic suitable for the mainstream. Conversely, especially his visual style and production design have left deep marks on the Goth subculture (see Spooner 2017, pp. 55–60 for a detailed discussion). Heavily intermixed with influences from circus and carnival, Burton's films can stand in as a primary example of what Catherine Spooner (2017, p. 22) calls "celebratory Gothic". It welcomes deviations from the norm and celebrates otherness, increasingly interweaves the Goth subculture with Gothic cinema, and exhibits comedic and romantic features. The eclectic, heterogeneous oeuvre of the filmmaker, who originally trained as an animator and concept artist at Disney, not only draws on a variety of genres from fairy tales to horror and science fiction to melodrama and children's literature, it also spans a variety of media from comics and cartoons to sculptures to film and television.

Helmut Merschmann (2000) particularly highlights Tim Burton as an *auteur* whose own biography is closely interwoven with his work. Prominent in his films are misunderstood, melancholic and sometimes neurotic loners. They often live secluded lives in typical Gothic locations such as ruinous mansions and leaky attics – Burton likes to stage empty spaces reminiscent of the fantastic films of German Expressionism, with acute angles marked by slanted roofs and hard shadows. As Catherine Spooner (2013) has shown, costumes are at the center of Burton's distinctive visuality (see Fig. 5.1): instead of following cinematic conventions by blending into the aesthetic environment, they draw attention to themselves, stand out, and function as narrative devices that emphasize the characters' status as outsiders. Children or young adults often play an important role in his films, cultivating a fearless and carefree approach to the unusual and supernatural that is more difficult for adult characters.

Burton draws inspiration from the entire film history of Gothic and horror – sophisticated productions as well as works that belong to the B-movie or trash. From this, he generates an original imagery (even beyond film) that seems like a glossy version of the B-movie aesthetic of the 1950s to 1980s. Referenced are, for example, Universal classics, the films of Roger Corman, whose star Vincent Price recorded the voice-over for Burton's animated short *Vincent* in 1982 and played the

Fig. 5.1 Miranda Richardson as Lady van Tassel in *Sleepy Hollow* (USA 1999), 01:28. (Netflix. Accessed: 09 December 2020)

creator of the title character in *Edward Scissorhands* in 1990. Christopher Lee, star of Hammer Gothic Horror, also appeared regularly in supporting roles in Burton's films. A strong reference to Gothic cinema is consistent and unmistakable in Burton's entire multimedia oeuvre.

The question of whether Burton's films actually belong to the Gothic canon, however, is a matter of debate. Most of his films can be described as Gothic hybrids: they blend Gothic cinema with the bio-pic (*Ed Wood*), the action blockbuster (*Batman* and *Batman Returns*), the comedy (*Beetlejuice, Dark Shadows*), or the musical (*Sweeney Todd*). Even the films outside of this group are clearly influenced by the Gothic. For example, the characters in *Alice in Wonderland*, which is set in a kind of post-apocalyptic version of the Wonderland of the literary original, are endowed with a traumatic past and thus stand in the tradition of the Gothic's interest in psychoanalysis and in psychopathologies. While films like *Mars Attacks!* or *Big Fish* are hard to classify as Gothic cinema, there is no question about *Sleepy Hollow* and *Corpse Bride* belonging to this category. The question of the classification of Burton's films points to a problem of definition of contemporary Gothic cinema, which I would like to outline below on the basis of two viewpoints on Tim Burton's work.

Often his films are understood as meta-Gothic because of their strong referentiality – that is, not Gothic, but films *about* Gothic. Jeffrey Weinstock (2013, p. 26) calls Burton's citation-saturated form of ironic, campy film-making "Gothic lite". With the exception of *Sweeney Todd*, he writes, Burton's films are not Gothic films, but "Gothic" in quotation marks. Through constant ciations and references, Burton's films celebrate the literary and cinematic tradition of the Gothic, but they themselves break the frisson through humor and sentimentality. Weinstock identifies nostalgia and irony as the two predominant narrative modes: the return to Gothic cinema, which Burton was fascinated by in his childhood, is a nostalgically transfigured homage in his films. An irony emerges in this retrospective, for the film-historical references in Burton's works underscore their own status as films, making them highly self-referential. This is supported by Burton's threefold predilections: his penchant for camp, for working with recurring actors (especially Johnny Depp and Helena Bonham Carter), and for thematizing film production itself (for example, in *Ed Wood* and *Frankenweenie*). This metatextuality, however, creates a distance that defangs the Gothic, so to speak. "Burton gives us Gothic plots," Weinstock (2013, p. 27) continues, "or at least Gothic plot elements – in non-Gothic universes". And this is precisely the reason for his outstanding success: In a world saturated with its elements after nearly a century of Gothic cinema, Burton's films offer viewers familiar components that evoke nostalgic memories of films from their youth. Instead of the horror of the originals, however, they deliver humor, sentimentality, and hope, and uphold honesty, integrity, and creativity as their ideals (Weinstock 2013, p. 27).

While a certain nostalgic, romantic transfiguration in Burton's works cannot be denied, this argument can be countered, as Catherine Spooner (2017, pp. 53 f.) does, because it implies, firstly, that contemporary Gothic cinema is merely a wistful look back at older works of a more "authentic" Gothic. As discussed in Sect. 2.5, however, Gothic has always referenced its (own) past and thus proves to be a succession of revivals. Early representatives already reference a tradition of folklore and fairy tale that recurs even more than a century later, for instance, in Guillermo del Toro's films. Even the first self-identified literary work of Gothic fiction, Horace Walpole's *The Castle of Otranto* (1765), purported to be a rediscovered medieval manuscript, referring to another, older (and fictional) "original." Second, Weinstock's argument assumes that this older original is characterized by its emotional and affective impact, which is that it evokes fear. This, however, would make Gothic congruent with horror, which on the one hand would render the term obsolete and on the other hand would contradict the characteristics of Gothic cinema as we have discussed in Chaps. 1 and 2.

Spooner therefore argues persuasively for reading Weinstock's understanding of Burton's "Gothic" cinema in quotation marks in terms of Susan Sontag's definition of camp, as "see[ing] everyhing in quotation marks" (2017, p. 54; original: Sontag 2013, p. 194). In this way, Burton's ironic distance reveals itself not as a contradiction to the mode of Gothic cinema, but as in harmony with its proximity to camp. This perspective proves productive not only with regard to Burton's films, but to contemporary Gothic cinema in general (Spooner 2017, p. 54). Burton's work is less oriented towards the narrative conventions of classic Gothic fiction, but rather creates its own visuality that not only echoes and cites the aesthetics of Gothic cinema, but also realigns them. Rather than devaluing it as "Gothic lite," the task is to take seriously its visual style, itself informed as much by Gothic cinema as by the sensibilities of the Goth subculture, as authoritative for contemporary Gothic, and conversely to adjust our definition of Gothic cinema (Spooner 2017, p. 66).

References

Literature

Abbott, Stacey. 2013. TV vampires. In *Gothic: The Dark heart of film*, ed. James Bell, 19. London: BFI.
———. 2016. *Undead apocalypse: Vampires and zombies in the twenty-first century*. Edinburgh: Edinburgh University Press.
Aldana Reyes, Xavier. 2020. *Gothic cinema*. London: Routledge.
Billson, Anne. 2013. Vampires. In *Gothic: The Dark heart of film*, ed. James Bell, 10–18. London: BFI.
Botting, Fred. 1996. Preface: The Gothic. In *The Gothic*, ed. Fred Botting, 1–21. London: Routledge.
———. 2014. *Gothic*. 2nd ed. London: Routledge.
Fürst, Michael. 2010. Zombies over the rainbow. Konstruktionen von Geschlechtsidentität im schwulen Zombiefilm. In *Untot. Zombie. Film. Theorie*, ed. Michael Fürst, Florian Krautkrämer, and Serjoscha Wiener, 99–120. München: Belleville.
Gaiman, Neil. 2002. *Coraline*. New York: HarperCollins.
Grilli, Alexandro. 2010. Ein ungeheuer zum Quadrat. Queer-Betrachtungen über den Film Gay Zombie von Michael Simon. In *Untot. Zombie. Film. Theorie*, ed. Michael Fürst, Florian Krautkrämer, and Serjoscha Wiener, 121–134. Munich: Belleville.
Kittler, Friedrich. 1993. Draculas Vermächtnis. In *Draculas Vermächtnis. Technische Schriften*, 11–57. Leipzig: Reclam.
Merschmann, Helmut. 2000. *Tim Burton*. Berlin: Bertz.
Meteling, Arno. 2006. *Monster. Zu Körperlichkeit und Medialität im modernen Horrorfilm*. Bielefeld: transcript.
Nazarian, Vera. 2010. A Kinder, Gentler Vampire. In *A taste of True Blood: The fangbanger's guide*, ed. Leah Wilson, 123–136. Dallas: Benbella Books.

Polidori, William. 1968. Der Vampyr, transl. Adolf Böttger. In *Von denen Vampiren oder Menschensaugern. Dichtungen & Dokumente*, ed. Dieter Sturm and Klaus Völker, 45–69. Vienna: Wiener Verlag. (first published in 1819).

Shelley, Mary. 1999. *Frankenstein, or the modern Prometeus*. London: Worsworth. (first published in 1818).

Sontag, Susan. 2013. Notes on „Camp". In *Against interpretation, and other essays*, 515–30. New York: Picador.

Spooner, Catherine. 2013. Costuming the outsider in Tim Burton's cinema, or, why a corset is like a codfish. In *The works of Tim Burton: Margins to mainstream*, ed. Jeffrey A. Weinstock, 47–63. Basingstoke: Palgrave Macmillan.

———. 2017. *Post-millennial Gothic: Comedy, romance and the rise of happy Gothic*. London: Bloomsbury Academic.

Walpole, Horace. 1765. *The castle of Otranto*. Project Gutenberg E-Book #696. https://www.gutenberg.org/files/696/696-h/696-h.htm. Accessed on: 7 May 2020.

Weinstock, Jeffrey A. 2013. Mainstream Outsider: Burton Adapts Burton. In *The works of Tim Burton: Margins to mainstream*, ed. Jeffrey A. Weinstock, 1–29. Basingstoke: Palgrave Macmillan.

Film

Alice in Wonderland. USA 2010. Directed by Tim Burton. Walt Disney Studios.

Batman. USA 1989. Directed by Tim Burton. Warner Bros./The Guber-Peters Company/PolyGram Pictures.

Batman Returns. USA 1992. Directed by Tim Burton. Warner Bros./PolyGram Pictures.

Beetlejuice. USA 1988. Directed by Tim Burton. The Geffen Film Company.

Big Fish. USA 2003. Directed by Tim Burton. Columbia Pictures et al.

Blade. USA 1998. Directed by Stephen Norrington. Amen Ra Films et al.

Braindead. New Zealand 1992. Directed by Peter Jackson. WingNut Films et al.

Bram Stoker's Dracula. USA 1992. Directed by Francis ford Coppola. American Zoetrope.

Buffy the Vampire Slayer. TV series. USA 1997–2003. Created by Joss Whedon. Mutant Enemy.

Coraline. USA 2009. Directed by Henry Selick. Focus Features/Laika Entertainment/Pandemonium.

Corpse Bride. USA/UK 2005. Directed by Tim Burton, and Mike Johnson. Warner Bros et al.

Dawn of the Dead. USA/Italy 1978. Directed by George A. Romero. Dawn Associates/Laurel Group.

Dracula Untold. USA/UK/Ireland 2014. Directed by Gary Shore. Universal Pictures.

Ed Wood. USA 1994. Directed by Tim Burton. Touchstone Pictures.

Edward Scissorhands. USA 1990. Directed by Tim Burton. Twentieth Century Fox.

Frankenweenie. USA 2012. Directed by Tim Burton. Walt Disney Pictures/Tim Burton Productions.

From Dusk Till Dawn. USA/Mexico 1996. Directed by Robert Rodriguez. Dimension Films et al.

Hotel Transsylvania. USA 2012. Directed by Genndy Tartakovsky. Columbia Pictures/Sony Pictures Animation.

Interview with the Vampire. USA 1994. Directed by Neil Jordan. Geffen Pictures.

Låt den rätte komma in. Sweden 2008. Directed by Tomas Alfredson. EFTI et al.

Mars Attacks!. USA 1996. Directed by Tim Burton. Tim Burton Productions/Warner Bros.

Martin. USA 1977. Directed by George A. Romero. Laurel Productions.

Near Dark. USA 1987. Directed by Kathryn Bigelow. F/M/Near Dark Joint Venture.

Night of the Living Dead. USA 1968. Directed by George A. Romero. Image Ten.

Nosferatu, eine Symphonie des Grauens. Weimar Republic 1922. Directed by Friedrich Wilhelm Murnau. Jofa-Atelier Berlin-Johannisthal/Prana-Film GmbH.

Only Lovers Left Alive. UK et al. 2013. Directed by Jim Jarmusch. Recorded Picture Company et al.

Pontypool. Canada 2008. Directed by Bruce McDonald. Ponty Up Pictures/Shadow Shows.

Rebel Without a Cause. USA 1955. Directed by Nicholas Ray. Warner Bros.

Sixth Sense. USA 1999. Directed by M. Night Shyamalan. Hollywood Pictures et al.

Sleepy Hollow. USA/Germany 1999. Directed by Tim Burton. Paramount Pictures.

Sweeney Todd: The Demon Barber of Fleet Street. USA/UK 2007. Directed by Tim Burton. Dreamworks Pictures.

The Blair Witch Project. USA 1999. Directed by Daniel Myrick and Eduardo Sánchez. Haxan Films.

The Haunting of Hill House. TV series. USA 2018. Created by Mike Flanagan. Flanagan Film et al.

The Hunger. UK 1983. Directed by Tony Scott. Metro-Goldwyn-Mayer/Peerford Ltd.

The Lost Boys. USA 1987. Directed by Joel Schumacher. Warner Bros.

The Name of the Rose. West Germany/France/Italy 1986. Directed by Jean-Jacques Annaud. Constantin Film et al.

The Nightmare Before Christmas. USA 1993. Directed by Henry Selick. Touchstone Pictures et al.

The Vampire Diaries. TV series. USA 2009–2017. Created by Julie Plec and Kevin Williamson. Outerbanks Entertainment et al.

True Blood. TV series. USA 2008–2014. Created by Alan Ball. Your Face Goes Here Entertainment/Home Box Office.

Twilight. USA 2008. Directed by Catherine Hardwicke. Summit Entertainment et al.

Vampire Sex Diaries. USA 2010. Directed by Gary Dean Orona. K-Beech Video.

Vincent. USA 1982. Directed by Tim Burton. Walt Disney Productions.

White Zombie. USA 1932. Directed by Victor Halperin. Victor & Edward Halperin Productions.

Wir sind die Nacht. Germany 2010. Directed by Dennis Gansel. Celluloid Dreams/Constantin Film/Rat Pack Filmproduktion.

Part III

Gothic Cinema After 2000

Between the Old and the New

6

In the twenty-first century, we are dealing with a Gothic cinema that can no longer be defined by the characteristics of the traditional Gothic novel. Instead of trying to apply a definition derived from eighteenth-century literature to contemporary works in other media and consistently excluding everything that does not meet it, it is more fruitful to observe and describe the metamorphoses of Gothic cinema. Chris Baldick (2009, p. xix), whom I have already quoted in Chap. 2, writes: "For the Gothic effect to be attained, a tale should combine a fearful sense of inheritance in time with a claustrophobic sense of enclosure in space, these two dimensions reinforcing one another to produce an impression of sickening descent into disintegration". Although this description primarily focuses on literature, it also applies to contemporary Gothic cinema, working equally well in view of Mary Shelley's *Frankenstein* and Guillermo del Toro's *Crimson Peak*. However, this definition would need to be expanded with regard to contemporary works to include, for example, as Catherine Spooner (2017) has convincingly argued, ironic, humorous, and family-oriented works. Only then will we arrive at a productive definition of the Gothic mode that does justice to the twenty-first century rather than fixating on time-honored works.

Around 2000, we can observe, on the one hand, the proliferation of remakes and revivals – whether that of Hammer Film Productions, the Universal Studios' attempt to reanimate its monster movies in the wake of the success of superhero movies, or the 2020 remake of *Rebecca*. On the other hand, Gothic aesthetics, monsters, and narratives have increasingly entered the mainstream in recent decades. They have long since found their way into popular film and television productions that appeal to mass audiences. For example, elements of Gothic cinema can be found in the *Harry Potter* film series, particularly *Harry Potter and the*

© The Author(s), under exclusive license to Springer Fachmedien Wiesbaden GmbH, part of Springer Nature 2023
K. Rein, *Gothic Cinema*, https://doi.org/10.1007/978-3-658-40721-6_6

Half-Blood Prince (2009), or in action films such as *Blade* (1998) or *Underworld* (2003). Contemporary Gothic cinema is, as a result, highly heterogeneous, hybridized, fragmented, and dispersed. In addition to conquering the mainstream, a wider distribution geographically as well as into other media can also be observed.

Just as Gothic transformed and diversified in the twentieth century under the conditions of cinema, it is now necessary to take into account the changed media conditions of our time. In the past twenty years, the descendants of what was described as Gothic cinema in the previous part are no longer limited to the cinema. Under the auspices of digitization, Gothic has invaded online streaming services such as Netflix and Amazon Prime Video, where, following its tradition of serialization and recurrence, we encounter it in the form of new adaptations of familiar works as well as new imaginings of familiar characters, motifs, and places. Thus, an expanded concept of Gothic cinema in the twenty-first century must also include artifacts beyond the format of film. Particularly with a view to the past 10 years, it even becomes clear that the characteristics of classic Gothic cinema are found less in film than in the series offered by online streaming services. Two of these are, for this reason, among the three representatives of Gothic cinema from the recent years, which are analyzed below as examples of its contemporary expression.

In particular, the traditional Victorian aesthetic has migrated – with a few exceptions such as *The Woman in Black* (2012) or *Crimson Peak* (2015) – from the screening context of cinema to serial formats for domestic consumption. To speak of television series in this context is not always accurate, as they are often produced for streaming services such as Amazon Prime Video or Netflix, which are not exclusively consumed via television sets. On a media-technical level, series like *The Haunting of Hill House* (2018), strictly speaking, have little to do with television technology in terms of production, distribution, or reception. For the sake of comprehensibility, however, I would still like to stick with the term "television series," which is still commonly used in research. The following chapters examine one example each, by means of which, not least due to numerous references, the motifs, locations, and characters of traditional Gothic cinema as well as its contemporary manifestation and their differences and similarities can be traced.

Example: Penny Dreadful (2014–2016)

One example of how recent television series attempt to shape the tradition of Gothic cinema according to contemporary discourses is *Penny Dreadful*, a series created by John Logan, which aired in the U.S. on Showtime and was available in Germany via Netflix. Already in its title, the series identifies itself with the popular serialized dime novels that were called "penny dreadfuls" in Victorian

England. Here, however, their characters and motifs merge with the high production value of so-called "quality TV", aimed at an audience of the educated middle
class (see Germaine Buckley 2019, p. 2). Displaying a historicist aesthetic, the
series brings together canonical characters from the literature of the Victorian
Gothic Revival: In season 1, the wealthy British explorer Malcolm Murray
(Timothy Dalton) and his African companion Sembene (Danny Sapani) team up
with the psychic occultist Vanessa Ives (Eva Green), the U.S. gunslinger Ethan
Chandler (Josh Hartnett), and Victor Frankenstein (Harry Treadaway) against
Dracula, who has kidnapped Malcolm's daughter Mina Harker (Olivia Llewellyn).
So, as in Stoker's novel, we meet a group of variously gifted protagonists (in the
style of *League of Extraordinary Gentlemen*) fighting against a monster. Other
characters include Dorian Gray (Reeve Carney), Frankenstein's creature (Rory
Kinnear), Dr. Henry Jekyll (Shazad Latif) and briefly Abraham van Helsing
(David Warner), who appears here as Frankenstein's mentor and is murdered by
the creature. Dr. Seward goes by the first name Florence here and is Vanessa's
psychotherapist in season three. She is unaware that her secretary Renfield
(Samuel Barnett) serves Dracula (Christian Camargo). The legendary Patti
LuPone not only appears in the role of Dr. Seward, but also plays Vanessa's mentor, the witch Joan Clayton, who is lynched by a mob in the second season. She
thus slips into a double role typical of Gothic cinema, and is also recognized as a
doppelganger by Vanessa.

While the series is set primarily in Victorian London, a classic setting for Urban
Gothic, the second season features extensive flashbacks to Vanessa's past with the
witch Joan Clayton, while the third takes us in part to Ethan Chandler's native
North America. In addition to the convolute of canonical characters from Victorian
Gothic literature, the series makes an effort to feature other stereotypical fictional
as well as cultural-historical characters from that period. These include, for example, the U.S. American who fought indigenous people in the Territorial Wars; the
psychoanalyst as a representative of a then novel form of therapy; the transgender
sex worker Angelique (Jonny Beauchamp) with whom Dorian Gray has an affair;
or Frankenstein's female creature Lily (Billie Piper) who becomes a twisted fighter
for the rights of women in her new life, after having been the Irish sex worker
Brona Croft and Ethan's lover before her death and resurrection. The eccentric,
queer Egyptologist Ferdinand Lyle (Simon Russell Beale) represents another typical character, being strongly influenced by the time's exoticism and Egyptomania.
Uniting all these characters in a sensual, neo-Victorian Gothic aesthetic, *Penny
Dreadful* proves to be a declaration of love to Victoriana as well as a tribute to the
literature of the Gothic Revival *par excellence*.

Accompanying this tribute, however, is a problem that Chloe A. Germaine has discussed in her essay "A Tale of Two Women: The Female Grotesque in Showtime's *Penny Dreadful.*" Striving to recreate Victorian narratives and characters while meeting the demands of twenty-first century audiences, *Penny Dreadful* attempts a balancing act that is not entirely elegant. In particular, the series imports the misogynistic image of the woman of the Victorian era, which it attempts to nestle into today's worldview without straying too far from typical Gothic characters and stories.

> *Penny Dreadful* constantly negotiates between feminist principles, the demands of a post-feminist media economy, and the misogyny coded into its visual tropes. The show puts female bodies on display, pathologizes those bodies and evokes problematic dualisms in its parade of female grotesques: prostitutes, femme fatales, madwomen and witches. (Germaine Buckley 2019, p. 3).

Central to Germaine's argument are the two female protagonists, Vanessa Ives and Brona Croft/Lily. She sees the figure of the "female grotesque" identified by Mary Russo at the core of the ambivalence that she identifies in *Penny Dreadful* – and in contemporary, postfeminist media culture in general. Drawing on Russo's concept as well as Julia Kristeva's notion of the abject and Barbara Creed's "monstrous feminine," Germaine attests that Vanessa and Brona/Lily are portrayed as deviant from mainstream gender ideology, exceptional, transgressive, and at times terrifying. While this affirms female rebellion in terms of a feminist gesture, it also evokes conflicting misogynistic notions of monstrous women (ibid., p. 3). The latter manifest themselves in the portrayal of the two women as witches, prostitutes, *femme fatales*, and hysterics. The persistence of such "monstrous women" illustrates the tenacity of such gender stereotypes to this day, even in seemingly feminist plots, Germaine writes (ibid., p. 18). *Penny Dreadful* thus comes into conflict in its stance between affirming contemporary feminist ideas and the misogyny of the historical models on which it draws (ibid., p. 3).

Other ideological conflicts are also revealed; for example, the series becomes entangled in class issues, which Germaine also demonstrates through the portrayal of the main female characters: Vanessa, as a member of the wealthy bourgeoisie, is depicted as a martyr. Although she is portrayed as abject during her episodes of "madness", she is eventually redeemed from this grotesque portrayal and finds her end in a transcendent narrative that symbolizes the perpetual struggle between good and evil (ibid., pp. 7–11). The sub-plot about the working-class Irish prostitute Brona, on the other hand, revolves around the "banal violence and tragedy faced by lower class women" (ibid., p. 12). Brona appears as a changeable character who embodies different female roles for different men – Chandler, Frankenstein,

Gray. Instead of revealing a character of her own, she is an empty shell that is filled with meaning by male characters at will. In the process, Brona/Lily also becomes more objectified: On the one hand, she is sexualized more clearly than Vanessa, and on the other hand, she is also staged as an object of male desire. Both are particularly evident in her role as Frankenstein's creature Lily, whom he coiffures, dresses, "educates," and eventually makes his mistress. Lily's escape from this relationship and her subsequent liaison with Dorian Gray initially appears as a process of (sexual) empowerment, however, as a result of it she is increasingly portrayed as violent, vengeful, and cruel (ibid., p. 14 f.). Female emancipation from male paternalism thus turns monstrous.

Under the weight of its literary templates, *Penny Dreadful* thus reproduces images which carry with it centuries of misogynistic discourse. Even in its most feminist moments, the series thus ultimately proves to be torn between a decidedly feminist and an anti-feminist position. Germaine (2019, p. 18) concludes:

> *Penny Dreadful* is replete with literary references and intertextual awareness, through which it comments on, but is also caught within, a post-feminist media economy that produces female bodies as objects of consumption and all-too-frequently reduces female experience to a side-show in favor of stories of masculine heroism and tragedy.

If this inconsistency between historicist Victorian *mise-en-scène* and contemporary political and ethical defensibility and capitalist marketability can be extended beyond the representation of gender roles, it similarly applies to other representatives of Gothic cinema. Aesthetically, too, contemporary Gothic cinema – insofar as it adheres to a historicist representation – performs a balancing act between the traditional visuality that has been well known since the films of Universal and Hammer and an audiovisual product that is exciting for twenty-first century-audiences. At best, the productions can be understood as adaptations of works to be read in their historical context, though the challenge remains to liberate them from outdated political ideologies.

Two of the examples examined below are direct adaptations of literary works dating from times whose political conservatism has long since become indefensible. The translation processes of literary works into contemporary adaptations are among the issues that will play a role in the analyses that follow. In accordance with the central role of the media in Gothic narratives, as identified in Chap. 2, a special focus on media emerges in the following three chapters. We begin with the house as a central motif in Gothic fiction (see Newman 2013): Mike Flanagan's series *The Haunting of Hill House* (2018), a Netflix adaptation of Shirley Jackson's 1959 haunted house classic, is examined as an example of haunted house narratives. I claim that the series interprets the haunted house as a medium that records events and replays them at a different time. Therefore, in the haunted house, multiple strands of time potentially exist parallel to one another, interacting and interrupting each other in singular events. In this case, this temporal structure also characterizes the series itself, which interweaves past events with present ones, increasingly mixing past, present, and future.

Next, the most recent adaptation of the paradigmatic vampire narrative comes into focus: *Dracula* (2020), a co-production of Netflix and BBC One, created by Mark Gatiss and Steven Moffat. Media already play a special role in Stoker's novel – not only is the novel told through a series of letters, diary entries, etc., but the plot itself depends to a large extent on just such entries and their bundling and processing (see Kittler 1993). The mini series of 2020 focuses especially on blood as a universal medium, with which the vampire here also absorbs and adopts central characteristics and abilities of his victims. For this reason, the analysis focusses on blood, while also discussing other central topoi.

The third example, Guillermo del Toro's feature film *Crimson Peak* (2015), proves to be a veritable catalog of the topoi of Gothic cinema as well as an homage to its history. It cites canonical films and combines typical characters and locations as well as narrative and story elements. Del Toro succeeds in creating a harmonious whole out of the juxtaposition of formative elements of the Gothic from about two centuries of literature and 120 years of film history, which unfolds its own concise visuality, conveyed especially through costumes as well as the striking, red, skeletal ghosts. Since central elements of Gothic cinema are repeated in the examination of this film, this chapter concludes this volume instead of a summary.

References

Literature

Baldick, Chris. 2009. Introduction. In *The Oxford book of Gothic tales*, ed. Chris Baldick, 3rd ed., xi–xxiii. Oxford: Oxford University Press.

Germaine Buckley, Chloe A. 2019. A tale of two women: The Female Grotesque in Showtime's *Penny Dreadful. Feminist media studies*.https://doi.org/10.1080/14680777. 2019.1583263. Accessed 26 Oct 2020.

Kittler, Friedrich. 1993. Draculas Vermächtnis. In *Draculas Vermächtnis. Technische Schriften*, 11–57. Leipzig: Reclam.

Newman, Kim. 2013. The Old Dark House. In *Gothic: The dark heart of film*, ed. James Bell, 96–102. London: BFI.

Spooner, Catherine. 2017. Post-millennial Gothic: Comedy, romance and the rise of happy Gothic. London: Bloomsbury Academic.

Film

Blade. USA. 1998. Directed by Stephen Norrington. Amen Ra Films et al.

Crimson Peak. Canada/USA/Mexico. 2015. Directed by Guillermo del Toro. Double Dare You/Legendary Entertainment.

Dracula. TV miniseries. UK. 2020. Created by Mark Gatiss, und Steven Moffat. Hartswood Films/British Broadcasting Corporation/Netflix.

Harry Potter and the Half-Blood Prince. UK/USA .2009. Directed by David Yates. Warner Bros. et al.

Penny Dreadful. TV series. Ireland/UK/USA. 2014–2016. Created by John Logan. Desert Wolf Productions/Neal Street Productions.

The Haunting of Hill House. TV series. USA 2018. Created by Mike Flanagan.

The Woman in Black. UK et al. 2012. Directed by James Watkins. Hammer Films et al.

Underworld. USA et al. 2003. Directed by Len Wiseman. Lakeshore Entertainment et al.

The Haunting of Hill House (2018)

7

7.1 Haunted Media and Mediums

Haunting phenomena, in which ghosts manifest themselves, are closely entangled with the history of communication media. For example, an increased interest in ghost phenomena can be observed around the middle of the nineteenth century – a time that was not only marked by media-historical caesura such as the invention of photography or the expansion of the telegraph network, but also by the emergence of modern spiritualism. It originated in March 1848 in Hydesville, New York, where the sisters Margaret and Catherine Fox began to communicate with the deceased by means of tapping. Their otherworldly interlocutor was identified as Charles B. Rosna, a former resident of the house, who claimed to have been murdered 5 years earlier and buried in the basement, where, indeed, human bones were found.

In this world, technical media, through their operations of recording, storing, and transmitting, have been realigning the parameters of time and space since the nineteenth century: Telegraphy and telephony detached communication from the physical presence of the communicating partners. Since the mid-nineteenth century, optical and acoustic media have preserved personal and collective moments in photography, phonography, and later in film. There is something ghostly about such records – be it photographs, about which Roland Barthes (1989, p. 81) wrote that they allowed us to enter the past; the phonograph, whose invention *Scientific American* announced with the message: "Speech has become, as it were, immortal" (Johnson 1877); or the cinema, which Maxim Gorky described in 1896 as a shadow empire inhabited by ghostly figures (Pacatus 1995; P(eško)v 1995).

Underlying spiritualism, John Durham Peters (1999, p. 139) writes, following Friedrich Kittler,[1] is the realization that in the age of technical media, the spirits inhabiting the realm of the dead are no longer only remembered, but also recorded and transmitted. Thus, as the media spectrum expands, so does the scope of the real and the conceivable – not only in relation to the world of the living, but also to that of the dead. The border between occultism and science was unclear in the nineteenth century, which entailed a dissolution of that between their real and fantastic possibilities. "Scientific advances only added to the air of mystery," writes Peter Lamont (2005, p. 39 f.):

> In the mid-1800s telegraph lines began to cover London's rooftops, providing a new form of communication that few understood and some viewed as almost magical. [...] In an environment that surrounded people with evidence of new technology that they did not fully understand, the possibility that another mysterious form of communication had been discovered must have seemed all the more plausible.

Electromagnetic telegraphy not only opened up a possibility of communication by means of discrete signals and a simple code, which recurs in the rappings of the Fox siblings 15 years after telegraphy's invention. It also provided a concept of instantaneous message exchange between physically absent entities, which spiritualists picked up and extended: If it was now possible to communicate by means of sound signals with persons elsewhere on earth, why not with persons in other spheres of existence? Following such and similar thoughts, spiritualists used telegraphy as a model to explain their supernatural communication. Louis Alphonse Cahagnet's *The Celestial Telegraph, or, Secrets of the Life to Come* (1851) and other spiritualist writings compare it to the kind of contact established in séances not only metaphorically but quite literally, when they, describe, for instance, Kate Fox's initial communication with the realm of the dead as the opening of a "spiritual telegraph" line. Designed and established in the afterlife according to scientific standards, this telegraph's purpose was to send signals to the world of the living (Hardinge 1872, p. 29). In spiritualist discourse, thus, a current technical communication medium was placed directly in the service of another, otherworldly form of contact. Spiritualist communication in the second half of the nineteenth century was not only metaphorically but very concretely inspired by telegraphy (see Sconce 2000, p. 22 f.).

The Fox sisters' rappings were preceded by almost a century by one of the most famous cases of alleged contact with the dead, the famous London "Cock Lane Ghost." Also communicating by means of knocks, this ghost claimed in 1762 that

---

[1] Kittler (1999, p. 24) states, "The realm of the dead is as extensive as the storage and transmission capabilities of a given culture."

Frances Lynes had been poisoned with arsenic by the widower of her deceased sister (who also haunted the house), with whom she had lived in a wild marriage. Several ensuing séances became city attractions. Among the visitors was Horace Walpole, who, 2 years later, published the paradigmatic Gothic novel *The Castle of Otranto* (1764). It later turned out that, like the Fox sisters a century later, it was the medium communicating with the "Cock Lane Ghost," Elizabeth Parsons, who produced the knocking signals. Such revelations, however, harmed neither the belief in ghosts nor the spiritualist movement.[2] Both cases contain typical elements of ghost stories revolving around missions to solve murders and inflict justice: In both cases, the haunting ended once the crime was solved and the deceased person's remains were buried in a cemetery.

This idea of redemption (among other iconic elements) appears already in the oldest mention of a haunted house, in a letter of Pliny the Younger to Lucius Sura from the first century C.E.: He describes that a house in Athens, in which the ghost of an old man in shackles and chains appeared nightly – an image we still find in Charles Dickens – was freed from the apparitions after a skeleton lying in chains was dug up in the courtyard and buried in a cemetery (Pliny 2010. epist., VII/27).

7.2   The Hill House from Jackson's Novel to Netflix

If the redemption of a person who has died of unnatural causes and cannot come to rest has long been the common explanation for haunting phenomena, Shirley Jackson's 1959 novel *The Haunting of Hill House* popularized a new one. This is one of two works whose adaptations and variations essentially defined the canon of twentieth-century hauntings (see Meteling 2006, p. 282). The second is Henry James' 1898 novella *The Turn of the Screw*. Consequently, while the first season of Mike Flanagan's haunting anthology series adapts Jackson's novel, the second one (that went online on Netflix in October 2020), *The Haunting of Bly Manor*, is based on James' novella. In *The Haunting of Hill House*, the apparitions are not caused by a crime and therefore do not end when it is solved. They are produced by the house itself, which is characterized as malevolent, soaked in its dark history and the sinister deeds of its former occupants. This kind of haunting can be neither explained nor resolved nor terminated. It is an abstract, uncontrollable threat to those who reside in the house – a threat that is always already within its walls and not "out there."

---

[2] The Fox sisters published a confession in October 1888; see *The New York World,* October 21, 1888; qtd. in: Houdini 1924, pp. 5–11; see also N.N. 1888.

The Haunting of Hill House has been previously adapted for film in 1963 and 1999 (both under the title *The Haunting*), and for the stage in 1964 and 2015 (respectively by F. Andrew Leslie and by Anthony Nielson). The third audiovisual adaptation took the form of a miniseries in 2018, created and directed by Mike Flanagan for the streaming service Netflix. As in the novel, here a group of people spend a summer in Hill House. In Jackson's novel, very much in the spirit of the 1950s, John Montague, an investigator of supernatural phenomena invites selected people to the presumably haunted house as part of an experiment. In the 2018 adaptation, the temporary inhabitants are a family with five children who stay there while the parents, both architects, renovate it to sell it for profit.

Hill House is labyrinthine, twisted, and sinister. Its disorienting structure is modeled on the Winchester House in San Jose, California, which is also mentioned in the novel as a possible architectural model for the fictional Hill House (Jackson 2009, p. 105).[3] In Hill House, the novel says, all the angles are a little crooked, which is why doors do not stay open but keep slamming shut, creating not only the haunting impression of autonomy, but also a prevailing darkness. The closed doors, however, do not stop the ever-present cold draft in the house. This is a central element of the haunting in the second half of the twentieth century: The historically mutable conceptualization of ghosts changed in the 1960s in such a way that ghosts turned into a feeling, as Roger Clarke (2013, p. 85) writes, "people now believe ghosts are a 'feeling' in a house – ghosts have become an emotion field." Jackson's atmospheric novel and its adaptations in film, with their depiction of cold places and haunting phenomena that do not visualize ghosts as anthropomorphic figures, have played their part in this shift. Rather than a figurative ghost, here it is the house itself that seems threatening, unsafe, and ghostly.

Jackson endows Hill House with a life of its own in a variety of ways, repeatedly describing it with attributes of the living: When the protagonist Eleanor Vance first catches sight of the house, she unwillingly stops her car and resists the impulse to turn back: "She shivered and thought, the words coming freely into her mind, Hill House is vile, it is diseased; get away from here at once" (Jackson 2009, p. 33). Before restarting her vehicle, she realises that she feels like the house is watching her: "it was enormous and dark, looking down over her" (ibid., p. 35). Other characters also feel observed by the house. At one point, the house is even compared to a predator, "waiting until we feel secure, maybe, and then it will pounce" (ibid., p. 152).

---

[3] The so-called Winchester Mystery House, built by Sarah Winchester, widow of the heir to one of the most successful gun and ammunition manufacturers of the era, was itself the subject of a 2018 Gothic film called *Winchester*.

The helplessness of the characters subjected to an unknown power is as typical of Gothic fiction as it is of Jackson's works, writes Darryl Hattenhauer (2003, p. 3): "Jackson's characters are not so much constitutive as they are constituted. [...] her characters experience agency as something form without." In this case, it is the house that has agency rather than its occupants. They tread carefully and quietly inside it, Eleanor feels "like a small creature swallowed whole by a monster, [...], and the monster feels my tiny little movements inside" (Jackson 2009, p. 42). This metaphor is also echoed in Flanagan's series, where the former residents are compared to an unfinished meal for the house, which will not rest until it has eaten them entirely. I argue, however, that the 2018 depiction of Hill House does not primarily aim at characterizing it as animated, but rather at endowing it with a different form of agency: Here it appears as a rogue recording medium: it stores characters, events, and places and plays them back at a different time. In the process, it increasingly confuses timelines by overlapping different time axes and turning timelines into loops. Thus, in Flanagan's *The Haunting of Hill House*, the psychological intactness of the characters becomes as disordered as the narrative structure and the integrity of the narration itself.

7.3   The Haunted House as a Dysfunctional Storage Medium

From a media studies perspective, the haunted house can be described as a storage medium that arbitrarily records events and plays them back with a time delay. It thereby creates disturbances in time. Here, past and present interfere in singular events in which they interact and conflict. Notably, in Flanagan's *The Haunting of Hill House* is that this time structure also guides the series itself. Here, the repetition of past occurrences, a basic figure of psychoanalysis, shapes both the main characters and the structure of the entire series. At the beginning of the series, five episodes each introduce one character with two parallel timelines showing events from the Crains' present life and the family's stay in the haunted house in the 1980s, which was prematurely ended by the death of the mother. In this way, repetitive structures are established, events that are 30 years apart are unfolded parallel to each other, interwoven through match cuts and other cinematic techniques. The time axes are disordered even more, because the plot of each individual event is not told chronologically, but in a fragmentary manner, by leaps and bounds. We see some events multiple times, from the points of view of different characters. The different narrative strands in themselves are increasingly enriched with flashbacks and flashforwards, allowing future events to mingle with present and past ones as the series progresses. The entire plot itself loops and consequently returns to its origin when both time and narrative line converge in Hill House at the end, where all main characters come together.

The series thus itself adopts the time structure of a haunted house, in which past and present exist in parallel and eventfully interrupt one other. Towards the end of the first season, the future is additionally thrown into the mix in individual sequences, for example in "Screaming Meemies" (ep. 09): here Olivia (Carla Gugino), the mother of the family, steps through a door in Hill House in the 1980s and, instead of finding herself in the room behind it, steps into the funeral home run by her adult daughter Shirley (Elizabeth Reaser) in 2018. A moment later, the adult version of her daughter Eleanor (Victoria Pedretti) appears dead on the autopsy table (00:09). She is joined by the corpse of her brother Luke (Oliver Jackson-Cohen), who, at this point, is still alive in the parallel, present narrative thread – so, from the viewer's perspective, his death in this sequence is either a fictional, or not-yet-occurred, future event. To Olivia, her twin children, whom she never sees as adults, also reappear as corpses later in the same episode: in the Hill House of the 1980s, she sees their faces in a mirror, which she smashes with her fist in horror (00:32). Here, Olivia unexpectedly gets a glimpse of future events that psychologically destabilize her, and eventually lead her to an attempt to murder her children (on toxic motherhood in *The Haunting of Hill House*, see Patterson 2019).

7.3.1   "The Bent-Neck Lady" (ep. 05)

In *The Haunting of Hill House*, time gets mixed up in more ways than one. Sometimes it runs circularly, which I would like to exemplify in this section through the examination of the fifth episode "The Bent-Neck Lady". It revolves around Eleanor, called Nell, who eventually returns to Hill House and commits suicide there. It was here that she, as a child, was first plagued by the nighttime apparition of a woman with a broken neck, hanging from her bedroom ceiling. Still haunting her in her adult life, this apparition is accompanied by a consciously experienced sleep paralysis, a sleep disorder often accompanied by visual, auditory, or tactile hallucinations, for which she seeks treatment. Called the "bent-neck lady" by the child, it appears especially in situations of crisis, such as when Nell's husband unexpectedly dies of a brain aneurysm in the night, and Nell, lying in bed paralysed, sees the apparition hanging from the ceiling in the marital bedroom (00:15 ff., see Fig. 7.1).

Because this apparition ties her back to Hill House, her psychotherapist advises Nell to return there and to seek confrontation with her fear. In doing so, he says, she

Fig. 7.1   Still from *The Haunting of Hill House,* ep. 05 "The Bent-Neck Lady" (USA 2016), 00:17. (Netflix. Accessed: July 10, 2022)

would realize that it is merely a house that was animated only by her imagination as a child and later turned into a memory which became exaggerated and distorted over the years. On her way to Hill House, Nell stops at a motel, where she again sees the "bent-neck lady." Upon her arrival at Hill House, she first enters the parallel timeline of her own past in the house. Here she encounters her siblings as children (00:57) and her parents as Nell remembers them from her childhood. The ghosts in the house include not only the family's mother, who died there, but also earlier versions of Nell's siblings who are still alive. The haunted house as a spiritualist storage medium records not only its own realm of the dead, but also the past of those who lived in it and have not yet died. It replays both at will, treating them equally and intermixing the past timeline with the present.

Here, Nell relives an incident that took place at Hill House during her childhood, which we have seen earlier in the same episode: in a reference to Jackson's novel, she finds herself addressed by writing on the wall that appears behind wallpaper (00:21–00:23, see Fig. 7.2). And as in the novel, a conflict ignites after the other characters accuse her of having produced this message herself. Upon adult Nell's arrival in Hill House, this scene from her past is replayed, but now it takes a different outcome than it did in her childhood. Now, when adult Nell takes the place of child Nell, her mother shows more understanding and absolves her of the crime she wrongly accused her of at the time (00:59). The spirits then welcome Nell and escort her to a reception, where she encounters another happy past: her adult siblings appear in the clothes they wore at Nell's wedding. They apologize

Fig. 7.2 Still from *The Haunting of Hill House,* ep. 05, 00:23. (Netflix. Accessed: July 10, 2022)

and thank her – fulfilling a need of Nell's that her real-life siblings outside the haunted house failed to fulfill. Nell's now-deceased husband also appears and dances with her until he vanishes into thin air again as the couple kisses – another sequence reminiscent of the novel, where Nell dances with the ghost of the Hill House's constructor, Hugh Crain, on her last night. In the TV series, these images alternate with ones in which we see the Nell walking or dancing alone through the dark and ruinous house – reminding us that the objective reality of this scene is different from the character's subjective perception. As viewers, we see both versions, which clearly differ in their lighting as well: while the world presented to Nell by the haunted house appears in warm light, the other is only sparsely lit by the moonlight entering through the windows.

Here, the haunted house first fulfills Nell's wishes by showing her versions of past events, altered in her favor, and thus resolving unprocessed conflicts: the incident from her childhood ends as she would have wished rather than as it actually occurred, and the following sequence not only revives her husband but gives Nell a reconciliation with her siblings that never took place. This episode is further transposed to the day she felt particularly happy – her wedding day.

Eventually, Nell's mother leads her and her child siblings along with a friend up a cast-iron spiral staircase – "come along, we're going to have a tea party" (01:05). As we learn in a later episode (in ep. 09, "Screaming Meemies"), this sequence occurred on the family's last night in the house, when Olivia, driven mad by Hill House, tried to poison her children. This time, the adult, present-day Nell replaces child Nell, and unlike in the earlier sequence (though this is not revealed to viewers until later), this time Nell does not make it to the tea party. Arriving at the top landing of the iconic spiral staircase that appears in all adaptations, the ghost of her mother presents Nell with a necklace that she had asked for as a child (and never received). On Nell's neck, it turns into the noose of a rope, and Nell suddenly finds herself standing outside the banisters. A motherly kiss on her forehead gives Nell the impetus to fall backwards down from the staircase landing. As we see her death by hanging from below, it is no longer bathed in the yellow light that characterized Nell's hallucinations, but in the cold, blue moonlight that illuminates the present, ruinous manor (01:07).

As the camera moves up to her face, we see that Nell's neck is broken but she is still conscious. She then appears to drop even lower, as if the rope she is hanging from had just elongated. As if falling through a ceiling, she falls into an earlier scene from the same episode. Here, Nell is at the motel, on her way to Hill House, when the "bent-neck lady" appears – a sequence we now see from the reversed point of view of the hanged woman. Hanged Nell continues to fall in this way, level to level, backwards in time, through all the moments in which we saw the "bent-neck lady" appear to Nell earlier. The traumatic time loop closes when the hanged woman confronts the youngest version of herself in her nursery at Hill House (see Fig. 7.3), letting out a desperate scream and disintegrating. We thus arrive at the primal scene of Nell's childhood traumatization, now reiterated from the other point of view. In this episode, time at Hill House creates a paradoxical circle of

Fig. 7.3   Still from *The Haunting of Hill House,* ep. 05, 01:08. (Netflix. Accessed: July 10, 2022)

events that evoke and cause each other: The apparition of the "bent-neck lady" that has accompanied Nell since her childhood leads to her return to Hill House, where she hangs herself/is hanged and becomes the "bent-neck lady" who appears to her former self as a ghost, and so on. Nell's becoming-a-ghost, then, is a consequence of her seeing a ghost who turns out to be herself. The ghost haunting Nell is Nell.

7.3.2 Repetitions of the Past

Nell's death stands at the beginning of the series and structures its further narrative by giving her siblings a reason to get in touch with one another, come together at the funeral, etc. If Jackson's novel, as a representative of the Female Gothic, focused on Eleanor's psyche and was told predominantly from her perspective, Flanagan's series is interested in the psyches of all the Crain siblings. Nell's fate thus exemplifies a problem that unites all the main characters: they are all haunted by their past in Hill House, which they each try to overcome in different ways, often getting caught in the ropes they themselves have laid out in the process.

"[T]he hallmark of Gothic that Jackson reinscribes most," Hattenhauer (2003, p. 5) writes, "is the motif of entrapment as a figure of power and powerlessness". Flanagan's series, too, centers this metaphorical entrapment, even outside of the haunted house: Taking the double meaning of "haunted" seriously – as in "haunted house" and the metaphorical "being haunted" (by traumatic events etc.), it unfolds not only the hauntings in Hill House itself but also their psychological aftershocks. This shifts the focus from the haunted house as a site of horror to the former occupants and their traumatic memories (see Robson 2019 for a detailed discussion). While the Crain siblings were plagued by the ghosts at Hill House some 30 years ago, their adult lives are controlled by their attempts to come to terms with that past. One way this becomes clear is in their choices of profession: Steven (Michiel Huisman), the eldest child in the family, is an author whose best-selling novel is about the haunting of Hill House. That this turns him into Shirley Jackson's double is underlined by the voiceover at the beginning of the first episode, which largely corresponds to the beginning of her novel, but is voiced by the actor playing Steven. Steven relives the traumatizing events of his childhood at Hill House over and over again by repeating them in his book, retelling them at readings, and acting as an expert in investigations of potential supernatural phenomena at other houses.

Also paying homage to the novel's author is his sister's first name, Shirley, who runs a funeral home as an adult. Not only has she made dealing with death her profession, she also insists on autopsying, restoring, and burying the body of her youngest sister, Nell. Her choice of profession not only shows an ongoing preoccupation with death, but is also revealed as a reenactment of a traumatic event from her own childhood: in the episode "Open Casket" (ep. 02), we learn that as a child Shirley found a litter of kittens on the grounds of Hill House and adopted them. However, they all died in her room. In particular the burial of the first of the deceased kittens in the garden is highlighted as a traumatic event for the girl (00:24–00:27), who perpetuates holding funerals as an adult.

In Jackson's novel, Theodora (Kate Siegel) is a "modern woman" who defies patriarchal structures and to whom Eleanor is attracted. If her homosexuality is only implied in 1959, it is explicit in 2018, when Theo openly lives in relationships with women, even though her fear of commitment gets in the way. The association of lesbian love and ghosts or the phantomization of homosexual women is a theme that, for reasons of space, can only be mentioned in passing here – I would like to refer in particular to Terry Castle's 1993 book *The Apparitional Lesbian* (with regard to *The Haunting of Hill House* specifically see also Munford 2016, p. 128 f.). Professionally, Theo works as a child psychologist in the series. She helps her patients to overcome traumas that have remained unresolved in their own families as well as in their own biographies. Here, as in the novel, Theodora is an over-empathetic character. While her "sixth sense" in Jackson's book is the reason for her invitation to Hill House, in the Netflix series she has a gift she inherited from her mother: Touching people or objects lets her share in their past, which is conveyed to her in a fragmented way. In the third episode, "Touch," she solves a child abuse case involving one of her patients by visiting the basement in the victim's parents' home. As soon as she lies down on the couch standing there, Theodora senses the rape of the girl that took place on it, and when she subsequently shakes hands with the father, she is able to identify him as the perpetrator. The fact that this gesture-centered gift creates an exhausting flood of information in everyday life is something Theodora copes with by always wearing gloves so as not to touch things and people directly. Thus, her visions of past impressions are also her constant companions, which she is also unable to get rid of.

We learn about Eleanor/Nell that she is consciously trying to come to terms with the consequences of her childhood experiences at Hill House in the context of psychotherapy. Her twin brother Luke, on the other hand, resorts to drugs in his attempts to get rid of the ghosts that are haunting him beyond the confines of Hill House and ends up addicted to heroin. As becomes clear in "The Twin Thing" (ep. 04), he is merely replacing one problem with another. His attempt to tame the ghosts by means of drugs leads to the loss of everything else – he quarrels with his siblings, loses his job and his apartment, and ends up in rehab. His life is no longer determined by the ghostly apparitions, but by the drug. And as soon as he stops using it, the apparitions return, until both together catch up with him.

Hugh Crain (Timothy Hutton/Henry Thomas), we eventually learn, the father of all these characters (in Jackson's novel, the designer and constructor of Hill House), has been accompanied at every turn since leaving the haunted house by the ghost of his deceased wife, with whom he has conversations ("Eulogy," 07). Hill House thus extends beyond its physical confines – including, but by no means limited to, Olivia's ghostly presence. It has inscribed itself in the minds of the former inhabitants and follows them everywhere. The haunted house here, then, not only records the events within it and the characters that enter it, it also inscribes itself in the imagination and psyche of these characters after they leave it. Luke and Nell in particular, as adults, are haunted by ghosts they saw in Hill House as children. The haunting has inscribed itself in the minds of the Crain family and lives on inside them, regardless of their whereabouts. The house and the events in it metaphorically stand in for a trauma, the memory of which "acts in the manner of a foreign body, which for a long time after its intrusion must be regarded as a presently acting agent" (Freud and Breuer 1895, p. 1). It has destroyed the characters themselves and especially their relationship to each other: since their departure from it, the remaining family has been at odds. The father has little contact with most of the children, just as they hardly socialize with each other.

Once the haunted house has recorded someone or something, it neither forgets nor releases. As a logical consequence of this, the season concludes with all the family members reuniting in the still uninhabited Hill House. Here, living characters also encounter deceased ones as well as past versions of themselves. They all coexist in Hill House simultaneously; they are all equally real (or unreal). They have all been recorded and stored by Hill House in its function as a spiritualist recording medium. Thus, it not only treats the realm of the living as equal to that of the dead, it also refuses to differentiate between separate timelines as well as between ontological states such as reality, dream, memory, and fantasy.

7.4   Ambiguity, Disorientation and Unreliability

7.4.1   Reality, Illusion or Imagination?

Not only past, future, and present, but also reality, imagination, and dream become indistinguishable in Hill House. This becomes clear when Olivia encounters Poppy Hill (Catherine Parker), the ghost of a previous 1920s Hill House resident, in "Screaming Meemies." To her question, "I'm dreaming, aren't I?", Poppy replies, "Of course, you are. I'm a dream and so are you and so are we" (00:15). Both are equally real or not – there can be no decision about this because reliable clues are missing. That ghosts here are identical to what might be called records of people – events from the past reproduced over and over again by the haunted house – underscores that our access to the world of ghosts has always been through media. Textually through stories in scrolls and books, visually at least since mirror and magic lantern projections, and since the séances of modern spiritualism also on an auditory and haptic level, media (and mediums) have been making ghosts appear, thereby shaping our experience and expectation of them (see Rein 2015). The ghosts we experience are mediumistic images. At the same time, media themselves become ghostly as a result. Not least, the term "medium" first referred to those who made contact with the dead in spiritualist séances, before it was applied to technical media that store, transmit, or process.

In haunted-house narratives, writes Arno Meteling (2006, p. 282), "the question is always asked: Is it real what the character and the spectator see or hear?" Flanagan's *The Haunting of Hill House* uses the possibilities of audiovisual media and the conventions established in their reception to blur the line between ghosts and the living. If a representation of ghosts as semi-transparent and/or luminescent has been established since Victorian times, the series dispenses with this visual marker. It thus robs viewers of the possibility of making a distinction between living characters and ghosts or hallucinations.

Shirley Jackson's novel also erases this difference, but by other means: After the first occurrence of the nocturnal knocking at Hill House, which Theo describes as "[s]omeone knocked on the door with a cannon ball" (Jackson 2009, p. 133), the characters converse about possible explanations for it. None of them believe in ghosts, Montague states, and yet they cannot deny that something extraordinary has occurred at night. The events cannot be classified as imagination, because this would affect only one character. That the others also perceive the haunting, he continues, distinguishes it from madness and places it on an objective foundation. Eleanor responds that the other characters, too, just like the haunting phenomena, could be part of her imagination. For Montague, this objection is a warning with regard to Eleanor's increasing loss of sense of reality (ibid., p. 139 f.). He then expresses a fundamental problem with the verifiability of events: While an outside perspective may objectify one's own perception, it can never be said with certainty whether the perception of others is not also unreliable.

In essence, Montague's own scientifically designed experiment is doomed to failure precisely because haunting phenomena cannot be objectified. They refuse to be measured scientifically. At another point in the novel, he identifies a cold spot outside the Hill House nursery and attempts to measure its temperature. Although the spot is so cold that his hand holding the gauge goes numb, the thermometer registers no change in temperature at all from its surroundings (ibid., p. 150). Thus, while all the characters clearly feel the cold spot, "like passing through a wall of ice" (ibid., p. 119), the measuring instrument refuses to register it.[4] Scientific criteria of judgment fail in the face of the disturbances caused by haunted houses. The cold spot is present because the characters feel it – it seems objectified because they all do – and at the same time it is absent because it cannot be measured with an objective measuring device. The data simply contradict each other and whether one's own sensation or the thermometer is more trustworthy cannot be decided. The ambiguity cannot be eliminated, and both possibilities are potentially disturbing. They would mean to question either one's own sensory perception, on which one relies for our daily orientation in the world, or science as the basis of our rational worldview.

7.4.2   Unreliable Narration

On a narrative level, the same unreliability is conveyed in Jackson's novel. Hattenhauer (2003, p. 4) writes in this regard:

> Jackson is […] an inchoate postmodernist in her extensive and complex use of unreliable narration. […] her first-person narrators are often delusional. Moreover, her third-person narration often affords only a delusional focalization because so many of her characters are decentered. The result is a rather undecidable world.

In Flanagan's series, the narrative perspective is also unreliable. It robs the viewers as well as the characters of the possibility to distinguish ghostly apparitions from visions and from real events. This happens visually, for example, in that ghosts are depicted as opaque and physical as the living. The characters' excursions into the past as the ghosts' time axes are thus visually indistinguishable from their experiences in the now. There is a lack of criteria by which reality could be differentiated from hallucinations, dream or imagination. In the last three episodes of the first season, all these ontological and temporal levels overlap in the same place. A watchmaker, who, we learn in "Witness Marks" (ep. 08), did not exist in the 1980s timeline (00:30 f.), can be seen repairing a watch several times (ep. 08, 00:06 and ep. 09, 00:08). He mingles with the workmen actually employed in the house at this time, from whom he is indistinguishable to the viewers as well as to the characters. The house produced a ghost and hid him in plain sight.

---

[4] In Flanagan's series, the cold spot is referenced in "Touch," where only Theo and Olivia feel it, but not the housekeeper Dudley, which alludes to a particular sensitivity on their part.

An example of the house interfering with this perspectival confusion is the infamous Red Room – an echo of the nursery from Jackson's novel, which is made out to be the heart of the haunting. The idiosyncratic accessibility of the Red Room is addressed several times when it temporarily refuses to be opened by the house's occupants. However, it is selectively open to different characters at different times, each time appearing as a different space. We learn, for example, that even the tree house in which we saw the children playing several times during the series did not exist (ep. 08, 00:32) but was a manifestation of the Red Room.

In the episode "Silence Lay Steadily" ep. 10), it serves as a dancing room for Theo. Here it creates a spatial and temporal distortion: as children, Shirley and Nell try to enter the ever-locked Red Room with the help of a master key. On the other side of the door, we see Theo, who is disturbed in her dance exercises by someone rattling at the door from the outside. When Theo looks under the door, however, she sees no shadow (00:00 f.). If in the novel the haunting manifests itself mainly in the form of an infernal banging and rattling on doors, this phenomenon is referenced in the series in this and other sequences. Here, from Theo's perspective, the event looks like a haunting phenomenon, but on the other side of the door are her sisters. The ghosts are other people. In "Screaming Meemies," it is, among other things, the visions of her dead adult twins that destabilize Olivia and drive her into a psychotic episode in which she attempts to poison her children – as if to erase this horror by preventing the twins from reaching adulthood. The ghosts are sometimes ourselves, too, as in the case of Nell and the "bent-neck lady." In the novel, too, Eleanor becomes a ghost herself, as it were, when on her last night at Hill House she knocks on the others' doors to make the same sound that had previously haunted them nightly. "Her characters," Hattenhauer (2003, p. 4) writes of Shirley Jackson, "are sometimes so restricted by place that they start to merge with it".

In this way, the unreliable narrative perspectives of the series disorient not only the viewers but also the characters themselves. The episode "Silence Lay Steadily" (ep. 10) opens with a flashforward in which we see Steven and his wife Leigh (Samantha Sloyan) in their shared apartment (00:03 ff.). Steven is writing about recent events for his next novel; Leigh is heavily pregnant. The child is to be named Eleanor. As Steven's writing reaches the point at which the narrative also broke off for the viewers in the previous episode, he notes that he (like us) cannot remember anything that happened after that – including how he got here (00:09 f.). The previous state of the plot was that Steven and his wife were separated. We also learned that he had a vasectomy while still in college because he doesn't want children. So what is presented here as a flashforward shows, to our knowledge, an impossible scene. This situation is finally resolved when Nell appears next to Steve on the couch and touches his forehead, whereupon he awakens in the Red Room at Hill

House. Luke has a similar experience a few minutes later, though this time it's an apparent flashback that fills in a gap from an earlier episode (00:14–00:17). This, too, ultimately proves to be a vision, one that leads to Luke injecting himself with an overdose of heroin – because, as Jackson (2009, p. 139) writes in the novel, "No ghost in the long history of ghosts has ever hurt anyone physically. The only damage done is by the victim to himself". Both sequences thus prove to be hallucinations that the haunted house creates in the minds of the characters and that are as indistinguishable from past, future, or present real events for them as they are for us viewers.

Here, not only timelines but also metaphysical states intermingle. The simultaneous existence of past, present, and future events, real and imagined places, and deceased and living characters establishes an unreliable narrative perspective that makes it as impossible to distinguish between time axes as between reality, delusion, and imagination. The dead interact with the living, and memories turn out to be unreliable, containing non-existent places or characters. Hill House is able to arrange or disarrange the past, present, and future, whose blending proves highly disturbing for the characters.

Like a recording medium, it has recorded and stored events, characters, and scenes, and reproduces them chaotically, at different times. As a recording medium, the haunted house (like photography, tape recording, or the video camera) does not distinguish between noise and signal. It therefore treats each type of input equally. Consequently, it mixes all the events it has ever witnessed. Instead of a linear timeline that has a completed past, an instantaneous present, and a future that has not yet occurred, the timelines in Hill House loop, interfere and interact with one another. The haunted house as a rogue medium automatically records events and randomly reproduces them, thereby instigating the central elements of the Gothic mode: disorientation, isolation, disease, madness, and death.

References

Literature

Barthes, Roland. 1989. *Die Helle Kammer. Bemerkung zur Photographie*, trans. Dietrich Leube. Frankfurt on the Main: Suhrkamp.

Castle, Terry. 1993. *The apparitional lesbian: Female homosexuality and modern culture*. New York: Columbia University Press.

Clarke, Roger. 2013. Spectres of the past. In *Gothic: The dark heart of film*, ed. James Bell, 84–92. London: BFI.

Freud, Sigmund, and Josef Breuer. 1895. *Studien über Hysterie*. Leipzig: Deuticke.

Hardinge, Emma. 1872. *Modern American Spiritualism*. New York: self-publ.

Hattenhauer, Darryl. 2003. *Shirley Jackson's American Gothic*. Albany: State University of New York Press.

Houdini, Harry. 1924. *A magician among the spirits*. New York: Harpers & Brothers.

Jackson, Shirley. 2009. *The Haunting of Hill House*. London: Penguin (first published 1959).

Johnson, Edward H. 1877. A wonderful invention. Speech capable of indefinite repetition from automatic records. *Scientific American* 37 (20): 304.

Kittler, Friedrich. 1999. *Gramophone, Film, Typewriter*. Translated, with an introduction by Geoffrey Winthrop-Young and Michael Wutz. Stanford, CA: Stanford University Press. (first published 1986).

Lamont, Peter. 2005. *The first psychic: The peculiar mystery of a notorious Victorian wizard*. London: Little, Brown.

Meteling, Arno. 2006. *Monster. Zu Körperlichkeit und Medialität im modernen Horrorfilm*. Bielefeld: Transcript.

Munford, Rebecca. 2016. Spectral femininity. In *Women and the Gothic: An Edinburgh companion*, ed. Avril Horner and Sue Zlosnik, 120–134. Edinburgh: Edinburgh University Press.

N. N. 1888. Spirit mediums outdone. Lively rappings in the Academy of Music. *New York Daily Tribune*, 22 October 1888.

Pacatus, I. M. [i. e. Maxim Gorky]. 1995. Flüchtige Notizen, transl. Jörg Bochow. In KINtop 4: Anfänge des dokumentarischen Films, ed. Frank Kessler, Sabine Lenk, and Martin Loiperdinger, 13–16. Basel: Stroemfeld/Roter Stern. (first published 1896).

Patterson, Mason. 2019. Waking up from the dream of motherhood in Netflix's *The Haunting of Hill House*. *Midwest Journal of Undergraduate Research* 11: 48–55.

P(eško)v, A. [i. e. Maxim Gorky]. 1995. Von der Gesamtrussischen Ausstellung (von unseren Korrespondenten). Der Kinematograph von Lumière, trans. Jörg Bochow. In KINtop, 4: Anfänge des dokumentarischen Films, ed. Frank Kessler, Sabine Lenk, and Martin Loiperdinger, 16–20. Basel: Stroemfeld/Roter Stern. (first published 1896).

Peters, John Durham. 1999. *Speaking into the air: A history of the idea of communication*. Chicago: University of Chicago Press.

Pliny the Younger (i.e. Gaius Plinius Caecilius Secundus). 2010. *Epistulae*, trans. and ed. Heribert Philips and Marion Giebel. Stuttgart: Reclam. (first published c. 100 CE).

Rein, Katharina. 2015. Gespenstische Medien und mediale Gespenster. Jules Vernes *Das Karpathenschloß* und Bram Stokers *Dracula*. In *"Lernen, mit den Gespenstern zu leben". Das Gespenstische als Figur, Metapher und Wahrnehmungsdispositiv*, ed. Lorenz Aggermann et al., 319–330. Berlin: Neofelis.

Robson, Melanie. 2019. Five shots, twice disappeared: Staging memory and trauma in *The Haunting of Hill House* (2018). *Mise-en-Scène. The Journal of Film & Visual Narration* 4 (1): 1–17.

Sconce, Jeffrey. 2000. *Haunted media: Electronic presence from telegraphy to television*. Durham: Duke University Press.

Film

The Haunting. UK 1963. Directed by Robert Wise. Argyle Enterprises.

The Haunting. USA 1999. Directed by Jan de Bont. Dreamworks Pictures/Roth-Arnold Productions.

The Haunting of Bly Manor. TV mini series. USA 2020. Created by Mike Flanagan. Amblin
    Television/Intrepid Pictures/Paramount Television Studios.
The Haunting of Hill House. TV mini series. USA 2018. Created and directed by Mike
    Flanagan. FlanaganFilm et al.
Winchester. Australia/USA 2018. Directed by Michael and Peter Spierig. CBS Films/
    Blacklab Entertainment/Imagination Design Works.

Dracula (2020)

8

8.1   The Vampiric Palimpsest

In 2020, Mark Gatiss and Steven Moffat, who had previously translated Arthur Conan Doyle's detective stories about Sherlock Holmes into the twenty-first century for a BBC series with great success, adapted Bram Stoker's *Dracula* for Netflix and BBC One. As with *Sherlock* (2010–2017), this is a heavily referential series, which becomes clear at the latest in the following exchange: Jonathan Harker (John Heffernan) has found refuge in a nunnery after his stay in Dracula's (Claes Bang) castle, and here he finds himself in conversation with Sister Agatha (Dolly Wells). When he mentions Dracula's statement "Blood is lives." she asks in amazement, "Lives? You are quite certain he did not say, 'Blood is life'? He said, 'blood is lives'?" which he confirms: with "He did." (E. 01, 00:16 f.). Here, Sister Agatha verbalizes the question of the viewers, who, as *Dracula* connoisseurs, also stumble over the plural in the prominent quotation. In Stoker's novel, the mantra "Blood is life" is repeated several times by the Dracula-serving inmate of John Seward's mental institution, Mr. Renfield; at the latest since Universal's 1931 adaptation, it has also been put into the mouth of the Count himself (here as "the blood is the life", 00:11).

The modified quotation with the plural "lives" and Agatha's reaction to it point to the fact that *Dracula* primarily comes to us through adaptations, citations, references, and quotations of quotations, rather than through direct reading of Stoker's novel – if it ever is read. Often, several layers of reference are involved. For example, two highly influential film adaptations, from 1931 and 1979, are based on the stage play by Hamilton Deane and John L. Balderston (1924/1927), the first adaptation authorized by Stoker's widow Florence Balcombe. In both cases, the leading actors played the title roles in Broadway productions before reprising them on film – Bela Lugosi in 1927 and Frank Langella 50 years later. These films, then, adapted an adaptation of Stoker's novel, which thus changed the medium for the third time. Mel Brooks' *Dracula: Dead and Loving It*, in turn, parodies these films, while non-parodic successors such as *Bram Stoker's Dracula* (1992) or *Dracula* (2020) refer back to it through quotations and references, thus continuing the chain of reference. Roger Luckhurst (2018, p. 1 f.) writes in this regard:

> Bram Stoker's *Dracula* is rarely approached except through the myriad adaptations, transpositions and revisions of the novel since it was first published in 1897. […] We come at *Dracula* as if it were always already 'found footage'. We somehow already know the arbitrary rules of vampirism and how to protect ourselves against it, we come decked out with crucifixes and garlic flowers, and we know the narrative arc of this story, from margin to center and back again.

Dracula, along with Joseph Sheridan Le Fanu's *Carmilla* the quintessential template for pop-cultural vampires, has been drowning in the noise of countless adaptations and references for the last century or so, while at the same time the novel's elements have been increasingly dispersed and popularized. "Like a palimpsest," Stacey Abbott (2018, p. 192) writes, "Dracula's various screen appearances build upon each other, operating as much in dialogue with their cinematic and televisual predecessors as they do with Stoker's original text". It is thus primarily the reference to other adaptations that determines our perception of *Dracula*, especially in the postmodern era. Accordingly, Gatiss' and Moffat's *Dracula* is brimming with quotations from, references to, and bows to predecessors such as the films of Tod Browning, Terence Fisher, John Badham, and Francis Ford Coppola, but is just as clearly interested in Stoker's novel as in its translation into the twenty-first century. The Netflix/BBC miniseries both joins and breaks a long tradition.

The first episode, "The Rules of the Beast," opens in 1897, the year Stoker's novel was published, with the Hungarian monastery where Jonathan is recuperating after his visit with and his escape from Dracula. The series thus decidedly does not begin in Transylvania, as most adaptations and the novel do. The very first image turns out to be a historical reference: the yellowed and scratched vignette is reminiscent of old film footage, the blood-red lettering "Hungary 1897" (see Fig. 8.1) recalls the striking opening sequence of Terence Fisher's *Dracula* by Hammer Film Productions (see Fig. 4.3). While the 1958 adaptation opened with shots of Dracula's monumental medieval castle, accompanied by dramatic, pompous music, the 2020 one presents us with an idyllic white building with a bell tower, surrounded by forests, mountains and white houses. The innocent and peaceful tinkling of a music box can be heard, which is drowned out by the ringing of bells and church choir singing as the monastery is approached – a soundscape

Fig. 8.1 Still from *Dracula*, E. 01 "The Rules of the Beast" (UK 2020), 00:00. (Netflix. Accessed December 07, 2020)

that seems downright cynical in comparison with the Hammer production. What is more, in light of the gruesome content that awaits us in this episode, this soundtrack can be understood as an ironic commentary.

The camera moves toward the idyllic monastery and eventually into its interior. The very first image inside contrasts with the idyllic music we just heard: it shows the inside of a window with a fly on it, that folkloric devil's companion that not only features prominently in the opening credits alongside blood cells and streams in this series, but also signals Dracula's presence throughout. Accordingly, flies are ubiquitous, especially in his castle. In this sequence, the fly seems to have accompanied Jonathan Harker to his place of refuge – as a harbinger of Dracula, as will soon become apparent. A short time later, a nun interrupts Harker's interaction with the fly. Her question, "Are you hungry, Mister Harker?" (E. 01, 00:00) suggests that she knows that Dracula's underlings like to feed on insects, as Renfield does in the novel.

8.2 Medial Transmission

After the patient has negated this, the nurse enters the room and suggests a conversation. She has read Jonathan's account of the events in Dracula's castle, she says, whereupon Jonathan insists that it contains the truth. As we later learn, the "report" titled "Dracula," which he wrote incessantly for a whole week after his arrival is a confused accumulation of endlessly repeated phrases such as "Dracula will rise," "Dracula is my master," or "Dracula is God" (E. 01, 00:52). Thus, while the existence of an account written down by Harker is established at the beginning and declared to be the impetus for the interview, it turns out after nearly an hour that the only account of events at Dracula's castle is the one Sister Agatha is receiving orally from Jonathan in this episode. A manuscript titled "Dracula" thus stands at the beginning of the series, suggesting a self-reflexive move which makes Harker assume the role of the author. In fact, we later learn, the manuscript seems to have been written more by a version of Renfield, of whom we see several variations in the miniseries.[1]

When Sister Agatha takes out the supposed report, we also get a glimpse of the other contents of her bag (E. 01, 00:01). Inside are several wooden stakes that identify her as a vampire hunter, even before Dracula and we learn her full name, Agatha van Helsing (E. 01, 01:16). Whereas in Stoker's narrative Sister Agatha is Jonathan's nurse at the monastery, who inscribes herself in the novel via a letter to his fiancée Mina, here she becomes a female version of van Helsing. Accordingly, before she begins her interview with the vampire, she also makes sure that his transformation has not yet progressed too far by asking if the sunlight is not too harsh for Jonathan.

Harker's narration, which begins after the opening credits, then takes us in flashback to the beginning of Stoker's novel and to a staple sequence of any *Dracula* adaptation: in a nocturnal landscape, a woman begs him to accept her crucifix, which he refuses, before finding himself alone some distance from his destination because the coachman refuses to drive closer to Dracula's castle and leaves with the remaining occupants of the coach. As Harker remains alone in the darkness pierced by wolf howls, we also hear the voice of his fiancée. In a reference to a similar sequence in Francis Ford Coppola's 1992 adaptation, she reads her letter to Jonathan. The fact that the novel *Dracula* is told through letters, diary entries and other media prompted Coppola to weave them into the film's narrative as well. Roger Luckhurst (2018, p. 4) has pointed out that Stoker adopted the narration qua a fictional assemblage of characters from Wilkie Collins' literature of the 1860s, but greatly expanded it. He also identifies it as a marker of modernity:

---

[1] In each episode, we meet a character who embodies certain aspects of Renfield: While in the monastery Harker takes on this role in his delusional worship of Dracula, in the second episode, on board of the Demeter, it is at times Lord Ruthven who sides with him. In the third episode, Mark Gatiss appears as Dracula's lawyer Frank Renfield, who, among other things, helps him procure victims and cover up his murders.

[It] turns *Dracula* into a breathless rendition of modernity itself, racing on with the whizz of trains and omnibuses, of letters and telegrams speeding through wires or voices caught in real time on wax cylinders. It might have felt crude and vulgar to cultivated aesthetic taste in the 1890s, but it makes *Dracula* part of the new century, not the old. (Luckhurst 2018, p. 4)

In keeping with this, Jonathan travels to Transylvania by rail, a mechanized, modern means of transportation, where he changes to the traditional horse-drawn carriage – a mode of transportation appropriate for Dracula, the centuries-old aristocrat. Accordingly, Dracula himself embarks on his journey to England in a pre-industrial manner: on the sailing ship Demeter, named after the harvest goddess on whom pre-modern agriculture was particularly dependent.

In Coppola's paradigmatic *Bram Stoker's Dracula*, the novel's multimedia arsenal translates into multiple visual overlays as soon as Harker (Keanu Reeves) arrives in Transylvania: during his train ride, he writes in his diary and then reads a letter he has received from Dracula. As he looks at the paper, its contents ring out as a voice-over spoken by Dracula (Gary Oldman), accompanied by the latter's eyes appearing outside, watching Harker menacingly from a sky coloured blood-red by the sunset (00:08). The glowing eyes reference Tod Browning's *Dracula* by Universal, in which the area around Bela Lugosi's eyes was particularly showcased by lighting and camera (see Fig. 4.4) – in contrast to later productions, which placed the focus in the vampire's face on the unusually long fangs. Afterwards, Harker looks at a photograph of his fiancée Mina (see Fig. 8.2), while we hear her read her diary entry. The image then follows the sound and shows Mina (Winona Ryder) sitting at the typewriter and looking at a photograph of Jonathan before she begins to write (00:09, see Fig. 8.3).

In 2020, we see a similar sequence, which is without a doubt a nod to Coppola's adaptation: while Harker reads Mina's letter, he holds a photograph of her next to it (see Fig. 8.4). Dissolves show her (Morfydd Clark) typing this letter on a typewriter (see Fig. 8.5, E. 01, 00:06 f.). What is surprising, however, is its open and progressive content, for in it Mina in advance absolves her future husband of possible flings during his travels. She follows this announcement with a list of the men who keep her company in the absence of her fiancé. Her progressiveness, established in Stoker's novel with the use of the typewriter, is here extended into the realm of morality and gender roles.

The role of the media in *Dracula* was elaborated by Friedrich Kittler in his essay "Dracula's Legacy." The characters in Stoker's novel – and this has long been overlooked in film adaptations – write and read: letters, diaries, notes. Dr. Seward records his diary on phonograph cylinders. Mina Harker, a stenographer, collects

Fig. 8.2 Keanu Reeves as Jonathan Harker in *Bram Stoker's Dracula* (USA 1992), 00:09. (Netflix. Accessed December 07, 2020)

Fig. 8.3 Winona Ryder as Mina Murray in *Bram Stoker's Dracula,* 00:09. (Netflix. Accessed: December 07, 2020)

and bundles all this data, types it up on her typewriter, and distributes copies to the group of vampire hunters, making everyone's information available to all. "Vampirism," writes Kittler (2012, p. 71 f.), "is a chain reaction, and can therefore only be fought with the techniques of mechanical text reproduction". The machine

Fig. 8.4 John Heffernan as Jonathan Harker in *Dracula*, E. 01, 00:06. (Netflix. Accessed: 07 December 2020)

Fig. 8.5 Morfydd Clark as Mina Murray in *Dracula*, E. 01, 00:06. (Netflix. Accessed: 07 December 2020)

text democratizes information and takes away Dracula's *raison d'être* as a symbolic figure of the attempted re-empowerment of the nobility. Only thanks to Mina's dossier can the vampiric count be defeated, which is why Kittler (2012,

p. 73) concludes that "Stoker's Dracula is no vampire novel, but rather the written account of our bureaucratization". The ensemble of vampire hunters emerges victorious in part thanks to means that seem regressive to Victorian Londoners, such as herbs and crucifixes, and in part thanks to state-of-the-art medicine (blood transfusions) and technology – in addition to those just mentioned, they also use rapid communication by telegraphy and faster travel by rail to their advantage.

In the 2020 adaptation, partly as a reference to Coppola's *Bram Stoker's Dracula,* we encounter some of the recording media that Kittler identifies as essential to the vampire hunt – only Seward's phonograph and Lucy's letters are replaced by smartphones. Lucy Westenra (Lydia West) and Jack Seward (Matthew Beard) appear in the third episode, which takes place in the present day and consequently updates its media technology.

The focus in *Dracula,* however, lies on a different transmission medium. As already becomes clear in the quote at the beginning, blood as the medium of vampirism and of the vampire narrative *par excellence* takes center stage here. Blood transmits genealogy and therefore determins all parameters of life in times of the estate-based society. It can transmit diseases and therefore decide over life and death. In *Dracula* it reaches the next level of escalation as a universal medium – here blood transmits the characteristics of the person concerned. It provides access to knowledge and skills (such as languages) as well as biographical information and character traits. For example, Dracula learns van Helsing's name when he licks her blood from his hand (E. 01, 01:18). On board the Demeter, he learns German by draining the German helmsman (E. 02, 00:16), and when he arrives in present-day England, he uses the blood of his first victim to acquire knowledge of contemporary culture and technology (E. 03, 00:04 f.).

Blood is the essence of people from which they can be reproduced. This is also shown by the fact that, in episode 3, Zoe Helsing (also Dolly Wells) increasingly adopts the idiom of her ancestor Agatha after drinking her blood via Dracula's blood. In Gatiss' and Moffat's *Dracula* "blood is life" becomes "blood is lives" because blood here is not just one life, but multiple lives. Their Count not only sucks the lifeblood out of his victims, but also their essence, thereby temporarily acquiring some of their characteristics and abilities. He chooses his victims purposefully not only because he is an epicure, but also, as he emphasizes repeatedly, to protect himself from characteristics he wants to avoid. The blood of his victims thus contains their lives in the plural – not only the biological ones, but also the biographical ones.

8.3   The Drinking of Blood and Its Consequences

The general occurences in Dracula's castle are well known, and the first episode of
Dracula begins comparatively traditionally. Dracula's castle in Stoker's novel as
well as in Universal's adaptation is, in typical Gothic fashion, an enormous medieval, partially ruinous structure – in Universal's 1931 adaptation even with missing
wall segments, (exotic) animals running loose inside it and huge cobwebs through
which Dracula walks like an immaterial ghost (00:09 ff.). In 2020 we are not dealing with a ruin, but with an elaborate, highly disorienting building of gigantic pro-
portions, "a rising labyrinth of stairs and doors and shadows" (E. 01, 00:13). There
are no maps of this "haunted prison without locks," Dracula says, in whose corri-
dors many souls have been lost (E. 01, 00:13). As the Count informs Harker upon
his arrival, the castle is the masterpiece of an architect who wanted it to serve as a
monument to his deceased wife and to the daylight he would never see again
(E. 01, 00:13) – a comment that raises the question of whether Dracula himself was
this architect, who also used it to build an elaborate trap for his victims. In this
labyrinth that could just as easily be found in a haunted house movie, Harker slips
into the role of a typical female heroine of the Gothic novel: like Emily St. Aubert
in Ann Radcliffe's *The Mysteries of Udolpho* (1794), he finds himself held in isolation by an older man in a mysterious castle. And like her, he makes it his mission
to explore this labyrinth, repeatedly gets lost in it, is attacked, faints, and always
regains consciousness dazed and weakened either in his own room or in Dracula's
dining hall.

The initially old count rejuvenates over the course of Jonathan's stay, his strong
accent gives way to perfect British English – all of which he always comments on
in an unmistakably ambiguous manner with statements like "your presence has
invigorated me. Fresh blood." (E. 01, 00:24). Later, he says to Jonathan: "Well, you
do look rather … drained," and responds to his surprised observation that he himself looks young: "And I owe it all to you. Thanks." (E. 01, 00:36). Moffat's and
Gatiss' eloquent dandy Dracula is bubbling over with puns, and tends to tell his
victims the truth straight out, which usually leaves them startled rather than running only because they either don't believe him or misunderstand his remarks.[2]
"The strength of the vampire," explains van Helsing (Edward Van Sloan) in
Universal's Dracula in 1931, "is that people will not believe in him." (00:43).

---

[2] For example, aboard the Demeter, he tells a young woman directly that he is a vampire
(E. 02, 00:31). She does not seem to understand this or thinks it is a joke and continues the
(highly erotically charged) conversation until Dracula repeats his statement and this time
confirms it by subsequently biting her neck.

Fig. 8.6   John Heffernan as Jonathan Harker in *Dracula,* E. 01, 00:03. (Netflix. Accessed December 07, 2020)

While Dracula absorbs Jonathan's youth with his blood, the latter ages rapidly and appears increasingly weak and confused. His physical deterioration is evident, for example, in his peeling fingernails (E. 01, 00:27). When he talks to Sister Agatha in the monastery, he is emaciated, pale as a sheet, and his skin is covered with ulcers (see Fig. 8.6). Here, Harker exhibits the typical appearance of a terminal AIDS patient, thus referencing a topos of Gothic cinema: the construction of vampirism and of monstrosity in general as a metaphor for disease. Agatha's question as to whether Harker had sexual intercourse with Dracula and her explanation also equates vampirism with an infectious disease: "Clearly, you have been contaminated with something. Any contact you've had with count Dracula, sexual or otherwise, is therefore relevant." (E. 01, 00:21). Thus, in the tradition of the 1958 Hammer adaptation, in which Abraham van Helsing (Peter Cushing) refers to vampirism as infectious (00:36), here Agatha van Helsing conceives of it as transmissible by means of bodily fluids including but not limited to blood. The comparison of monstrosity to infectious diseases, and specifically AIDS, was particularly virulent in the body horror and Gothic of the 1980s and 1990s, such as in David Cronenberg's films, which were characterized by tumor-like growths on bodies and body parts.

Another topos taken up in *Dracula* is the construction of vampirism as addiction, which was previously prominently featured, for example, in Abel Ferrara's *The Addiction* (1995). In the second episode, "Blood Vessel," Agatha learns that the Count can hardly resist the sight and smell of blood and quickly loses control of himself. As in previous vampire films and series, his facial features and teeth visibly transform as soon as he smells blood, his eyes turn red like those of Christopher Lee in the Hammer adaptation. This happens several times aboard the Demeter, for example when a crew member falls from the lookout onto the deck and suffers an open fracture to his leg (E. 02, 00:39). This event, too, unfolds as a flashback during an interview with a vampire: At the beginning of the second episode, Sister Agatha questions Dracula about the events on the Demeter during his passage to England, while he sits across the table from her, a chessboard between them. At this point in the narrative, when it becomes clear that Dracula is losing control in the presence of blood, Agatha states: "You can't control yourself in the presence of blood. It's not just sustenance. It's an addiction." (E. 02, 00:39 f.). Since he himself repeatedly compares blood to wine, he also moves into the proximity of an alcoholic who faces potential loss of control by being exposed to just the smell of the drink. Accordingly, Dracula equates different people with different vintage wines, the higher quality ones of which should be enjoyed and the inferior ones avoided (E. 02, 00:47). "Agatha, you're exquisite!" he proclaims when, about halfway through the second episode, he turns the tables on the interviewer (00:48) – or rather, when Agatha and we realize that the tables had been turned all along. As it now turns out, she herself is also aboard the Demeter, sedated by Dracula's "kiss" and locked in his cabin. The narrative frame of the interview turns out to be a vampirically induced dream, which ends as Agatha regains consciousness aboard the ship.

Also in this scene, Dracula repeats the phrase that Bela Lugosi immortalised in 1931: "I never drink ... wine" (00:15) – preferably saying it while holding a wine glass filled with the blood of the person he is addressing (E. 01, 00:35; E. 02, 00:47). The symbolic interchangeability of wine and blood articulated here in an ironic way derives from the Catholic mass, where red wine symbolizes the blood of Christ. Drinking blood as an inverted communion turns vampiric blood consumption into a blasphemous parody of the Eucharist (see Bale 2018, p. 108). It also points to the Eucharistic Controversy, one of the central disagreements between the Protestant view, which in *Dracula* would be represented by the British protagonists, and the Catholicism dominant in the vampire's homeland. The aforementioned famous quote "the blood is the life", too, is a religious reference. In Stoker's novel, Renfield explains it to Mina Harker in a lucid moment:

The doctor here will bear me out that on one occasion I tried to kill him for the purpose of strengthening my vital powers by the assimilation with my own body of his life through the medium of his blood – relying, of course, upon the Scriptural phrase, 'For the blood is the life.' (Stoker and Klinger 2008, p. 333)

This, too, is an inversion – Renfield is referring here to a passage from Deuteronomy that is the source of the prohibition of the consumption of blood in the laws of kashrut. In the English standard translation it reads: "Only be sure that you do not eat the blood, for the blood is the life, and you shall not eat the life with the flesh" (Deut. 12:23). Renfield – or, in the case of those adaptations that put the phrase in Dracula's mouth, he – takes the passage to mean the contrary: a reason to consume blood in order to absorb the life force of other creatures (see Bale 2018, p. 109 f.).

Drinking blood as sacriledge underscores Dracula's blasphemous existence – all the more so when he is wasteful with human blood. Dracula's consumption is not merely for sustenance; it is exuberant, passionate, decadent, and celebratory. If, in parts, the HBO series *True Blood* and even more so the *Twilight* tetralogy established the temperate restraint of the ethically responsible, abstemious, "vegetarian" vampire, then *Dracula* positions itself as the antithetis to moderate vampirism. While the Cullens in *Twilight* feed exclusively on non-human blood and the responsible among the vampires in *True Blood* gulp down microwaved, bottled, synthetic blood, Dracula in this series passionately sinks his teeth into the necks of his victims and enjoys it to the fullest. Not only does he delight in sadistic practices like the massacre at the nunnery (E. 01, 01:22 ff.), he also lavishly lets the blood run down in streams and form puddles, for instance, until it drips through the deck onto a passenger sleeping on the lower deck of the Demeter (E. 02, 01:32). *Dracula* thus declares war on the anti-pleasure, chaste Cullens as well as on the hypocritical, (at least outwardyly) ethically responsible vampires fighting for integration into human society in *True Blood*. Dracula wallows with relish in his superiority as a supernatural being and as a strategist and manipulator with 400 years of experience. As a decadent dandy, he celebrates his lust unrestrainedly and provocatively, enjoying the games he plays with his victims as much as their literal incorporation.

8.4   (Homo)Sexuality

Dracula's lust is also exuberant in sexual terms. Among the passengers who find themselves aboard the Demeter with him in the second episode is a certain Lord Ruthven – a reference to a literary predecessor of Dracula: this is the name of the vampire in William Polidori's short story "The Vampyre" (1819), which originated at the same meeting at the Villa Diodati in 1816 that also produced Mary Shelley's *Frankenstein*. Modeled on Lord Byron, Polidori's seductive and murderous, aristocratic vampire may have been a model for Stoker's Dracula. In Polidori's short story, the odd, strikingly pale aristocrat suddenly appears in London society – just as Dracula plans to do in Stoker's novel. He marries the daughter of a friend with whom he has previously traveled Europe and murders her on her wedding night (just as Frankenstein's creature murders his bride on her wedding night). In Gatiss' and Moffat's *Dracula*, Lord Ruthven is aboard the Demeter with his young bride and a male companion with whom he is obviously engaged in a homosexual love affair. The only passenger who seems to register the homoeroticicm of this couple is Dracula. In addition to allusions to Ruthven's fiancée and her sex life, he openly articulates his affection when he aggressively grabs the thigh of a distraught Ruthven in the company of others (E. 02, 00:24).

Various representations of Dracula and his kind have been heavily eroticized in the past – in particular, the 1979 film adaptation starring Frank Langella in the title role was groundbreaking in this regard. Heike Bauer has pointed out that Stoker wrote his novel at a time when sexology was being established as a new field. Particularly for psychiatry and criminology at that time, it was important to observe and categorize deviations from normative sexual behavior in order to be able to decide, simply put, which cases required therapy and which ones a trial (Bauer 2018, p. 76). At the same time, deviant sexuality increasingly became a topic in literature and philosophy, which in turn left their mark on sexual science, for example in the naming of sadism and masochism based on the writings of the Marquis de Sade and Leopold von Sacher-Masoch, respectively (see Bauer 2018, p. 76 f.). Stoker's *Dracula*, too, needs to be seen in this cultural-historical context as a work that articulates sexual fears as well as desires, especially in light of the social construction of homosexuality and heterosexuality as well as of binary gender identity. Bauer (2018, p. 77) writes:

> *Dracula* addresses key concerns in discourses of sexuality at the fin de siècle including questions about the integrity, violation and potentially dangerous reproduction of certain bodies, and anxieties about an increasingly unstable gender binarism that was nevertheless considered crucial to social life. The novel seems less about sexual orientation than about desire as such, and pulses with fears and fantasies clustered specifically around the implications of reproductive sex.

In 1895, 2 years before the publication of *Dracula*, homosexuality gained enormous social visibility when Oscar Wilde, at the height of his fame, was sentenced to 2 years imprisonment with hard labor in the penitentiary for his affair with Lord Alfred Douglas. Stoker and Wilde were both from Dublin and knew each other personally. Florence Balcombe who was known all over Dublin for her beauty had rejected Wilde's wedding proposal before marrying Stoker. Nina Auerbach (1995, p. 102) has argued that Dracula can be read as a fictionalized, monstrous incarnation of Wilde: a deviant, sexualized figure crippled by arbitrary rules – whether the social prohibition of same-sex love or Dracula's restrictions, such as the commandment to sleep in native soil or the destructive force of garlic and the crucifix. Homosexuality was also long conceptualized as similar to a contagious disease, as if homosexuals were always on the lookout for new "victims" to seduce and bring "over to their side", long before AIDS was falsely stigmatized as a "gay disease."

Xavier Aldana Reyes (2018, p. 126) argues for reading the character Dracula not as much as homosexual or heterosexual but rather as queer – a representative of a deviant sexuality that must take place in secret because the dominant societal view is hostile to it. This set of themes becomes explicit in *Dracula* when the vampire here does not (as in Browning's, Fisher's, or Coppola's adaptations) go on a heterosexual prowl, specifically targeting, seducing, and trying to bring Mina Harker "over to his side." In 2020, he does not discriminate because of gender – Dracula refers to Jonathan Harker as his "bride" as naturally as to his other victims who become vampires – not only because he thereby demasculinizes him, but also because Dracula does not think in terms of "heterosexual or homosexual." Consistently, Dracula's leap from Victorian England to contemporary Western society means that he can be more open about his sexuality. Now Dracula appears as a decadent, pansexual bon viveur who, naturally, flirts as vigorously with Lord Ruthven as he does with Ruthven's bride Dorabella.

"The kiss of the vampire is an opiate," he explains to Agatha van Helsing (E. 02, 00:47). He thus analogizes vampirism not only to drug use in general, but also to intoxication as a shared, potentially romantic experience. Unlike the loss of self-control in the face of blood described above, this is intoxication for two, subject to Dracula's control. While he enjoys the blood of his victims, his "kiss" intoxicates them to the point of unconsciousness, inducing dreams and hallucinations. Agatha's aforementioned question of whether Jonathan had sex with Dracula is implicitly answered by insertions of his nocturnal fantasies of his fiancée Mina, who, however, transforms into Dracula for a few single frames (E. 01, 00:20; 00:36). Ecstatically hallucinating as a result of Dracula's "kiss," Harker finds himself at his mercy. Whether it is when he makes Jonathan his "bride," or when he promises to satisfy Dorabella's lust unfulfilled by her homosexual husband, Dracula's bite is erotic, if not sexual. Similarly, when the injured helmsman has an erotic dream about the beautiful Dorabella, he awakens to find that instead of her, Dracula is sitting on top of him, who immediately not only bites his neck, but literally tears him to pieces (E. 02, 00:45–00:46). As in the sexual encounter with Jonathan, the polymorphic vampire here slips into the role of the desired person regardless of gender in order to satisfy his own lust as much as the lust of his victim.

8.5   Society and Transgression

Finally, in the third episode, "The Dark Compass," Dracula fulfills the dark desire of young Lucy Westenra, who appears in 2020 London as a much-courted, dazzling party girl, played for the first time by an actress of colour, Lydia West. As in Stoker's novel, Lucy sneaks out at night to give herself to Dracula on lonely park benches and cemeteries – but unlike in the novel, she does so willingly. In turn, Dracula satisfies her longing for recognition as well as her hedonistic-self-destructive lust by becoming a secret lover, father figure, and drug dealer all at once. At their meetings, Lucy offers Dracula her blood in exchange for the intoxication of his "kiss." "What do you want to dream about tonight?" he merely asks her before sinking his teeth into her neck. "Put me somewhere beautiful," the world-weary party girl replies, "where no one can see me, where I don't have to smile" (E. 03, 00:55). As a result of her nocturnal encounters with Dracula, Lucy dies and subsequently returns as another one of his vampiric brides. And also as in the novel, she finds her true death soon after – though under different circumstances – by a wooden stake rammed into her chest by a loving man, in this case Jack Seward (E. 03, 01:21).

Sexual appetite and thirst for blood, intoxication and feeding, love and death all fall into one for Dracula. His victims, whom he turns into vampires, he calls his brides, regardless of their gender. Agatha's view that Jonathan may have been "infected" with vampirism through sexual intercourse with Dracula also blurs the distinction between sexual penetration and that through Dracula's elongated, phallic fangs. This is also where the line between human and animal becomes blurred. "Dracula is otherness itself," writes Jack Halberstam (1993, p. 334),

> a distilled version of all others produced by and within fictional texts, sexual science, and psychopathology. He is monster and man, feminine and powerful, parasitical and wealthy; he is repulsive and fascinating, he exerts the consummate gaze but is scrutinized in all things, he lives forever but can be killed. Dracula is indeed not simply a monster, but a technology of monstrosity.

Halberstam identifies Dracula not only as the paradigmatic monster, but as the paradigm of monstrosity *par excellence*. As the embodiment of the Other in general, he exists outside of human societies and their rules. In Gatiss' and Moffat's adaptation, too, he knows no rules set from the outside. He follows exclusively the rules by which he himself must live (such as the repeatedly thematized fear of the crucifix). Dracula's desire also recognises no socially imposed barriers – his sexuality just as little as his lustful thirst for blood. The two often go hand in hand: by taking literal the desire to assimilate and unite with a person he desires, Dracula inevitably murders the objects of his unbridled lust. "And all men kill the thing they love," wrote Oscar Wilde (2004, V. 649, 653 f.) after his prison sentence, 1 year before the publication of *Dracula* in *The Ballad of Reading Gaol,* "[t]he coward does it with a kiss, the brave man with a sword!".

The British protagonists in Stoker's novel counter Dracula's exuberant, animalistic instincts with their civilized rationality and bureaucracy. Reading and writing – the proud achievements of Western European literacy around 1900 – seem to be a safe alternative to the transgressive sexuality of the vampire in Stoker's novel (Halberstam 1993, p. 336). For example when John Seward notes: "After lunch Harker and his wife went back to their own room, and as I passed a while ago I heard the click of the typewriter. They are hard at it" (Stoker and Klinger 2008, p. 323). Whether writing here is an alternative occupation of the newlyweds to sexual activity or a metaphorization of the same remains unclear. In *Bram Stoker's Dracula* as well as in the 2020 adaptation, too, Mina's energetic typing seems to be a substitute for sexual activity – whether while her fiancé is traveling or while he is hunting the eroticized vampire with the other male protagonists in order to stake him, which in turn can be interpreted as a homoerotically connoted group activity.

8.5.1   Narrative Perspectives

Reading and writing, in turn, represent power and knowledge and were therefore subject to controlled production and reception in Victorian England: *Dracula,* as an epistolary novel, consists of the accounts of only four middle-class characters: Mina and Jonathan Harker, John Seward, and Lucy Westenra. The foreigner van Helsing, the aristocrat Lord Godalming, Renfield, who is classified as insane, and Dracula, who is identified as the enemy, are given no voice of their own. "The activities of reading and writing, then," concludes Jack Halberstam (1993, p. 336),

> are crucial in this novel to the establishment of a kind of middle-class British hegemony and they are annexed to the production of sexual subjectivities. Rather than being seen as essential to only certain kinds of bodies, sexuality is revealed as the completely controlled, mass-production of a group of professionals – doctors, psychiatrists, lawyers.

As described in Chap. 5, a humanization of the vampire can be observed since the 1990s. In the course of this, Dracula is, for example, increasingly identified with the historical voivode Vlad III Drăculea – an association that Raymond T. McNally and Radu Florescu already made in 1972 in their seminal work *In Search of*

Dracula. This linkage back to a real historical figure already helped to give the vampire more character compared to Stoker's Dracula, who is relatively one-dimensional in the novel and who is not given a voice of his own. His point of view, motivations, and emotional world remain inaccessible because everything we learn about him is from characters who are hostile to him.

In Coppola's 1992 adaptation, on the contrary, Dracula's perspective sets the tone. Stacey Abbott (2018, p. 203) argues that while the film reproduces the narrative perspective of Mina and Jonathan Harker, John Seward, and Lucy Westenra, conveyed through letters, diary entries, etc., it also adopts Dracula's point of view on an aesthetic level:

> The rich colors, layering of imagery through superimpositions and Gothic orchestral score that are used throughout the film convey his emotional register, including anger and betrayal, passionate blood lust, and romantic longing. In particular the film's use of costume and make-up as Dracula adopts different personas, not only suggests the otherness of his vampiric state but significantly his self-loathing.

By articulating Dracula's point of view through the grotesque splendor of its soundtrack, costumes, and imagery, Coppola's film not only makes him accessible to us, it forces us into his complicity. Accordingly, this adaptation also emphasizes Dracula's romantic side, his self-sacrifice and his yearning love for his deceased wife, which here becomes the motivation for his journey to England in the first place. "This shift toward rendering Dracula sympathetic within film and TV," Abbott (2018, p. 203 f.) writes, "does not necessarily defang Stoker's monster but rather highlights the tension between monstrosity and humanity as he embodies the liminal space between the two."

In the 2020 adaptation, the dominance of Dracula's point of view becomes even more explicit. Here, the title character is indisputably also the protagonist. While the series does not follow a personal narrative perspective, Dracula is the only character that remains consistent throughout all three episodes. None of the other characters figure in all episodes, with the exception of van Helsing, who appears in the third episode in flashbacks and as an apparition/hallucination as well as in the shape of her descendant and doppelganger Zoe. Dracula determines the entire plot of the series – even its place and time are subject to his perspective as we travel 123 years into the future together with him at the end of the second episode. While our initial encounter with Dracula is determined by Harker's narration, the second episode, which is staged as a chamber play aboard the Demeter, is even orchestrated by Dracula: In the course of it, it turns out that he, under a pseudonym, has arranged for the passengers to find themselves in this constellation on this ship – he has thereby put together a menu for himself for the long voyage to England. Gatiss and Moffat do not portray Dracula as the radically other that has to be erased. Nor is, unlike her male equivalent in Stoker's novel and most adaptations, his antagonist Agatha van Helsing (respectively, her descendant Zoe Helsing) out to destroy the vampire. Rather, she is driven by scientific curiosity and seeks to explore and understand Dracula as a vampire as much as a person. Thereby she, too, entices us to take Dracula's point of view and sympathize with him rather than to regard him as an enemy.

Together with her, we come closer and closer to Dracula: while we initially experience him through Harker's report, he subsequently makes his own appearance. In the second episode, Agatha interviews the Count herself before becoming an actor in the very story he just told her. At the end of this episode, van Helsing blows up the Demeter and goes down with the ship, together with Dracula to prevent him from reaching England. After 123 years at the bottom of the sea, however, the comatose vampire is brought back to life by a diving research crew and goes ashore on the British coast in 2020. Here, Agatha's descendant, Zoe Helsing, awaits him. As we later learn, she works as a scientist at the Jonathan Harker Foundation, which was founded by his fiancée Mina around 1900 and is dedicated to the research of vampirism.

Zoe Helsing takes a blood sample from the vampire before he can free himself from imprisonment in the research facility with the help of his lawyer Renfield (Mark Gatiss) and by invoking human rights. Giving in to her desire to understand the vampire, instead of bringing Dracula's blood to the lab, Helsing drinks it. In doing so, she places Dracula's mantra "blood is lives" above her professional ethos as a scientist and thereby reveals that her actions, too, are ultimately subject to the will of the series' protagonist. And since blood is a universal storage medium here, it gives her access to Dracula's world of memories, which also includes her deceased ancestor Agatha. Consequently, Zoe not only sees her in visions and speaks to her, she also increasingly adopts Agatha's features and accent.

Together with Agatha van Helsing/Zoe Helsing, we get to know Dracula. This intimacy reaches its climax at the end of the series, when the two become one through the mutual consumption of their blood. Moreover, they become so in death – while Zoe succumbs to her advanced cancer, Dracula drinks her blood, which is poisonous to him. In doing so, he not only sweetens her death through his intoxicating "kiss," but also chooses his own, along with her. Agatha died in 1897 to incapacitate Dracula, causing the sinking of the Demeter with him and herself aboard. At the same time, she thus saved herself from a vampiric existence, the first signs of which she had already observed. Similarly, Dracula now escapes vampiric immortality, while at the same time sweetening and hastening Zoe's demise. The final sequence shows the sun, which he feared for centuries until Zoe convinced him that its light would not harm him. So, just before both of their deaths, he experiences the sunlight he longed to see for centuries. In a final bow to the history of the vampire film, the final images cite a sequence from John Badham's *Dracula* from 1979, which features a love scene between Dracula and Lucy in which their silhouettes merge against a glowing red background (00:59 f., see Fig. 8.7). In 2020, it is the union of Zoe Helsing and Dracula in the eroticized vampire bite at the moment of their joined dying (E. 03, 01:29, see Fig. 8.8), which is cross-cut with astronomical images of the sun with visible protuberances (see Fig. 8.9). Similar solar shots we find at the end of Badham's film, cross-cut with Dracula's (supposed) death by burning, where the sun's visiblity seems to converge with his increasing agony (01:39 f.) until we see it greatly magnified (see Fig. 8.10). Sunlight at the end of the vampire film stands in the tradition of *Nosferatu*, the first (albeit unlicensed) adaptation of Stoker's famous novel. In terms of media technology, this is only logical, because sunlight also puts an end to the medium of film itself – at least as long as analog film was still being shot on film stock, whose images simply disappeared in the light if handled carelessly before they were developed.

When all of Dracula's attempts to procreate fail and none of the vampires he creates survive for long, on the one hand this shows that the Count, as the only one of his kind, is condemned to eternal loneliness. On the other hand, Gatiss and Moffat show that after 123 years of reception and adaptation of *Dracula*, all his descendants fade and disappear after a short time, while Dracula alone survives time, always metamorphic, flexible and eager to learn. He determines life, death and undeath, reality and dream, beginning and end. The storyline may span 123 years, but it simply does not take place without Dracula – the time he spends comatose at the bottom of the sea is also blanked out for us. If the plot begins when Harker approaches Dracula's castle, shortly before Dracula himself makes his first appearance, it ends when Dracula departs.

Fig. 8.7 Frank Langella as Dracula and Kate Nelligan as Lucy in *Dracula* (USA/UK 1979), 00:59. (DVD, Winkler Film, Germany 2009)

Fig. 8.8 Claes Bang as Dracula and Dolly Wells as Zoe Helsing in *Dracula*, E. 03 "The Dark Compass" (UK 2020), 01:29. (Netflix. Accessed September 03, 2020)

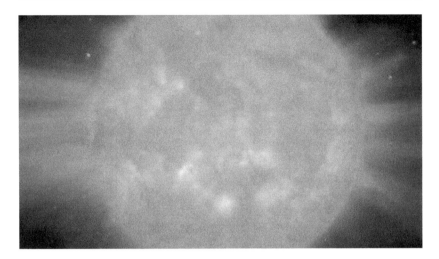

Fig. 8.9 Still from Dracula (UK 2020) E. 03, 01:29. (Netflix. Accessed: 03 September 2020)

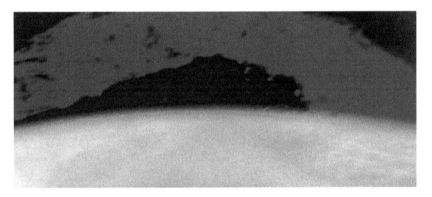

Fig. 8.10 Still from *Dracula* (USA/UK 1979), 01:40. (DVD, Winkler Film, Germany 2009)

References

Literature

Abbott, Stacey. 2018. Dracula on film and TV from 1960 to the present. In *The Cambridge companion to Dracula*, ed. Roger Luckhurst, 192–206. Cambridge: Cambridge University Press.
Aldana Reyes, Xavier. 2018. Dracula queered. In *The Cambridge companion to Dracula*, ed. Roger Luckhurst, 125–135. Cambridge: Cambridge University Press.
Auerbach, Nina. 1995. *Our vampires, ourselves*. Chicago: University of Chicago Press.
Bale, Anthony. 2018. Dracula's blood. In *The Cambridge companion to Dracula*, ed. Roger Luckhurst, 104–113. Cambridge: Cambridge University Press.
Bauer, Heike. 2018. Dracula and sexology. In *The Cambridge companion to Dracula*, ed. Roger Luckhurst, 76–84. Cambridge: Cambridge University Press.
Deuteronomy 12:23. Bible study tools. https://www.biblestudytools.com/esv/deuteronomy/12-23.html. Accessed 13 December 2022.
Halberstam, J. 1993. Technologies of monstrosity: Bram Stoker's "Dracula". *Victorian Studies* 36 (3): 333–352.
Kittler, Friedrich. 2012. Dracula's legacy. In *Friedrich A. Kittler. Essays. Literature. Media. Information systems*, ed. and introduced John Johnston, 50–84. Abingdon, Oxon: Routledge (first published in 1993).
Luckhurst, Roger. 2018. Introduction. In *The Cambridge companion to Dracula*, ed. Roger Luckhurst, 1–8. Cambridge: Cambridge University Press.
Polidori, William. 1968. Der Vampyr, trans. Adolf Böttger. In Von denen Vampiren oder Menschensaugern. Dichtungen & Dokumente. Lizenzausgabe, ed. Dieter Sturm and Klaus Völker, 45–69. Vienna: Wiener Verlag (first published in 1819).
Radcliffe, Ann. 1794. *The Mysteries of Udolpho*. Girlebooks E-Book.
Stoker, Bram, and Leslie S. Klinger. 2008. *The new annotated Dracula*. New York: Norton.
Wilde, Oscar. 2004. The ballad of Reading Gaol. In Oscar Wilde in prison, ed. Hans-Christian Oeser, 5–40. Stuttgart: Reclam (first published in 1896).

Film

Bram Stoker's Dracula. USA 1992. Directed by Francis Ford Coppola. American Zoetrope.
Dracula. TV miniseries. UK 2020. Created by Mark Gatiss and Steven Moffat: Hartswood Films/British Broadcasting Corporation/Netflix.
Dracula. UK 1958. Directed by Terence Fisher. Hammer Films.
Dracula. USA 1931. Directed by Tod Browning. Universal Pictures.
Dracula. USA/UK 1979. Directed by John Badham. Universal Pictures.
Dracula: Dead and Loving It. USA 1995. Directed by Mel Brooks. Gaumont/Castle Rock Entertainment/Brooksfilms.
The Addiction. USA 1995. Directed by Abel Ferrara. Fast Films.
True Blood. TV series. USA 2008–2014. Created by Alan Ball. Your Face Goes Here Entertainment/Home Box Office.
Twilight. USA 2008. Directed by Catherine Hardwicke. Summit Entertainment et al.

Crimson Peak (2015)

9

Guillermo del Toro's *Crimson Peak* is a neo-Gothic film *par excellence,* referencing a plethora of topoi and characters typical of Gothic cinema and citing various predecessors throughout film history. *Crimson Peak,* which Xavier Aldana Reyes (2018, p. 171) has called a love letter to Gothic cinema, is at once cliché, homage, and pastiche, and equally a coherent film with its own distinctive aesthetics. The young protagonist Edith Cushing (Mia Wasikowska), visited by warning ghosts in desicive moments, is introduced as the comparatively emancipated daughter of a wealthy U.S. entrepreneur. Similar to the Gothic heroine *par excellence,* Emily St. Aubert in Ann Radcliffe's *The Mysteries of Udolpho,* she becomes the center of intrigue and manipulation after the murder of her father (Jim Beaver). After marrying the handsome, mysterious Thomas Sharpe (Tom Hiddleston), she accompanies him to his native England, where he lives with his sister Lucille (Jessica Chastain) in a ruinous Gothic mansion. Sitting on a hill of scarlet clay, the mining of which once ensured the family's wealth, the estate is nicknamed Crimson Peak. As Edith gradually discovers the two siblings' plan to poison her for her fortune, she is unable to escape the remote, snowed-in mansion, thus serving another trope of classic Gothic fiction: the imprisoned female protagonist (see Germaine Buckley 2015). Eventually, she manages to incapacitate the murderous siblings and leave Crimson Peak, along with her longtime friend and secret admirer Alan McMichael (Charlie Hunnam), who has also uncovered the Sharpes' plan and come to Edith's rescue.

Not only in terms of characters, motifs, plot, and aesthetics, but also on a cinematographic-aesthetic level, *Crimson Peak* rolls out a rich tapestry of references to the entire history of Gothic cinema. It brings back the iris diaphragms of silent film and the chiaroscuro of German Expressionism (00:03, see Fig. 9.1, as well as 00:21 and 00:31) as we know them from *The Cabinet of Dr. Caligari* (1920)

© The Author(s), under exclusive license to Springer Fachmedien Wiesbaden GmbH, part of Springer Nature 2023
K. Rein, *Gothic Cinema,* https://doi.org/10.1007/978-3-658-40721-6_9

Fig. 9.1 Iris diaphragm closing in on a wall lamp with a moth and near-compelementary contrast of green/orange in *Crimson Peak* (CA/USA/MX 2015), 00:03. (Blu-Ray Disc, Universal Studios, Germany 2016)

or *Nosferatu – A Symphony of Horror* (1922), or the characteristic illumination in complementary color contrasts of the Italian Gothic, as used by Dario Argento or Mario Bava (see Fig. 9.1). The protagonist's maiden name pays homage to Peter Cushing, one of the stars of British Hammer Gothic horror. The opulent, striking costumes recall Eiko Ishioka's Academy Award-winning creations for Francis Ford Coppola's *Bram Stoker's Dracula* (1992).

In a list published in *Rookie Mag*, Guillermo del Toro revealed which works inspired him while working on *Crimson Peak*. Among them are various classics of Gothic fiction from Matthew Lewis' *The Monk* to Charlotte Brontë's *Jane Eyre* and Emily Brontë's *Wuthering Heights* to Henry James' haunted house novella *The Turn of the Screw* and Edgar Allan Poe's *The Fall of the House of Usher* (del Toro 2015). But in *Crimson Peak*, he succeeds not only in weaving a tapestry of motifs, characters, and images from Gothic cinema, but also in reinterpreting them (see Aldana Reyes 2018, pp. 172 ff.), thereby inscribing himself in an original way in the list of iconic Gothic films.

9.1   The Old and the New World

Just as personal and aesthetic influences have migrated across the Atlantic and back several times throughout the history of Gothic cinema, this route is also travelled by the protagonists of *Crimson Peak*. The Sharpes travel to the New World in search of money and a new bride for Thomas. Even before his arrival at the com-

Fig. 9.2   Lucille (Jessica Chastain) accompanies her brother's (Tom Hiddleston) and Edith's (Mia Wasikowska) dance on the piano, *Crimson Peak,* 00:20. (Blu-Ray Disc, Universal Studios, Germany 2016)

pany of Edith's father, whom he hopes to recruit as a sponsor, the mysterious young man becomes a topic of conversation – not least because all the young women except Edith seem to immediately consider the handsome European a good catch (00:05). At an evening reception, the Sharpes become the main attraction: here, in a scarlet dress, Lucille accompanies her brother on the piano as he dances the waltz "European style" (00:18, Fig. 9.2). In this scene, which could equally figure in a work by Jane Austen or Lev Tolstoy,[1] several young women are obviously hoping to be asked to dance with Thomas. His choice, however, falls on Edith, who hesitantly agrees under the envious gazes of her rivals. Here, a difference between the two romantically involved characters already becomes apparent: When Thomas suggests that closing one's eyes in view of the unpleasant makes it easier, Edith replies: "I don't wanna close my eyes. I wanna keep them open" (00:19). While he, as a stereotypical Gothic protagonist, practices repression and denial and, as we learn later, passively inserts himself into his sister's horrifying scenarios, Edith is investigative, risk-taking, and willing to face fears and problems. She thus proves to be a variation on the Final Girl as identified by Carol Clover (1992).

---

[1] Thomas' declaration of love "I feel as if a link exists between your heart and mine, and should that link be broken, either by distance of by time, then my heart would cease to beat and I would die" (00:36) is also reminiscent of Austen's *Pride & Prejudice*. Even his expression of emotion is a cliché.

At the same time, the characters are juxtaposed as stand-ins for the Old and the New World – a contrast that often plays a role in the Gothic. The Sharpes are at home in the birthplace of the Gothic. They are sophisticated, reserved, and shrouded in mystery. Edith notes that Thomas' clothes, while elegant and tailored, are at least a decade old (00:11 f.). Lucille's Victorian gowns are out of fashion and seem like a relic from the past amidst the Edwardian garb of the Buffalo society. The Sharpes have inherited the financial hardship that drives them, as well as the Gothic ruin in which they live and their psychological traumas. Their economic misery is a burden of their family past that they cannot shed, their psychopathologies partly the result of childhood abuse. Their past determines every aspect of their lives: their financial situation, their relationship to each other as well as to others. At one point, the forward-looking, energetic Edith notes her husband's orientation toward the past: "You're always looking to the past. You won't find me there." (01:10). Thomas proves to be a typical Gothic character in his inability to live in the present because he cannot detach himself from his past. What Edith interprets as a romantic, dreamy attitude is in fact a reference to the economic and moral degeneration of the Sharpe family. Last but not least, Thomas' past includes his three previous wives, whom he and Lucille murdered, and who appear as Edith's predecessors and doppelgangers.

Edith quickly realizes that Thomas is an idealistic inventor and visionary. As it turns out, he is also a Mad Scientist who marries wealthy young women in order to fund his machine to extract clay and then murder them. In typical Gothic fashion, Lucille and he are representatives of the parasitic European gentry – Edith even explicitly refers to Thomas as a parasite before meeting him (00:05) because of his title of nobility, "baronet," which sounds so foreign to Americans that it is commented on several times. Instead of exploiting serfs and servants, however, the Sharpes sacrifice Thomas' brides to a machine that replaces human labor. The offering that capitalist industrialization requires is human sacrifice. That he and his technology are drenched in the blood of virgins[2] is symbolized in a sequence in which Thomas works on his machine: As he walks away from it, the snow takes on the red color of clay under the pressure of his feet, so that he literally leaves a blood-red trail (01:15).

As we learn later, Edith's father is justifiably skeptical of the Sharpes. Suspense plays an important role here, a typical narrative element of the Gothic, that Alfred Hitchcock has formulated as "the rule that the audience is provided with informa-

---

[2] We learn from Lucille that Thomas did not have sex with any of his brides before Edith (01:37). Consequently, Edith, who is no longer a virgin, is the only one to survive the marriage with him.

tion the characters in the picture don't know about." (Truffaut 1985, p. 114). While we learn early in the film that Edith's father is concerned to keep Thomas away from his daughter because he has incriminating files on the Sharpes, his sudden murder hardens suspicions just as it prevents this information from becoming known to the other characters for the time being.

9.2 Allerdale Hall

The Sharpes' house that Edith is taken to after marrying Thomas is a Gothic ruin *par excellence*. It is also a hybrid architectural monster, reminiscent in part of a Gothic cathedral and in part of wood carvings in medieval churches (see Fig. 9.3), the structure is labyrinthine and fragmentary. Neither we nor the characters have any sense of its totality: even Thomas, who grew up in the house, tells Edith upon her arrival that he does not know how many rooms it contains (00:40). Adding to the mysterious and oppressive atmosphere of Allerdale Hall is the fact that Edith – in the tradition of Emily St. Aubert in *The Mysteries of Udolpho* as well as the protagonist in Hitchcock's *Rebecca* – cannot move freely within it. Lucille justifies the fact that various rooms are inaccessible to her with the fact that the house is partially in danger of collapsing and therefore not safe for exploration. As guardian of the keys and caretaker of the house, Lucille stands in the tradition of the tyrannical

Fig. 9.3 The entrance area of Allerdale Hall in *Crimson Peak*, 00:41. (Blu-Ray Disc, Universal Studios, Germany 2016)

housekeeper Mrs. Danvers in *Rebecca*. Lucille's power over the house manifests itself in the bunch of keys repeatedly shown dangling from her belt – that Thomas does not have a copy either becomes clear when he asks her to hand a key to one of the workers so he can fetch coal to power his machine (01:18).

Another reference is *Bluebeard*. As in this fairy tale written by Charles Perrault, the bride is forbidden to move freely about the house – Lucille denies Edith the keys that she would need to do so (00:44) and Thomas instructs her never to take the elevator to the lowest level (00:42). While Bluebeard's bride finds the bloody corpses of his six murdered wives in the forbidden chamber, this lowest level of Allerdale Hall holds six tanks, which contain the crimson clay of the stagnant mine. Floating in them are the skeletons of Edith's predecessors and the Sharpes' mother. Unlike in Perrault's fairy tale, here we are dealing with a murderous, tyrannical landlady in whose plan the groom is only a pawn. Lucille is the driving force behind the murders: When she asks Thomas at the end to also get his hands dirty for once by murdering Alan (01:36), we can conclude that until now she has always administered the death blow.

"The house embodies the Gothic in *Crimson Peak*:" writes Laura Kremmel (2015), "it is the very structure on which the film is built, disintegrating yet obstinately reinforced by its perverse histories and by the blood that has been shed again and again within its walls". This blood manifests itself in the form of the red clay that the house is literally soaked in throughout the film. As soon as the bride and groom arrive, the crimson earth is visible, working its way through the floor in the entrance hall. As Thomas steps onto a broken floor board, the clay oozes out from underneath, as if the floor had been laid directly on top of the earth during construction (00:41, see Fig. 9.4). Increasingly, the red clay also runs down the walls of the house like a stream of viscous blood, where it forms large red stains (visible, for example, in 01:14 and 01:44, see Fig. 9.5). These are reminiscent of Oscar Wilde's ghost story *The Canterville* Ghost (1887), in which a family moves into a haunted house wherein a blood-red stain reappears on the floor every night after its removal. As it turns out, this refers to the murder committed by Sir Simon, the Canterville ghost, on his wife. In this way as well as through its references to *Bluebeard*, the red stains in Allerdale Hall point to the fate of Thomas' previous wives.

The earth around the Sharpes' house appears a shade of terracotta at the beginning, and by the end of the film stains the snow a blotchy blood red. In the final sequence, Allerdale Hall looks as if it were standing in the middle of a gigantic pool of blood like the one covering the floor of Bluebeard's forbidden chamber. The clay as a motif, as well as the color scheme of black, white, and (blood) red that dominates the set and costumes, especially in the final sequence, is reminiscent of *Snow White*, another fairy tale in which a mother figure bullies a half-orphan. In

Fig. 9.4 The red clay spilling into the house in *Crimson Peak*, 00:41. (Blu-Ray Disc, Universal Studios, Germany 2016)

Fig. 9.5 As Lucille storms down the stairs to murder Edith, the red clay flows down the walls in streams, *Crimson Peak*, 01:44. (Blu-Ray Disc, Universal Studios, Germany 2016)

del Toro's film, too, she contrasts with the deceased birth mother, who is depicted as protective and benevolent: The ghost of Edith's mother appears to her several times and delivers a warning: "Beware of Crimson Peak" (00:03; 00:14 f.). Unfortunately, Edith learns too late what "Crimson Peak" means – when she already lives with her husband who explains that the red clay earned Allerdale Hall this fairy-tale name (01:01).

Fig. 9.6 Allerdale Hall surrounded by blood-red snow, *Crimson Peak*, 01:50. (Blu-Ray Disc, Universal Studios, Germany 2016)

It is striking that the house merges with its surroundings and is not clearly delineated from the outside world. Not only does the red clay ooze in through the floor and trickle down the walls; in several places – most prominently in the entryway – there are gaping holes in the roof through which leaves, rain, and snow fall. The outside world enters the house, reliably indicating the change of the seasons in the foyer. From below, from above, and from the sides, the elements spill, flow, blow, and fall into Allerdale Hall, which merges with its immediate surroundings at the end of the film: The bloody finale that takes place inside spreads to the environment as the snow around Allerdale Hall turns red from the clay. Visually, this creates an effect as if the house were standing in a huge bloodstain (see Fig. 9.6).

Much more than a home, Allerdale Hall is an accumulation of Gothic imagery and topoi. With its gaping hole in the roof and ubiquitous red clay, it is uninhabitable. It is pure aesthetics and metaphor. It represents the past whose weight lies heavy on the Sharpes and it materializes the threat to Edith. "The house is sinking," Thomas says as he steps onto the broken parquet flooring, crimson clay oozing toward him through the cracks (00:41, see Fig. 9.4). The house literally sinking into the ground is reminiscent of Edgar Allan Poe's *The Fall of the House of Usher*, in which the couple of incestuous siblings sinks into the swamp that here turns from metaphorical to literal. It thus manifests the "seeping descent into disintegration" that Chris Baldick (2009, p. xix) identified as an effect of the Gothic in his introduction to the *Oxford Book of* Gothic *Tales*.

This bloody labyrinth not only knows no boundary between inside and outside, it also knows no boundary between the world of the living and that of the dead. Not only do ghosts appear to Edith, warning and guiding her, but the dog of Edith's predecessor, believed dead, also re-appears and becomes Edith's companion.[3] While the house is, on the one hand, labyrinthine, disorienting, dark and partially locked, it is, on the other hand, open – to the outside world, to the beyond, and of course to the lady of the house, Lucille, the only one who owns keys and thus the privilege of appearing anywhere in the house at (in)appropriate moments. As noted in Sect. 7.2, since the 1960s, hauntings have been conceived of as a feeling in a house (see Clarke 2013, p. 85), which includes a sense of being watched. While the real threat to Edith comes from the living, ghosts seem to move freely in Allerdale Hall just like the lady of the house.

In a self-reflexive reference to the tapestry of gothic motifs and clichés rolled out in the film, Thomas asks upon Edith's first glimpse of the house's interior, "Does it look the part?" (00:41). Allerdale Hall indeed not only looks the part, it plays it well. As the central topos of the Gothic, the titular house is the real protagonist. Its creaks and howls, at times indistinguishable from human noises, characterise the auditory atmosphere: "The house breathes," Thomas comments on the sounds the wind makes in duet with the architecture (00:48). Crimson Peak doesn't just set the tone of the film aesthetically – like Shirley Jackson's Hill House and other Gothic houses, it is a soulful house with its own agency. With its ghosts and clues, it significantly guides Edith's uncovering of the Sharpes' backstory and, by extension, the plot. For example, as Thomas says, the elevator has "a life of its own" (00:43) and seems to set itself in motion independently at will. Among other things, it does so to transport Edith to the next clue (01:15) or to serve as a refuge from and a weapon against Lucille (01:43 f.). The elevator thus proves to be one tool among many that the house seems to use to help Edith.

9.3   Colors and Costumes

The use of color in *Crimson Peak* is also striking. The sequences in Edith's home appear in warm shades of brown (see Fig. 9.7) – green light mingles with the warm light only when either ghosts or the Sharpe siblings are present. Allerdale Hall, on the other hand, is dominated by shades of green that frequently split into blue and yellow (see Fig. 9.8). Thomas' workshop alone – in one of the paradigmatic locations of the Gothic, the attic that is psychoanalytically associated with the Id –

---

[3] Thomas, hoping for the dog's imminent death, had previously locked it out (01:22).

Fig. 9.7 Charlie Hunnam as Alan McMichael and Mia Wasikowska as Edith Cushing in *Crimson Peak,* 00:05. (Blu-Ray Disc, Universal Studios, Germany 2016)

Fig. 9.8 Edith in her shiny canary yellow dress contrasting with Lucille's matte blue velvet dress. Edith's sleeves and the shape of her armchair are reminiscent of butterfly wings. The chair and wall in the background is green, the color that blue and yellow add up to, *Crimson Peak,* 01:19. (Blu-Ray Disc, Universal Studios, Germany 2016)

appears in brown hues and thus not only friendlier, but also as a reminder of Edith's home. It is in this comparatively light-filled room that the bride and groom's only romantic encounter in Allerdale Hall takes place, though it is interrupted by Lucille when she enters unannounced to serve poisoned tea to Edith. The only sequence marked by undisturbed intimacy and warmth is the one outside of Allerdale Hall, when Thomas and Edith have to spend the night away from home due to a snow-storm – warm shades of brown dominate this sequence as well. The rest of the house is dark, and we find the green hues that permeate it in the couple's bedspread, for example, as well as in the lighting or in the costumes of the female protagonists.

Colors also play a significant role in Kate Hawley's costume design for *Crimson Peak*. If the Sharpe siblings are often paired by their clothing – for example, when they both wear the same color (usually black or blue) – Edith presents the greatest possible contrast to Lucille not only in terms of character, but also visually – whether through a black/white or complementary contrast (see Fig. 9.8). When the brunette sister appears in a dull shade of blue, the blonde bride appears in bright canary yellow (00:79). The costumes of the two women are also marked by another typical Gothic motif: moths and butterflies. Edith's Edwardian, voluminous puffy sleeves are reminiscent of colorful butterfly wings that stand out against the dark surroundings (see Fig. 9.8), while Lucille is dressed in costumes reminiscent of a moth that adapts to the darkness. At the end of the film, Lucille's Victorian heavy velvet gown falls that was also symbolically concealing her true nature like a cur-tain. Now that Lucille's incestuous relationship with Thomas is exposed, so are her cleavage and shoulders. The voluminous sleeves of her chemise hang down like the wings of a moth (01:29 f.). The butterfly/moth motif also appears elsewhere in the film: In addition to the credits, moths accompany, for example, the first ghostly apparition in Edith's childhood (00:02 f.). Edith's (or formerly Enola's) dog is a Continental Toy Spaniel – a breed of which two varieties are distinguished depend-ing on the shape of their ears: Phalène and Papillon, French for "moth" and "but-terfly." Naturally, Edith's dog belongs to the latter. At the beginning of the film, Lucille tells Edith that there are only black moths at her house that feed on butter-flies, anticipating her power over Edith (00:24 f.). In fact, the attic in Allerdale Hall, where Lucille's room is located, is inhabited by moths.

9.4   The Ghosts of Crimson Peak

Another striking feature is the ghosts, whose visuals are anticipated by Lucille's costume at the ball at the beginning of the film: In her blood-red dress, she appears as a foreign body in a company of women dressed in pastel shades and men in

Fig. 9.9 The ghost of Edith's mother warns her about Crimson Peak, 00:03. (Blu-ray Disc, Universal Studios, Germany 2016)

black (00:16–00:20, see Fig. 9.2). Not only does this represent the red clay of Crimson Peak, but the long lacing in her back also traces her spine, creating a skeletal impression and echoing the red, skeletal ghosts that appear to Edith in Allerdale Hall.

The ghosts in *Crimson Peak* have the shape of skeletons with long fingers, some of them being shrouded in smoke. Most of the apparitions in Allerdale Hall are as crimson as the clay pots in the forbidden part of the house, where their decaying corpses are stored. Only the ghosts of Edith's mother (see Fig. 9.9) and Lucille are black. The sequences in which Edith is visited by her mother's ghost are particularly striking. They resurrect the lighting of the 1960s and 1970s Italian Gothic film, guided by bright colors and complementary contrasts. This apparition is accompanied by typical phenomena: the clock stops, a door creaks. Picking up on the iconic image from Murnau's *Nosferatu*, long fingers – first as shadows, then as physical figures – push their way into the frame (00:02). The ghosts in *Crimson Peak* are not white, transparent figures. But they seem at once ethereal and corporeal when, skeletal yet seemingly made of wisps of smoke, they rise from the floor or peer out of the closet. Sometimes they are physically maimed. Some move zombie-like, crawling forward (00:58), others hover (the ghost of Edit's mother in 00:02 f., another in 01:28). That the red ghosts in Allerdale Hall appear virtually in the guise of the actual state of their corpses gives them a zombie-like quality. They also prove corporeal in that they touch Edith (00:03) or yank her to the ground (01:03 f.), jerk doorknobs and locks (00:13), or shut doors (00:58).

With their bold color palette of scarlet, pitch black, and white, reminiscent of Snow White, they clearly differ from the stereotypical visuality of ghosts. The only exception to this is Thomas' ghost, appearing white and semi-transparent before he vanishes into thin air (01:48 f.). While he is also visible to Lucille, all the other ghosts seem to be perceptible only to Edith. She shows herself to be open to their communication, and in one sequence even tries to actively make contact instead of waiting for the apparitions, when she holds out her hand and calls out in typical spiritualist fashion: "If you're here with me, give me a signal" (01:03). The spirits warn her, leading her to signs and clues that allow her to uncover the Sharpes' murderous scheme, and thus saving her from becoming one of them (prematurely).

9.5 Ghostly Media

Following the clues of the ghosts in the house, Edith discovers the machinations of the Sharpes. In the process, not only she herself becomes a spiritualist medium herself, but so do also the recording mediums around her that play a central role in this Gothic film. For example, an apparition (presumably of Thomas' previous wife Enola) leads Edith to a closet containing phonograph cylinders. The wayward elevator transports her to the forbidden basement, where she finds Enola's luggage, including a matching record player. A tech-savvy Final Girl, Edith knows how to assemble and operate it (01:20 ff.).[4] The reels contain Enola's phonographic diary, which reminds us of that of John Seward in Stoker's *Dracula*. Unlike Seward, however, Thomas' ex-wife has documented her own history of illness rather than someone else's. As in Renfield's case, this report reveals the way in which she increasingly falls prey to a monster. "They're killing me. I'm dying. The poison. It's in the tea," the dead woman's voice says to Edith, sounding from the mechanical medium (01:22). This key sequence takes place in a typical Gothic location, the library. Here, in front of a gigantic window behind which winter rages, surrounded by stacks of books, Edith hears the revealing recording of her predecessor. Technical media in *Crimson Peak* also prove to be spiritualist mediums: While at the beginning of the film, Alan shows spirit photographs to Edith (00:22 f.) and explains that ghosts are stored in places, Edith learns about the fate of Thomas' former wife Enola through the phonograph recordings.

Non-technical recording media also play a role in the uncovering of the Sharpes' murder plans: Alan learns of the murder of the Sharpes' mother from a newspaper article. Before that, it is a letter that provides Edith with a piece of the puzzle: As it

---

[4] Edith's father also owned a phonograph, which we have seen in min. 31.

turns out, the letter addressed to "Lady E. Sharpe" that she receives at the post office (01:10) is intended for Enola, who becomes recognizable as Edith's doppelganger through this mix-up as well as based on her previous role.

Edith herself has an affinity for books and for Gothic fiction. She is introduced as a writer – in her first appearance, we see her holding her own manuscript (see Fig. 9.7) – of ghost stories, emulating Mary Shelley (on female authorship in the Gothic, see, for example, Haefele-Thomas 2016, p. 169 f.). When her father gives her a pen, she says, she would rather write her novel on a typewriter, thus following in the footsteps of Stoker's Mina Harker. With this pen, she later signs, coerced by Lucille, the order for the last transfer of her fortune to the Sharpes and thus her own death warrant. However, since Edith is not only a Gothic heroine, but also a Final Girl, she immediately uses the pen as a sword and stabs Lucille with it, thus avenging the murder of her father, which Lucille has just confessed to her (01:40).

9.6 Tyrannical Mothers and Incestuous Love

The psychoanalytically symbolic spaces of the basement and the attic are, not surprisingly, also prominent in this haunted house. While corpses are literally found in the basement, the attic is the site of the Sharpe siblings' deviant desires. In a reference to the iconic nursery in Shirley Jackson's Gothic classic *The Haunting of Hill House,* Lucille has previously told her brother's bride that as children they " were confined to the nursery in the attic" (00:50). It is in this room that Edith eventually finds the two of them, as adults, in the midst of a sexual act (01:29). If Lucille previously appeared as a sexually transgressive woman, making sex a topic of conversation with Edith and showing her a pornographic picture accompanied by the suggestion of "secrets everywhere" (00:51), she now reveals herself as a jealous, incestuous sister. Her heavy, dark, high-necked, Victorian velvet gowns in this scene are exchanged for a chemise reminiscent of lascivious Renaissance paintings, slipping off her shoulder and draping her body in opulent, light, white masses of fabric (see Fig. 9.5).

The jealous Lucille murders her brother/lover when he reveals his feelings for Edith to her. While his emancipation from her – for example, when he warned Edith not to drink the poisoned tea (01:25) – was already implicit earlier, it becomes explicit in this sequence. After killing her own mother in her youth, Lucille has taken on the role of the tyrannical mother – another typical Gothic character. When Thomas and Edith stay away overnight, Lucille responds with rage against the bride on the next morning (01:12 ff.). She reveals an emotional mix of the jealousy a wife would feel toward a lover and a mother's worry about the couple not returning home. In addition, there is a fear of loss similar to that a mother might feel when facing the emancipation of a child whose emotional attachment to another person may result in the abandonment of the mother. And like a psychologically unstable mother, immediately after lashing out, Lucille offers Edith a cup of tea when she says she doesn't feel well. Fittingly, this sequence takes place in the kitchen, a room dominated by Lucille and in which, particularly in this sequence, the blood-red clay runs visibly down the wall (01:14).

With the role of the tyrannical mother, Lucille, Laura Kremmel (2015) points out, also takes on a typically male role: Lucille controls the keys, manages the family home and finances, and dominates the male heir. The painting of mother Sharpe watches over the adult children after her death – the portrait of a grim old lady being another topos that runs through Gothic fiction from Radcliffe to Poe. Edith's sentence beginning with "She looks quite …" is completed by Lucille with "… horrible? Yes. It's an excellent likeness", She proceeds to explain, in an allusion to her incest and murders: "I like to think she can see us from up there. I don't want her to miss a single thing we do." (00:50 f.).

Like the house itself, the old lady is also more of a topos than a character. If the mother was murdered by 12-year-old Lucille, she would have to be significantly younger than the old woman we see on the wall. The portrait thus shows her at an age she never reached. In this sequence, Edith notices that the ring Thomas has put on her finger adorns their mother's finger in the portrait. In a previous sequence, we saw Lucille reluctantly pull it off her own finger, hand it to Thomas, and say that she had earned it and that she expected to get it back (00:25). As becomes clear· later, she "earned it" by removing it, along with the finger itself, from the hand of the murdered mother, whose ghost is now missing a ring finger (00:47). The tyrannical mother is thus present in the Gothic even after her death – not only in the shape of her all-seeing portrait and her ring, which is passed down as a blood-stained family heirloom, but especially in the shape of Lucille, who has assumed her role as mistress of the house (and to whom the ring returns after each murder of one of Thomas' brides). In other works of Gothic, the tyrannical mother also returns after her death, for example in the form of the hauntings that remind Eleanor of her mother in Jackson's *The Haunting of Hill House*, or in the form of her mummified corpse combined with Norman Bates' split personality in *Psycho*.

In another scene, Lucille feeds oatmeal to the now weakened, bedridden Edith, producing irritating scratching noises with her spoon. Meanwhile, she recounts that she nursed her mother – as Eleanor in *The Haunting of Hill House* nursed her tyrannical mother until her death. Her father hated her mother, she says, and broke her leg, from which she never recovered (01:24). In this sequence, Lucille not only reveals to her sister-in-law a piece of the violence that reigned in that family, but also establishes her mother as another doppelganger of Edith: in this sequence, it is Edith who lies in bed and is fed by Lucille – as it later turns out, with poisoned porridge. Lucille tells her she will take care of her the same way she took care of her mother (whom she murdered). Shortly thereafter, Edith is given the wheelchair that presumably previously served to transport the mother when she had a broken leg. We saw it before in a shot in the attic, wafted by ghostly wisps of mist that formed bony hands (00:53) as well as in one of the photographs Edith found in Enola's suitcase (01:21). It is in this wheelchair, then, that Edith sits – even before breaking a leg when Lucille pushes her down from the gallery (01:30). It is therefore consistent that at the end of the film Lucille takes out the axe with which she murdered her mother and goes after Edith with it (01:45 f.). The repetition of events and biographies identified by Freud (1999, p. 246 ff.) as a central manifestation of the Uncanny (along with doppelgangers) is a central motif of the Gothic, which is also taken up many times in *Crimson Peak*.

9.7   Gothic Fiction About Gothic Fiction

As Gothic heroine and Final Girl, Edith is also a modern, emancipated woman. While she finds herself isolated in a labyrinthine haunted house and surrounded by mysterious characters and events, she is not a passive, surrendered fairy-tale princess waiting for a male savior like Bluebeard's bride. Her long-time friend and physician Alan comes to the rescue in time to treat Edith after Lucille has thrown her down the stairs, but he ultimately fails in his mission to take her away and instead ends up being the one *she* takes out of the house. The final duel is fought between the two women – Thomas is already dead, his ghost stands by passively, unable to respond to Edith's call for help (01:48), while Alan is inside the house, badly wounded. It is the pragmatic, self-determined and active Edith who kills Lucille with a shovel blow to the head. She dryly responds to Lucille's dramatic, repeated announcement that she would not stop until one of them was dead with "I heard you the first time" (01:49), reminding us of the wisecracking Buffy, the vampire slayer from Joss Whedon's series of the same name.

After all of the Sharpes' dark secrets have been revealed and they themselves have died, Edith stands in the snow outside Allerdale Hall, with tears in her eyes, her white nightgown stained with blood like the blotchy red snow around her. Accompanied by the rhythmic sound of Thomas' hoisting machine, the images and Edith's voiceover from the beginning of the film are repeated: "Ghosts are real. This much I know." While we first heard this line accompanying her mother's funeral at the beginning, it now sounds to Edith's and Alan's exit from Crimson Peak. At the gate, Edith looks back and with her gaze sends the camera into the house, past the crimson snow, past the stain of Alan's blood in the front entrance, past the fireplace, whose blaze has taken on a life of its own over the course of the film, following the mood of the house, to the piano in the parlor where Lucille's ghost is sitting (01:51). Lucille played the piano in her first appearance (00:16). She now does so again but as a black ghost, with the bunch of keys on her belt, in a shot that Chloe Germaine (2015) has called "[t]he most horrifying and haunting image". If Thomas' white ghost dissipates immediately after his death, implying redemption, it now becomes apparent that Lucille is doomed to eternally repeat her actions. While Edith and Alan survive and leave Allerdale Hall at the end, Lucille remains trapped there in death as she was while alive, woven into the house's ruinous, decaying structure.

Del Toro not only manages to masterfully play the keys of Gothic cinema in *Crimson Peak*, retrieving central motifs, characters, and images to create what Aldana Reyes (2018, p. 172) calls "a mosaic of Gothic cognates". As in his other films, he weaves these together with fairy tale motifs to create a coherent overall image. Visually, he draws on the entire history of Gothic cinema as well as on canonical literary works, presenting a body of work that takes deep bows to this tradition while simultaneously amalgamating its components into an aesthetic of its own.

Edith's novel, which is thematized several times in the film, points not only to the fact that much of the canon of Gothic fiction was written by women, but also to the difficulties they faced. During their undisturbed night outside Lucille's sphere of influence, Thomas, referring to the main character in Edith's novel, says, "This fellow Cavendish, your hero, there's a darkness to him, I like him." and asks if he survives to the end, to which Edith replies that it depended entirely on him. The characters in a novel develop, change, and make decisions, she explains (01:09). In this sequence, Thomas realizes that he too can decide against murdering his new bride and that this decision would also significantly change his own life. As he identifies with the main character in Edith's novel, it also becomes clear that she is writing a Gothic novel – a romance, as she says at the beginning, in which ghosts appear, without calling it a ghost story (00:06). Thomas *is* the protagonist in it. The work that Edith writes is *Crimson Peak*.

References

Literature

Aldana Reyes, Xavier. 2018. Guillermo del Toro's *Crimson Peak*. In *The Gothic: A reader*, ed. Simon Bacon, 169–175. Oxford: Peter Lang.
Baldick, Chris. 2009. Introduction. In *The Oxford book of Gothic Tales*, ed. Chris Baldick, xi–xxiii, 3rd ed. Oxford: Oxford University Press. Accessed 26 Oct 2020

Clarke, Roger. 2013. Spectres of the past. In *Gothic: The dark heart of film*, ed. James Bell, 84–92. London: BFI.

Clover, Carol J. 1992. *Men, women, and chain saws: Gender in the modern horror film*. Princeton: Princeton University Press.

Freud, Sigmund. 1999. Das Unheimliche. In *Gesammelte Werke. Chronologisch geordnet. Werke aus den Jahren 1917–1920*, ed. Anna Freud, vol. 12, 229–268. Frankfurt on the Main: Fischer. (first published in 1919).

Germaine Buckley, Chloe. 2015. *Crimson Peak* – A Gothic Romance that takes us back to the feminine early days of horror. *The Conversation*. 20 December. https://theconversation.com/crimson-peak-a-gothic-romance-that-takes-us-back-to-the-feminine-early-days-of-horror-49396. Accessed 27 May 2023.

Haefele-Thomas, Ardel. 2016. Queering the Female Gothic. In *Women and the Gothic: An Edinburgh companion*, ed. Avril Horner and Sue Zlosnik, 169–183. Edinburgh: Edinburgh University Press.

Jackson, Shirley. 2009. *The Haunting of Hill House*. London: Penguin (first published in 1959).

Kremmel, Laura. 2015. Piano keys to the house: *Crimson Peak*, the Gothic Romance, and feminine power. *Horror Homeroom.* 7 December. https://www.horrorhomeroom.com/piano-keys-to-the-house-crimson-peak-the-gothic-romance-and-feminine-power/. Accessed 26 Oct 2020.

Lewis, Matthew. 1998. *The Monk*, ed. Christopher MacLachlan. London: Penguin (first published in 1796).

Poe, Edgar Allan. [1839]. The Fall of the House of Usher. *The Poe Museum*. https://www.poemuseum.org/the-fall-of-the-house-of-usher. Accessed 22 Nov 2020.

Radcliffe, Ann. 1794. *The Mysteries of Udolpho*. Girlebooks E-Book.

Toro, Guillermo del. 2015. Guillermo del Toro'sguide to Gothic Romance. *Rookiemag*. 29 October. https://www.rookiemag.com/2015/10/guillermo-del-toros-guide-gothic-romance/. Accessed 26 Oct 2020.

Truffaut, François. 1985. *Hitchcock*. Rev. ed. New York et al.: Simon & Schuster.

Film

Bram Stoker's Dracula. USA 1992. Directed by Francis Ford Coppola. American Zoetrope.

Crimson Peak. Canada/USA/Mexico 2015. Directed by Guillermo del Toro. Double Dare You/Legendary Entertainment.

Das Cabinet des Dr. Caligari. Weimar Republic 1920. Directed by Robert Wiene. Decla Film-Gesellschaft.

Nosferatu, eine Symphonie des Grauens. Weimar Republic 1922. Directed by Friedrich Wilhelm Murnau. Jofa-Atelier Berlin-Johannisthal/Prana-Film GmbH.

Psycho. USA 1960. Directed by Alfred Hitchcock. Shamley Productions.

CPSIA information can be obtained
at www.ICGtesting.com
Printed in the USA
LVHW051220020723
751358LV00003B/187

9 783658 407209